ASIAN ECONOMIC HANDBOOK

ASIAN ECONOMIC HANDBOOK

EUROMONITOR PUBLICATIONS LIMITED
87–88 Turnmill Street, London EC1M 5QU

THE ASIAN ECONOMIC HANDBOOK
First edition 1987

Other titles in this series:

The African Economic Handbook
The Pacific Basin: An Economic Handbook
The Caribbean Economic Handbook
The Third World Economic Handbook
The East European Economic Handbook
The USSR Economic Handbook
The China Economic Handbook
The South American Economic Handbook
The Middle East Economic Handbook

Published by
Euromonitor Publications Limited
87–88 Turnmill Street
London EC1M 5QU

Telephone: 01–251 8024
Telex: 21120 MONREF G

British Library Cataloguing in Publication Data

Wong, John
  Asian economic handbook.
  1. Asia —— Economic conditions —— 1945–
  I. Title
  330.95'0428   HC412

  ISBN 0–86338–141–3

Phototypeset by Photoprint, Torquay, England
Printed by St Edmundsbury Press Limited, Bury St Edmunds, Suffolk

FOREWORD

THE ASIAN ECONOMIC HANDBOOK continues a new series of macro-economic studies on the world's developed and developing regions. As with previous titles, the handbook presents an economic overview of the region as a whole within the context of the world economy; discusses recent economic growth and development by sub-region and country; and assesses future growth and development.

The traditional vitality of the Asian population is finding new expression in commercial pursuits which are resulting in strong economic growth within many Asian countries, especially the ASEAN nations and other New Industrialised Countries (NICs).

With the rapid development of the Pacific Rim economy, and the dynamic growth currently experienced by many Asian countries, Asia will have a significant impact on the development of the world economy into the next century and the future pattern of international trade and investment. This timely new study offers an opportunity to assess the structure and development of this role over future decades.

The principal contributor to the handbook is John Wong, currently Associate Professor of Economics at the National University of Singapore, who has written extensively on Asian economic affairs. Regional and national studies were contributed by Michael Wilson, Robert Adams and Trevor Maggs, who are all journalists specialising in political and economic issues. The datafile is by Euromonitor.

CONTENTS

Chapter One

ASIA IN A WORLD CONTEXT

I Introduction

Asia is a huge continent, surpassing all the others in area, population, size and resource base. It has rich and varied heritages and is the home of the world's two oldest civilisations: China and India. Beyond culture and history, the vitality of the Asian peoples now finds its new expression in economic pursuits as epitomised in GNP increases, industrial growth and trade expansion. Thus Asia has given rise to a modern Japan, which is the only non-Western country to have successfully industrialised and become affluent. Also in Asia there has emerged a number of small but extremely dynamic economies which have had an impact on the world market with their highly competitive manufactured exports.

Just as it has in the past distinguished itself by its cultural pre-eminence, Asia is now noted for its dynamic economic growth. As can be seen in Figure A the Asian economies as a whole have continued to maintain high growth despite the world recession and have clearly out-performed the other country groups. For the dynamic Asian economies the deteriorating international economic environment might have subdued their economic growth but has not denied their long-term growth potentials.

For many Asian countries high economic growth is not a recent phenomenon, and some have in fact experienced fast growth for a sustained period of over two decades. This has led to the creation of the notion that global economic dynamism will gradually shift from the North Atlantic to the Asian rims of the Pacific. Whether or not such Asia-Pacific era will come about soon, Asia is already undergoing rapid economic transformation with more and more Asian countries gearing up to export expansion as their main engine of growth. This in the long run will certainly produce profound impact on the pattern of world trade and global financial flow.

II Asian development typologies

Asia is also an extremely diverse continent in terms of culture, history,

FIGURE A   DEVELOPING COUNTRIES, GROWTH OF REAL GDP, 1983–1985[1]

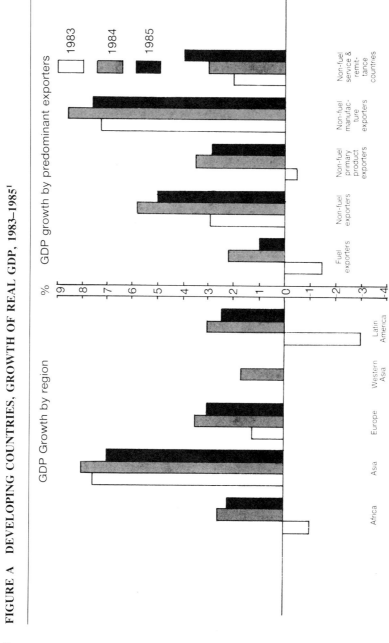

Source: IMF, *World Economic Outlook* (Washington, D.C., 1985)

Note: [1] Except where otherwise indicated, arithmetic averages of country growth rates weighted by the average United States dollar value of GDPs over the preceding three years; preliminary estimates for 1985.

language, ethnicity, religion and traditions. Diversity is similarly pronounced among the Asian economies in terms of their stages of growth and systems of economic and social development. Geographically speaking, however, Asia can be neatly divided into three clear-cut regions: East Asia, Southeast Asia and the Indian Sub-Continent, with each region containing an assortment of countries following fairly similar development strategies. A particular development strategy pursued by a particular country conditions not only its pattern of economic growth but also the manner in which it interacts with the world economy. Hence three distinct development typologies are identified to correspond with the three broad geographical regions.

III East Asia

Thus in East Asia are China, Japan, North Korea, and the three well-known 'Newly Industrialised Countries' (NICs), namely, South Korea, Taiwan and Hong Kong. This book concentrates on the NICs, North Korea and Macao in this region. Japan is a world-class economic giant, second only to the United States. With exports taking up 14% of the world market, Japan's external economic influence is clearly on a global scale. Increasingly the Japanese economy is asserting its leadership role as a new source of capital and technology as well as a locomotive for Asian economic growth.

China and North Korea are socialist countries which are supposed to operate their economies, in principle, on the basis of central planning with minimal reliance on market forces. For almost three decades, the Chinese economy was developed first along the Soviet-type central planning and then on the Maoist variant of the socialist development strategy. In recent years, however, the Chinese economy under the present leadership of Deng Xiaoping has taken a radical turn by following a more outward-looking development path. This is being achieved by opening up the economy to more foreign trade and foreign investment on the one hand and by undertaking extensive economic reforms on the other. The Chinese economy is now back on the path of high economic growth, which, coupled with its open-door policy, will lead to the increasing integration of the Chinese economy with other Asia-Pacific economies.

In contrast, North Korea has not undergone similar political and economic liberalisation to that in China, though North Korea has had more stable economic growth because it has not experienced such upheavals as Mao's Cultural Revolution. The North Korean economy is still rigidly socialistic and remains largely inward-looking so that it is not in a position to have significant interaction with the world economy, not even with its Asian neighbours.

In East Asia, therefore, the NICs tend to dominate the economic scene. Throughout the 1960s and the 1970s, they have registered on the average a near double-digit rate of economic growth, based primarily on the expansion of manufactured exports.

Broadly speaking, the Asian NICs are land-scarce and resource-poor countries. As city-states, Hong Kong and Singapore have no natural resources to speak of except for their geographical location. For South Korea and Taiwan, the only creditable 'resource' base before their industrial take-off was perhaps their well-developed agricultural sector. Nonetheless, the lack of natural resources in these NICs, as in Japan, has not impeded growth and development in these economies, which have striven to overcome such a constraint by intensifying the development of their human resources through cultivating higher levels of skills, entrepreneurship and industrial discipline. It has recently been re-emphasised that the mainstream cultural traditions of East Asia as embodied in Confucianism could well have produced a direct bearing on the economic growth of these NICs in the same way attempts by the Chinese Communists to supplant it by Maoism in the 1960s could have contributed to the economic stagnation of China in this period. Confucianist ethics, which puts heavy stress on educational achievements, hard work and self-discipline but does not deplore individual wealth possession and material acquisition, gives rise to a social milieu conducive to the type of economic development currently taking place in these densely populated countries. Such an achievement-orientated social structure, coupled with the political necessity of economic progress for national survival, provides a compelling exogenous explanation of the dynamic economic growth in East Asia. As a result of sustained economic growth, the Asian NICs as a group are now clearly in the upper middle-income category of the developing countries whilst Hong Kong, with its per-capita income (currently at US$ 6500) equivalent to that of Italy but higher than that of Spain and Ireland, is on the verge of crossing over to developed country status.

IV Southeast Asia—ASEAN and Indochina

Southeast Asia as a broadly defined geographical region comprises the socialist countries in Indochina (Laos, Kampuchea and Vietnam) and the 'semi-socialist' Burma, in addition to Brunei, Indonesia, Malaysia, the Philippines, Singapore and Thailand, which together constitute the Association of Southeast Asian Nations (ASEAN). Politically the Indochina states have barely established a semblance of order and stability and economically they are still in the process of rehabilitating their economies from the long period of war ravages and dislocation. Their economies remain stagnant and their trade has not fully recovered. Burma may fare considerably better in terms of growth and development. But the Burmese economy has not yet fully emerged from its self-imposed economic isolation. Consequently, Burma, like the socialist economies of Indochina and North Korea, will remain largely secluded from the main current of the world economy.

The mainstay of the Southeast Asian economy is therefore centred on the outward-looking ASEAN countries. With the average growth rates of 6–8% during the last two decades, the ASEAN economies are still impressive growth performers, though a little less 'dynamic' than the East Asian NICs. In contrast to the NICs, ASEAN is noted for its rich resource endowment. Together the ASEAN economies export the bulk of the world's natural rubber, tin, palm oil and coconut products, in addition to a high proportion of other commodities of agricultural and mineral origin, including petroleum and natural gas, rice and sugar. The continuing export of these geographic-specific primary commodities has provided the ASEAN economies with a vital source of foreign exchange earnings needed to maintain their economic growth, although in recent years manufactured exports have increasingly become a new source of their economic growth. As a result of the spurt of high growth in the 1970s, the ASEAN economies now all belong to what the World Bank has categorised as the middle-income developing countries, except for the tiny Brunei whose inordinately high per-capita income of US$ 20,000, buoyed by high oil revenue, would put it more appropriately among a handful of extremely high-income oil sheikhdoms of the Middle East.

V Indian Sub-Continent

The Indian Sub-Continent basically comprises the low-income countries centred on the Indian Sub-Continent. By comparison, these economies with their moderate average growth rates of about 4% in the 1960s and 4.5% in the 1970s are clearly much less 'dynamic' than both the NICs

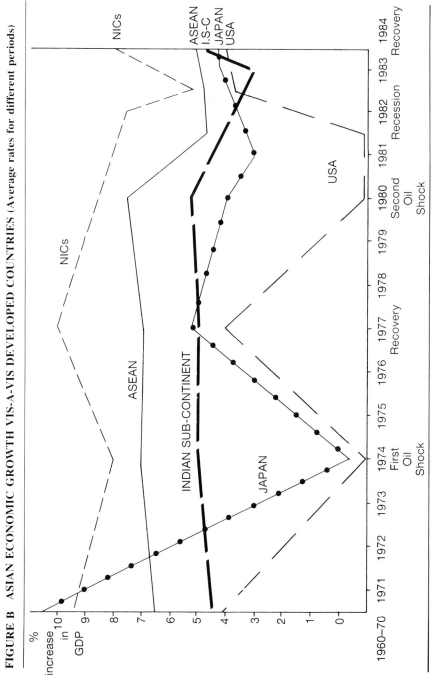

FIGURE B ASIAN ECONOMIC GROWTH VIS-A-VIS DEVELOPED COUNTRIES (Average rates for different periods)

and ASEAN. The Indian Sub-Continent economies differ considerably in resource endowment and in their economic structures, e.g. Pakistan and India are quite industrialised while Sri Lanka and Bangladesh still depend heavily on primary exports. As a group, however, they are not nearly as resource-rich as the ASEAN economies. In fact, they are on the whole endowed with a small resource base relative to their population size, much like the NICs. At the same time, they have not yet succeeded in developing a dynamic export-oriented industrial sector to propel their economies for high growth, as have the NICs. Nor have they developed a strong agricultural sector to provide a stable precondition for the industrialisation thrust, as in South Korea and Taiwan. In some parts of the Indian Sub-Continent industrialisation has barely started, while in others, the process of industrialisation is trapped in the prolonged phase of import substitution. In varying degrees, all the economies are still preoccupied with their domestic problems of poverty and unemployment. Furthermore, most of the countries pursue inward-looking development strategies. It is actually this inner-directed orientation in their economies, more than their low income and low growth, that has in the past constrained their capacity to interact with the world economy in the manner that has characterised the development processes of the more open economies of the NICs and ASEAN.

This characterisation of the distinct structural features of the Asian economies in terms of different development typologies helps put the economic growth and development of the various Asian countries in proper perspective as well as providing a useful framework to analyse their respective linkages with the world economy at large.

The economic growth patterns of different Asian economies are summarised in Table 1.1. Their social development as reflected in the selected socio-economic indicators is presented in Table 1.2. It is evident that the economically more well-developed East Asian NICs have achieved a relatively higher level of social development in terms of education, health-care and desirable demographic trends. By comparison, the low-income countries in the Indian Sub-Continent have on the whole accomplished less social progress, and hence effectively neither fast growth nor better distribution. Sri Lanka may be an exception in that its slower economic growth has been traded off for the better provision of basic needs to its people. The ASEAN countries as a group seem to stand in the middle range for both economic growth and social development while the socialist or semi-socialist economies, reflecting

7

TABLE 1.1   GROWTH PERFORMANCE OF ASIAN ECONOMIES

	Population million mid-1983	GNP per capita US$, 1983	Average % growth rate of GDP, 1960–70	Average annual growth rate (%), 1973–83				Export GDP ratio, 1983 (%)	Average inflation rate, 1973–83 (%)
				GDP	Agriculture	Manufacturing	Services		
Japan	119.3	10,120	10.5	4.3	–1.6	(5.5)	8.3	13.8	4.7
China	1,019.1	300	5.0	6.0	3.5	(8.4)	4.5	8.1	1.7
North Korea	19.2	923	7.8	n.a.	n.a.	n.a.	n.a.	n.a.	n.a.
East Asian NICs									
South Korea	42.0	2,010	8.5	7.3	1.5	11.8	6.8	31.9	19.0
Taiwan	18.6	2,457	9.2	8.6	1.3	11.1	8.5	50.3	7.4
Hong Kong	5.3	6,000	10.0	9.3	1.1	(8.2)	9.8	79.8	9.9
ASEAN									
Brunei	0.2	20,800	n.a.	n.a.	n.a.	n.a.	n.a.	n.a.	n.a.
Indonesia	155.7	560	3.5	7.0	3.7	12.6	9.0	27.0	18.0
Malaysia	14.9	1,860	6.5	7.3	4.4	(8.7)	8.2	48.3	6.5
Philippines	52.1	760	5.1	5.4	4.3	5.0	5.2	14.1	11.7
Thailand	49.2	820	8.2	6.9	3.8	8.9	7.6	15.8	8.7
Singapore	2.5	6,620	8.8	8.2	1.5	7.9	8.1	131.2	4.5
Indochina									
Vietnam	58.5	n.a.	n.a.	n.a.	n.a.	n.a.	n.a.	n.a.	n.a.
Laos	3.7	140	n.a.	n.a.	n.a.	n.a.	n.a.	n.a.	n.a.
Kampuchea	6.1	n.a.	n.a.	n.a.	n.a.	n.a.	n.a.	n.a.	n.a.
Burma	35.5	180	2.6	6.0	6.6	6.1	5.1	6.1	6.5
Indian Sub-Continent									
Bangladesh	95.5	130	3.6	5.2	3.2	(8.1)	7.4	6.8	9.6
India	733.2	260	3.6	4.0	2.2	4.3	6.1	5.1	7.7
Pakistan	89.7	390	6.7	5.6	3.4	7.0	6.3	11.9	11.1
Sri Lanka	15.4	330	4.6	5.2	4.1	3.4	6.0	22.3	14.5
For comparison									
Low-income economies	—	260	3.9	5.0	2.9	(7.1)	5.0	—	5.4
Middle-income economies	—	1,310	6.0	4.7	2.5	4.9	5.3	—	29.3

Sources: World Bank, *World Development Report* (1985); Asian Development Bank, *Key Indicators of Developing Member Countries of ADB* (April 1985); Executive Yuan, Taiwan, *Statistical Yearbook of the Republic of China* (1985) and Far Eastern Economic Review, *Asia Yearbook 1985*.

Note: n.a. = not available

TABLE 1.2   SELECTED SOCIAL INDICATORS FOR ASIAN ECONOMIES

	Population growth rate, 1973–83 (%)	Total fertility rate, 1983	Life expectancy 1983 (years)	% of labour in agriculture, 1981	Urban population, 1983 (%)	Infant mortality rate, 1983	Population per physician, 1980	No. enrolled, in 1982, in secondary school, as % of age group	Literacy rate, 1980 (%)
Japan	0.9	1.7	77	12	76	7	780	92	n.a.
China	1.5	2.3	67	74	21	38	1,740	35	n.a.
North Korea	2.5	4.0	65	49	62	32	430	n.a.	n.a.
East Asian NICs									
South Korea	1.6	2.1	67	34	62	29	2,990	89	93
Taiwan	1.9	2.1	75	19	50	9	1,268	87	90
Hong Kong	2.5	1.8	76	3	92	10	1,210	67	90
ASEAN									
Brunei	2.6	n.a.	66	5	n.a.	13	n.a.	n.a.	n.a.
Indonesia	2.3	4.3	54	58	24	101	11,530	33	62
Malaysia	2.4	2.4	67	50	31	69	1,320	49	60
Philippines	2.7	4.2	64	46	39	49	7,970	64	75
Thailand	2.3	3.4	63	76	18	50	7,100	29	86
Singapore	1.3	1.7	73	2	100	11	1,150	66	84
Indochina									
Vietnam	2.7	4.9	64	71	20	53	4,190	48	87
Laos	2.2	6.4	44	75	15	159	n.a.	18	44
Kampuchea	n.a.	n.a.	n.a.	n.a.	n.a.	n.a.	n.a.	n.a.	n.a.
Burma	2.3	5.3	55	67	29	93	4,680	20	66
Indian Sub-Continent									
Bangladesh	2.4	6.0	50	74	17	132	7,810	15	26
India	2.3	4.8	55	71	24	93	3,690	30	36
Pakistan	3.0	5.8	50	57	29	119	3,480	14	24
Sri Lanka	1.7	3.4	69	54	26	37	7,170	54	85
For comparison									
Low-income economies	2.0	4.0	59	73	22	75	5,556	30	n.a.
Middle-income economies	2.4	4.6	61	44	48	75	5,995	42	n.a.

Sources: World Bank, *World Development Report* (1985); Asian Development Bank, *Key Indicators of Developing Member Countries of ADB* (April 1985); Executive Yuan, Taiwan, *Statistical Yearbook of the Republic of China* (1985) and Far Eastern Economic Review. *Asia Yearbook 1985*.

Note: n.a. = not available

9

their emphasis on the non-economic objectives in development, have achieved some social progress at the expense of economic growth.

It follows that rapid economic growth seems to offer the best chance for a poor country to achieve its goals of social development. This is being increasingly recognised by the governments of the Indian Sub-Continent countries, which have accordingly modified their main development strategies in favour of growth. For the relatively high-income NICs and ASEAN, there is still the general perception that continuing high growth is the only means to generate the required resources for meeting the growing material aspirations of their populace. 'Growthmanship' has now spread to virtually all the non-socialist Asian economies.

VI International aspects of Asian economic growth

Except for the socialist or semi-socialist group of economies like the Indochina states which chose to follow a more self-reliant development strategy, international economic forces had played a pivotal role in the growth of the developing market economies, especially for the export-oriented NICs and ASEAN. Even countries on the Indian Sub-Continent, which used to be introverted, have increasingly turned outward-looking. All the NICs and ASEAN have a high export-GDP ratio, as shown in Table 1.1. In brief, trade has been their main engine of growth.

VII Trade patterns

Except for India, Pakistan and Indonesia, all the Asian economies are small to medium size. Small economies are unlikely to be self-contained as economic units, and they have to develop a specialised production structure for the export market in order to exploit their comparative advantage. It can further be argued that the high trade dependency of the Asian economies stemmed from their past colonial legacies. All these countries (except perhaps Thailand which strictly speaking had also been a kind of 'semi-colony') had been (and Hong Kong still is) colonies of the industrial powers. Colonial domination led to the development of 'dependent' production structures in these countries (e.g. the growth of the plantation sector in ASEAN), and rendered their economies oriented towards the industrial countries of the West

TABLE 1.3 FOREIGN TRADE OF ASIAN ECONOMIES

| | Average annual growth rate (%) | | | | Direction of exports (% of total) | | | | | | | |
| | Exports | | Imports | | Industrial market economies | | East European socialist economies | | High income oil exporter | | Developing economies | |
	1965–73	1973–83	1965–73	1973–83	1965	1983	1965	1983	1965	1983	1965	1983
Japan	14.7	7.4	14.9	1.3	49	50	3	2	2	8	47	39
China	n.a.	n.a.	n.a.	n.a.	47	42	12	5	2	2	40	52
North Korea	n.a.	n.a.	n.a.	n.a.	n.a.	n.a.	n.a.	n.a.	n.a.	n.a.	n.a.	n.a.
East Asian NICs												
South Korea	31.7	14.8	22.4	7.5	75	65	0	0	*	10	25	25
Taiwan	31.7	30.8	13.1	1.4	74	71	0	0	n.a.	4	n.a.	25
Hong Kong	11.7	10.3	10.5	12.0	67	61	*	*	1	3	32	35
ASEAN												
Brunei	n.a.	n.a.	n.a.	n.a.	n.a.	n.a.	n.a.	n.a.	n.a.	n.a.	n.a.	n.a.
Indonesia	11.1	1.4	13.9	9.8	72	73	5	1	*	1	23	26
Malaysia	8.0	4.9	4.4	7.3	56	50	7	3	*	1	36	47
Philippines	4.2	7.5	3.1	1.3	95	77	0	2	*	1	5	20
Thailand	6.9	9.0	4.4	3.3	44	56	1	2	2	5	53	37
Singapore	11.0	—	9.8	—	28	42	6	1	2	5	64	52
Indochina												
Vietnam	−7.9	−8.3	−8.9	−4.2	n.a.	n.a.	n.a.	n.a.	n.a.	n.a.	n.a.	n.a.
Laos	n.a.	n.a.	n.a.	n.a.	9	n.a.	0	n.a.	0	n.a.	91	n.a.
Kampuchea	n.a.	n.a.	n.a.	n.a.	36	n.a.	6	n.a.	0	n.a.	58	n.a.
Burma	−4.8	4.9	−6.7	−0.6	29	34	8	3	1	2	62	61
Indian Sub-Continent												
Bangladesh	−6.5	1.7	−8.2	4.1	n.a.	43	n.a.	8	n.a.	1	n.a.	47
India	2.3	4.9	−5.7	2.8	58	55	17	12	2	7	23	26
Pakistan	3.7	8.1	−2.9	5.7	48	35	3	4	4	22	45	39
Sri Lanka	−4.7	2.6	−3.2	4.7	56	46	9	5	3	6	33	44

Sources: World Bank, *World Development Report* (1985); Asian Development Bank, *Key Indicators of Developing Member Countries of ADB* (April 1985); Executive Yuan, Taiwan, *Statistical Yearbook of the Republic of China* (1985) and *Far Eastern Economic Review, Asia Yearbook 1985*.

Note: *Amount insignificant   n.a. = not available

and Japan. Such an orientation has also enabled these trade-oriented Asian economies to obtain access to the markets of the industrially advanced countries.

As can be seen from Table 1.3 the merchandise trade of most of the developing market economies in Asia grew at a high rate in the 1960s and the 1970s, particularly for the NICs. During their period of industrial take-off, 1965–73, South Korea and Taiwan had experienced a phenomenally high rate of export growth of 32% per year. Several ASEAN countries, riding on the crest of the commodity booms in the 1970s, had also registered high trade growth. With the notable exception of Pakistan, trade, however, did not expand so rapidly on the Indian Sub-Continent and some of the countries even experienced a decline over the same period. Clearly the NICs and ASEAN are highly trade-oriented economies with their growth mainly propelled by expansion of exports.

For the non-socialist Asian economies, especially for the NICs and ASEAN, their exports are mainly destined for the markets of the industrial countries of the West and Japan. Such high market concentration on the industrial economies is due to the fact that these advanced countries happen to be the major consumers of the primary commodities from Asia and at the same time provide the main market outlet for the manufactured exports from the latter. In return, the industrial countries supply the Asian economies with most of their requirements of capital goods and consumer durables. Of the markets of the industrial countries, the United States in particular absorbs the bulk of Asia's manufactured exports while Japan alone takes up a large proportion of Asia's primary exports. For most of the non-socialist Asian economies, their strong trade links with the industrial countries thus render them highly vulnerable to the economic fluctuations originating from the latter.

For some Asian countries like Taiwan, South Korea, the Philippines and Indonesia, their market dependence on industrial countries has become excessively high, to the extent of over 70%. This is because Taiwan, South Korea and the Philippines have strong historically-rooted bilateral trade with the United States. Likewise, Indonesia has strong trade links with Japan, which absorbs the bulk of Indonesia's primary exports.

Other countries like Singapore and those on the Indian Sub-

Continent have developed a more diversified trade pattern and hence a relatively lower share in their total trade with the industrial countries. This is because these Asian economies have established stronger trade relations with their neighbours (and hence a higher market share with the developing countries, as can be seen from Table 1.3). The overall trade pattern clearly points to the fact that greater regional trade among the Asian economies will be an effective means for them to diversify their existing market concentration.

VIII Financial flows

Apart from trade, the Asian economies have another critical link to the international economy via a complex system of financial flows. All developing countries are faced with the immense task of mobilising sufficient financial resources to fill their savings and foreign exchange shortfalls if their economies are geared to high growth. It is almost always the case that such additional real resources have to come in the form of external flows, usually from the capital-surplus OECD countries.

As shown in Table 1.4 there has been a very significant increase in the total net financial flows from all sources between 1972 and 1983 for the non-socialist Asian economies. The size of the increase is much larger for ASEAN and the Indian Sub-Continent than for the NICs, indicating that the NICs, on account of their 'graduation' from development, are increasingly more capable of meeting their own financial needs through their domestic savings efforts. Indeed, Taiwan in recent years has become a capital-exporting country as a result of sustained trade surpluses.

The pattern of financial flows to Asia is revealing. Whilst the Indian Sub-Continent and the socialist countries depend almost exclusively on official financial flows in concessional terms (i.e. development assistance) for their external financing, the NICs tend to be much more dependent on private sources of external financial flows. Again this is because the NICs have already progressed to the extent that they are no longer eligible for development assistance. By comparison, ASEAN has a mixture of both official and private financial flows, with these sources complementing one another.

Private financial flows mainly take the form of either foreign private

TABLE 1.4 NET FLOWS OF FINANCIAL RESOURCES

US$ mn	Total net flows from all sources			Official aid from all sources			Net private flows from OECD countries			Net direct foreign investment (US$ mn)	
	1972	1980	1983	1972	1980	1983	1972	1980	1983	1970	1983
East Asia NICs											
South Korea	559	823	1,312	366	139	8	92	236	271	66	−57
Taiwan	192	439	−48	6	−4	8	113	50	−49	n.a.	n.a.
Hong Kong	279	910	1,109	3	11	9	216	879	1,105	n.a.	n.a.
ASEAN											
Indonesia	824	1,180	3,126	503	950	744	242	459	1,584	83	289
Malaysia	212	689	1,760	50	135	178	109	472	1,400	94	1,370
Philippines	217	975	1,576	164	304	424	21	442	289	−29	104
Thailand	47	1,114	1,283	54	418	434	−7	382	250	43	348
Singapore	149	752	184	30	14	15	101	709	216	93	1,389
Indochina											
Kampuchea	66	282	37	67	281	37	−2	1	—	—	—
Laos	68	40	30	67	41	30	2	−1	—	—	—
Vietnam	581	202	90	577	229	106	4	−25	−16	—	—
Burma	51	403	329	44	309	301	5	89	29	—	—
Indian Sub-Continent											
Bangladesh	222	1,259	1,112	224	1,262	1,072	−2	6	6	—	—
India	585	2,517	2,176	614	2,127	1,720	−8	129	163	6	—
Pakistan	268	1,226	775	305	1,040	720	3	114	−10	23	31
Sri Lanka	63	434	537	58	393	470	−2	38	32	0	38

Sources: OECD, *Geographical Distribution of Financial Flows to Developing Countries* (Various Issues), and *World Development Report 1985*.

direct investment or foreign commercial lending, which includes short-term credits from banks and export credit agencies as well as medium-term loans from commercial banks. Because of their open economic structures, the NICs and ASEAN have been able to attract large amounts of external financial flows from private sources. In the NICs, South Korea relies heavily on foreign borrowing while Hong Kong depends on foreign investment. In ASEAN, the Philippines tends to be more dependent on borrowing. In theory, the two are complementary and even substitutable. In practice, the financial flows, given the overall international economic environment, are largely responsive to specific domestic economic policies adopted by the recipient countries.

This raises the pertinent point on the relative advantage of the different external financial flows to the Asian economies. Development assistance or other official financial flows at concessional rates of interest are still the most advantageous form of external financing. However, as the OECD donor countries continue to suffer from their protracted recession and develop into a kind of 'aid fatigue', aid has increasingly become an unreliable source of external development finance, with serious implications for the aid-dependent Indian Sub-Continent. On the other hand, the difficulty of debt servicing in recent years has also cast doubt on the long-term advantage of private borrowing as a source of development finance. This seems to leave foreign investment as a more attractive option for the future and the positive aspects of this vehicle in development have gained increasing recognition in Asia. Some Indian Sub-Continent countries which in the past were not receptive to foreign investment for fear of its negative effects have in recent years turned around to devise policies to attract foreign investment. For the more open and outward-looking NICs and ASEAN, foreign investment has been actively promoted for some time. Foreign investment is viewed not just as a transfer of external financial resources but as a potential contribution to development in terms of technology transfer, improved management knowledge and expansion of export markets. On balance, foreign investment has also responded well to meeting the major economic objectives of these countries, which goes far to explain why the NICs and ASEAN will continue to operate a pro-multinational economic policy.

Much of the foreign investment in the NICs and ASEAN originally stemmed from a colonial background, initially connected with primary resource exploitation and trading. Later, as these countries started their industrialisation, more American capital flowed in so that American

TABLE 1.5   DIRECT INVESTMENT MATRIX OF ASIA, 1980

US$ mn	Japan	USA	Hong Kong	Taiwan	South Korea	Singapore	NICs	Thailand	Malaysia	Philippines	Indonesia	ASEAN	Asia Total
Japan	0.0	1,611.6	73.1	18.9	0.0	0.0	92.0	0.0	0.0	0.0	0.0	0.0	92.0
USA	4,225.0	0.0	0.0	0.0	0.0	0.0	0.0	0.0	0.0	0.0	0.0	0.0	4,225.0
Hong Kong	120.9	218.2	0.0	5.6	0.0	16.0	21.6	13.4	0.0	16.8	0.0	46.2	172.7
Taiwan	457.7	776.3	0.0	0.0	0.0	0.0	0.0	0.0	0.0	0.0	0.0	0.0	457.7
South Korea	612.3	231.8	12.5	0.6	0.0	0.0	13.1	0.0	0.0	0.0	0.0	0.0	625.4
Singapore	517.5	957.8	0.0	0.0	0.0	0.0	0.0	0.0	0.0	0.0	0.0	0.0	517.5
NICs	1,708.4	2,184.1	12.5	6.2	0.0	16.0	34.7	13.4	0.0	16.8	0.0	46.2	1,773.3
Thailand	76.6	28.3	17.2	31.5	0.0	3.2	51.9	0.0	7.8	0.9	0.0	11.9	137.2
Malaysia	225.9	79.7	119.0	0.0	0.0	277.1	396.1	0.0	0.0	0.0	0.0	277.1	622.0
Philippines	299.1	752.1	84.2	4.2	6.0	12.7	107.1	0.0	0.0	0.0	0.0	12.7	406.2
Indonesia	3,372.4	575.2	1,062.3	128.6	84.8	145.1	1,420.8	0.0	60.4	292.6	0.0	498.1	5,146.2
ASEAN	4,491.5	2,393.1	1,282.7	164.3	90.8	438.1	1,975.9	0.0	68.2	293.5	0.0	799.8	6,829.1
ASIA TOTAL	5,682.4	5,231.0	1,368.3	189.4	90.8	454.1	2,102.6	13.4	68.2	310.3	0.0	846.0	8,176.9

Source: 'Direct Investment in the Pacific Basin: Interim Report', prepared by the Direct Investment Task Force chaired by Sueo Sekiguchi, Japan Center for International Exchange, Tokyo (April 15, 1983).

Notes: Inflow investment in home currency terms are converted into US dollars at the year-average exchange rates. Adding these figures to the 1976–end amount, cumulated approval or cumulated investment levels for 1980 were calculated. Figures for Malaysia are for the year 1979.

interests soon came to dominate foreign economic sectors in these countries. In recent years a growing Japanese presence has been felt. In fact, in some countries Japanese investment has already become predominant, and this trend is bound to accelerate as Japan continues to expand its economic influence in Asia. (See Table 1.5.) Another emerging trend, now already visible, is the increasing flow of foreign capital from the NICs to ASEAN and, in future, to the Indian Sub-Continent as well. Such an increase in inter-regional flow of resources will bring about greater economic integration in Asia.

IX   Growth and interdependence

It thus becomes clear that most non-socialist Asian economies, in varying degrees, are drawn into the international economy by an intricate web of trade, capital, finance and technology. For the high-performance economies of the NICs and ASEAN, their linkages with the international economy at large are especially strong and extensive, which they have forged by consistently maintaining an open and outward-looking development strategy. In pursuit of such an outer-directed development policy, these Asian economies have been able to capture the forces of international capitalism to maximise their growth potentials through utilising capital, technology and market outlet of the advanced capitalist economies.

The structure of the international economic system since the 1970s has actually undergone tremendous transformation, and changes are reflected in the emerging pattern of economic relationship between the Asian economies and the developed countries. Prior to the 1970s, the economies of the NICs and ASEAN, closely tied to the economic system of the developed countries, virtually swung with the latter in the process of growth and fluctuation. Thus between 1960 and 1970, when the developed countries as a group grew at the average rate of 5.1%, the NICs and ASEAN grew respectively at 9.1% and 5.8%, giving the NICs and ASEAN a margin of 4.0% and 0.7% over the developed countries. But when the economic growth of the developed countries plummeted to 2.4% during 1970–82, the NICs and ASEAN were still able to maintain growth at the average rates of 8.4% and 6.7% respectively, thereby increasing the spreads to 6.0% and 4.3%. This serves to indicate that economic growth of the NICs and ASEAN is not wholly dependent on the progress of developed countries.

The structure of Asia's economic dependence on the industrial

17

economies was radically transformed during the turbulent 1970s, when the world economy was hit by a series of economic crises. Figure 1.2 brings out the interesting interaction of the growth patterns of the Asian economies *vis-à-vis* that of the industrial countries. First, as growth of the US and Japanese economies collapsed in the early 1970s after being severely hit by the world's first oil shock, economic growth of the NICs also dipped but did not break down while the ASEAN economies emerged from the oil crisis unscathed as they were actually accelerating their growth on the back of the raw material boom and high energy prices. Secondly, the same pattern repeated itself during the second world oil crisis in the late 1970s. By this time, however, there had been basic changes in the international economic system with the emergence of economic superpowers: Western Europe and Japan. Consequently, these sectors became the focus of attention for trade, in particular ASEAN. This was clearly demonstrated during 1980–81 when the US economy turned into a nose-dive whereas the ASEAN economies were still on the relatively high growth track, at least in part fuelled by continuing good performance of the Japanese economy.

The growth pattern of the Indian Sub-Continent economies is, as to be expected, different from the NICs and ASEAN. As a result of pursuing a more diverse export strategy (i.e. less trade dependence on developed countries) these economies have followed a low level of stable growth—though India as a net importer of oil and food did experience considerable difficulties during the first oil crisis. Once these economies started to open up in the early 1980s, they too were susceptible to adverse international economic conditions and their growth similarly came down.

Chapter Two

REGIONAL OVERVIEW

This chapter serves to highlight the salient features of the patterns of growth and development of the different groups of Asian economies.

I Export-oriented growth of the NICs and ASEAN

The dynamic economies of the NICs and ASEAN have followed an open, outward-looking strategy which has enabled them to maximise their economic growth potential through reaping the gains from trade and specialisation. Given their internal economic constraints (e.g. small domestic markets) and the existing international economic conditions, such a development strategy may be considered optimal for them, and their past records of growth performance have eminently proved this.

It should, however, be stressed that export orientation by itself may be a necessary but not a sufficient condition to induce growth. An economy can grow only when the endogenous conditions are also conducive. The 'missing link' is found in such direct determinants of economic growth as the appropriate rates of capital formation and technological progress. These Asian economies have succeeded in recording high growth precisely because they were not lacking in those favourable 'real' factors of growth.

As shown in Table 2.1, the NICs and ASEAN in 1983 committed a high proportion of their GDP to domestic investment, ranging from the unusually high rate of 45% for Singapore to the still high 24% for Indonesia. These economies have in fact consistently maintained high levels of domestic investment during the past decade or so, as reflected also in their high rates of growth of investment, 1973–83. Furthermore, their gross domestic investment is matched mostly by their equally high rates of domestic savings. Where the difference exists, the 'resource gap' is filled by the inflow of foreign capital, mainly in the form of either direct foreign investment (as for Singapore, Indonesia and Malaysia) or foreign borrowing (as for South Korea and the Philippines). And the operation of an outward-looking development strategy has made it possible for such inflows of external financial resources.

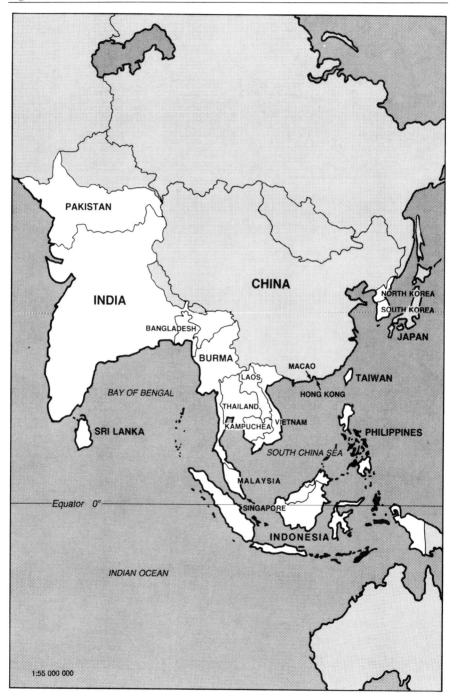

TABLE 2.1   SAVINGS AND INVESTMENT OF THE ASIAN ECONOMIES

% of GDP

	Gross domestic investment		Gross domestic savings		Resource gap		Average annual growth of domestic investment (%)
	1965	1983	1965	1983	1965	1983	1973–83
North Korea	n.a.	n.a.	n.a.	n.a.	n.a.	n.a.	n.a.
NICs							
South Korea	15	27	8	26	−7	−1	9.1
Taiwan	17	26	20	29	3	3	8.0
Hong Kong	36	27	29	25	−7	−2	10.8
ASEAN							
Brunei	n.a.	n.a.	n.a.	n.a.	n.a.	n.a.	n.a.
Indonesia	7	24	6	20	−1	−4	12.3
Malaysia	18	34	23	29	5	−5	11.9
Philippines	21	27	21	21	0	−6	7.3
Thailand	20	25	19	20	−1	−5	6.2
Singapore	22	45	10	42	−12	−3	9.2
Indochina							
Vietnam	n.a.	n.a.	n.a.	n.a.	n.a.	n.a.	n.a.
Laos	n.a.	n.a.	n.a.	n.a.	n.a.	n.a.	n.a.
Kampuchea	n.a.	n.a.	n.a.	n.a.	n.a.	n.a.	n.a.
Burma	19	22	13	17	−6	−5	14.1
Indian Sub-Continent							
Bangladesh	11	17	8	2	−4	−15	4.2
India	18	25	16	22	−2	−3	4.2
Pakistan	21	17	13	7	−8	−11	4.9
Sri Lanka	12	29	13	14	1	−15	15.7
For comparison							
Low-income economies (excl. China and India)	15	13	11	17	−4	4	4.4
High middle-income economies	23	22	24	23	1	1	3.8

Sources: *World Development Report* 1985; and *Statistical Yearbook of the Republic of China*, 1985.

It is relevant to note that the pattern of savings and investment for the different groups of Asian economies is quite closely correlated to the pattern of their economic growth. Thus it can be seen that the high rates of economic growth in the NICs have been sustained by their high levels of savings and investment. On the other hand, the low levels of savings and investment for the Indian Sub-Continent correpond to their low rates of economic growth.

As a result of sustained growth, the economies of the NICs and ASEAN have undergone significant structural changes, marked by a

TABLE 2.2   STRUCTURAL TRANSFORMATION OF THE ASIAN ECONOMIES

Sectoral share of GDP, %									Value-added in manufacturing (mn 1975 US$)		Manufacturing export as % of total exports
	Agriculture		Industry		Manufacturing		Services				
	1965	1983	1965	1983	1965	1983	1965	1983	1970	1982	1982
NICs											
South Korea	38	14	25	39	18	27	37	47	2,368	11,492	88
Taiwan	24	7	30	45	26	40	46	48	n.a.	n.a.	90
Hong Kong	2	1	40	30	24	22	58	69	1,914	3,679	92
ASEAN											
Indonesia	59	26	12	39	8	13	29	35	1,517	6,072	4
Malaysia	30	21	24	35	10	19	45	44	1,022	3,287	23
Philippines	26	22	28	36	20	25	46	42	2,659	5,510	50
Thailand	35	23	23	27	14	19	45	44	1,675	4,837	29
Singapore	3	1	24	37	15	24	73	62	827	2,431	57
Indochina											
Burma	35	48	13	13	9	9	52	39	287	496	8
Indian Sub-Continent											
Bangladesh	53	47	11	13	—	—	36	40	647	1,294	54
India	47	36	22	26	15	15	31	38	10,232	16,210	45
Pakistan	40	27	20	27	14	19	40	46	1,492	2,967	59
Sri Lanka	28	27	21	26	17	14	51	47	556	748	27

Sources: *World Development Report*, various years. For Taiwan, *Statistical Yearbook of the Republic of China*, (1985).

sharp rise of the manufacturing and modern service sectors at the expense of the traditional primary sector, as shown in Table 2.2. At this point the NICs start to show substantial structural difference from ASEAN in both quantity and quality aspects. The NICs have built up a much bigger manufacturing sector than ASEAN, particularly for Taiwan and South Korea whose manufacturing sector in 1983 accounted for 40% and 27% of GDP respectively. In the case of Hong Kong and Singapore there is already a diversification of manufacturing activities into modern services (e.g. banking and finances). But in ASEAN, with the exception of the Philippines, the primary sector remains dominant. In fact, industrialisation in the NICs markedly differs from that of ASEAN and the Indian Sub-Continent in scale, intensity and in its nature. The manufacturing activities of the NICs are primarily export-oriented. This is reflected in the extremely high proportion of manufactured goods in the total exports of the NICs: 88%, 90% and 92% for South Korea, Taiwan and Hong Kong respectively. The proportions for ASEAN and South Asia are generally smaller.

II Industrialisation processes

A few Asian countries started their industrialisation as early as in the 1950s. India and the Philippines launched their industrialisation programmes shortly after their independence, though real progress was achieved much later. Hong Kong commenced industrialisation in the early 1950s when its traditional role as an entrepôt trade centre for China was brought to an abrupt end with the formation of the People's Republic of China in 1949. The other NICs started their industrialisation drive in the early 1960s, built up momentum in the late 1960s or early 1970s, and sustained it through the 1970s. The other ASEAN countries started to industrialise in earnest somewhat later, and that associated with the Indian Sub-Continent is a relatively recent phenomenon.

For most Asian economies, as for many other developing countries, industrialisation is not simply an option but a necessity. It was mounted in order to provide a 'dynamic' and a more stable source of economic growth. This was clearly the case for the resource-poor NICs. For the resource-rich ASEAN countries, industrialisation was introduced as economic diversification measures for the purpose of reducing their dependence on primary exports, which was widely considered undesirable because of the price fluctuation of primary commodities as well as the potential deterioration in their terms of trade. For the densely populated countries of the Indian Sub-Continent industrialisation was primarily promoted in order to create employment for their rapidly growing labour force.

With the exception of Hong Kong, all the Asian economies started industrialisation with import substitution. Today some countries of the Indian Sub-Continent are still trapped in this phase of industrial development while the more successful ASEAN countries have already made the transition from import substitution to export expansion. But the NICs have progressed even further in building up an internationally-competitive manufacturing sector.

TABLE 2.3   CHANGING STRUCTURE OF ASIA'S MERCHANDISE EXPORTS

% share of total merchandise exports

	Fuels, minerals & metals		Other primary commodities		Textiles & clothing		Machinery & transport equipment		Other manu- factures	
	1960	1982	1960	1982	1960	1982	1960	1982	1960	1982
NICs										
South Korea	30	1	56	7	8	21	*	28	6	43
Taiwan	1	—	49	—	30	—	7	—	13	—
Hong Kong	5	2	15	6	45	34	4	19	31	39
ASEAN										
Indonesia	33	85	67	11	0	1	*	1	*	2
Malaysia	20	35	74	42	*	3	*	15	6	5
Philippines	10	12	86	38	1	7	0	3	3	39
Thailand	7	7	91	64	0	10	0	6	2	13
Singapore	1	30	73	13	5	4	7	26	14	28
Indochina										
Burma	4	—	95	—	0	—	0	—	1	—
Indian Sub-Continent										
Bangladesh	—	2	—	36	—	47	—	4	—	11
India	10	7	45	33	22	24	1	7	9	19
Pakistan	0	6	73	34	23	46	1	2	3	12
Sri Lanka	*	14	99	59	0	17	0	2	1	8

Sources: *World Development Report* 1983 and 1985; For Taiwan, *Statistical Yearbook of the Republic of China* (1985).

Note: *Amount not significant

Table 2.3 serves to bring out the structural transformation of the manufacturing sector of the Asian countries as reflected in the changing composition of their exports. Thus the NICs, starting off on labour-intensive manufactures, primarily textiles and clothing, are now diversifying into more capital- and skill-intensive activities, as manifested in the rise of the share for 'machinery and transport equipment' in their export trade. On the other hand, the manufacturing exports of the Indian Sub-Continent are still heavily concentrated in the labour-intensive products, although India is exporting some capital-intensive items. It appears that some NICs, especially Hong Kong, still retain a large textiles and clothing sector, which is, however, structurally different from that in existence in the Indian Sub-Continent. The textiles industry is also capable of technical progress in terms of sophisticated production process and innovative designs. In reality, the East Asian textiles industry is increasingly moving into high value-added and less labour-intensive activities. It is these efficient producers (East Asian) who have actually posed a threat to the textiles industry in the advanced countries, prompting trade protective measures from the latter.

III East Asian NICs

Rapid industrialisation of the NICs is a classic case of the dynamic process of capital accumulation. As noted earlier, the NICs mobilised tremendous resources, both domestic and external, to capital investment in order to fuel their industrial expansion. Fixed investment embodying new and more productive technology thus became the driving force of their industrial growth. In this way, they built up their export-oriented manufacturing sector.

Capital must be combined with labour, in its required quantity and quality. All along the NICs have depended on upgrading their human resources as a means to overcome the shortages of natural resources by emphasising education and training. Over the years along with the industrialisation process and growing modern sector employment, the NICs have succeeded in building up a pool of skilled labour, highly intelligent and trainable. The high level of human resource development of the NICs can be easily inferred from the social indicators in Table 1.4 (e.g. their high adult literacy rates). It may further be suggested that Confucianist values, with their stress on hard work, thriftiness and self-improvement, have contributed significantly to the qualitative enhancement of the labour force of the NICs. Hence also their high labour productivity.

The success of the NICs in their human resource development is manifested not just in their pool of skilled labour, but also in the availability of a large number of good entrepreneurs. The supply of entrepreneurship is admittedly conditioned by some very complex institutional and cultural factors. Suffice it to say that these East Asian societies have very open social structures (much so in comparison with those on the Indian Sub-Continent) and permit easy upward social mobility through the accumulation of wealth. Business success and rewards from risk taking are well protected—the NICs have no capital gains tax. In short, the NICs have built-in institutional and social conditions conducive to the operation of dynamic entrepreneurship. This is especially true of Hong Kong and Taiwan where the export drives are typically mounted by numerous small- to medium-size firms under conditions of high risk and uncertainty. The exports they handle have short product cycles (e.g. consumer electronics) or are subject to frequent changes in style and fashion (e.g. clothing).

In accounting for the industrialisation success (or the lack of it) of the Asian economies, the vital institutional preconditions should not be left out. Hong Kong is still a British colony, with its *laissez-faire* form of industrialisation deriving little direct support from government or political structure. Stripped of all the political rhetoric, the political systems of these NICs are actually not truly democratic in the Western sense, with the overall political style tending to be, in varying degrees, authoritarian in character. Conversely some countries in the Indian Sub-Continent have indeed followed closely the Westminster-style of democracy; but their political structures tend to consume too much social energy in contentious politics, instead of providing a consensus for rapid economic development.

In contrast, the political leaderships of the NICs have a strong sense of purpose and are highly committed to the single-minded pursuit of economic growth. In South Korea, for instance, real power is in the hands of the military, who may be high-handed at times but mostly pragmatic and managerial in character. Lack of political participation is amply compensated for by more social and economic freedom, which is, after all, more relevant for industrial development. At the same time, the political leaderships are under constant pressure to 'perform' and 'to deliver the goods' in terms of higher GNP growth and more export

26

markets, and this they have accomplished with the support from elites as well as the numerous technocrats.

Along with the spread of education the governments of the NICs have become increasingly technocratic. Some of the crucial policy break-throughs were actually the product of sound technocratic decisions, e.g. the shift towards an outward-looking strategy in Korea's First Five-Year Economic Development Plan, 1962–66 and the establishment of Taiwan's first Export Processing Zone in Kaoshiung in 1965. Today, indefatigable technocrats are posted to manage export growth by assisting the private sector in developing new markets and improving their international competitiveness. In Indian Sub-Continent countries, by comparison, much of their institutional and bureaucratic resources are dissipated unproductively in managing foreign exchange control, licensing systems and the like, which are created to maintain the inward-looking import substitution industries.

IV ASEAN

Though the level and intensity of industrialisation vary among the ASEAN countries, they have followed broadly similar patterns of industrial development. They all started off with a small industrial base, composed of a variety of food processing and traditional resource-based industries. Except for Thailand, all the ASEAN countries were under long periods of colonial rule, existing primarily to serve as sources of raw materials for the industrial countries. Serious attempts at industrial-isation were only made after they had gained independence. And they all began with the import substitution strategy.

The Philippines led the industrialisation of the region by setting up import-substituting industries in the early 1950s. But its domestic industries, under conditions of heavy protection and price distortion, soon exhausted their growth potentials and became stagnant. It was not till the early 1970s when the Philippine economy was re-oriented outward that the manufacturing sector started to take off.

Both Malaysia and Thailand launched their import substitution industrialisation endeavours around 1960, but the growth momentum gathered only in the 1970s when a clear switch-over to export orientation was made. By comparison, Indonesia was a late-comer to the industrialisation scene, and serious efforts at industrialisation were attempted only in the early 1970s when stable conditions were established. Because of its large domestic market, industrial development in Indonesia was exclusively import-substituting in nature, and it has only been during the last few years, after a sharp decline in the oil revenue, that the Indonesian industries have started to adopt an outward-looking orientation.

It thus becomes clear that the critical juncture in the industrialisation processes of the ASEAN countries was not the initial launching of their respective national industrialisation programmes but rather their adoption of the export-oriented strategies. In the Philippines, this crucial policy departure can be traced to the Export Incentives Act of 1970, and to the Investment Incentives Act of 1968 for Malaysia and the Export Promotion Act of 1972 for Thailand. It should be noted that the adoption of export orientation for the ASEAN countries did not mean outright abandonment of import substitution, which continued to exist in a parallel fashion. But once export-oriented industries were established, they produced dynamic effects on the less efficient import substituting industries through resource reallocation.

Why have the ASEAN countries started the transition from import substitution to export expansion earlier than many 'Less Developed Countries' (LDCs), especially those in the Indian Sub-Continent? One of the reasons has been the level of foreign investment. Virtually all the important export-oriented industries of ASEAN such as the electronics components industries in Malaysia and the textiles industry in Thailand were set up by foreign investors. It may be argued that part of ASEAN's manufactured exports represents merely 'intra-firm trade' on the part of the multinationals and its effects on the domestic economies of ASEAN are certainly less 'dynamic' than if it were carried out by local entrepreneurs as in Hong Kong and Taiwan. Nonetheless, any export activity will carry direct and indirect spillovers to the economy just the same.

V Indian Sub-Continent

These countries are economically and socially diverse, although they all share one common feature of having low per-capita income, ranging from $130 for Bangladesh to $390 for Pakistan for the year 1983. Low average incomes generally mean a low level of development. Thus on the whole these economies are less developed than those in Southeast

Asia and much more so than those in East Asia. However, per-capita income companions often do injustice to big economies like India and Pakistan and belie their considerable domestic industrial capacity. Indeed, some parts of India and Pakistan are quite well-developed while certain industries in India are technically quite sophisticated and even internationally competitive.

Two characteristics pervade all the Indian Sub-Continent countries which have retarded economic growth and industrial exports. The first is the dominance of agriculture in these economies, as reflected in its high sectoral share, from 47% for Bangladesh, 36% for India, to 27% each for Pakistan and Sri Lanka (Table 2.2). In terms of the labour force, the share for agriculture is even higher, ranging from 93% for Nepal to 54% for Sri Lanka.

The second important common feature of the economies is the high degree of government involvement in economic activity. All these economies take to some form of planning as their main development strategies with the state playing a particularly dominant role in the manufacturing sector. Thus state enterprises have proliferated in every aspect of economic life. Where the private sector has been allowed to exist, it has been subject to extensive government regulations and control. This, coupled with the import-substitution nature strategies, has been mainly responsible for the past poor performance of their manufacturing sectors.

In recent years two encouraging trends have emerged in the region providing a platform for sustained growth. First, there has been consistently good performance in the agricultural sector for most of the economies, thanks to the success of the Green Revolution. Apart from some cash crops like tea, jute, sugar and cotton, which are produced for the international markets, agricultural activities in the region are mainly concerned with food crop production for peasant subsistence. It is in food crop production that some marked technical transformation, in terms of wider adoption of high yielding varieties and more uses of modern inputs for production, has occurred during the past decade.

As shown in Table 2.4, rice productivity in East Asia is much higher than in the rest of the region; but agriculture is no longer an important sector in the economies of the NICs. In ASEAN, Thailand is the only large food surplus country while Indonesia used to be the largest importer of rice. For years, the Indian Sub-Continent had been a net

TABLE 2.4   GENERAL AGRICULTURAL PERFORMANCE INDICATORS

	Yield of rice (kg per ha)			General index of agricultural production (1974–76 = 100)			General index of per-capita food production (1974–76 = 100)		
	1975	**1980**	**1984**	**1975**	**1980**	**1984**	**1975**	**1980**	**1984**
East Asia									
South Korea	5,324	4,308	6,142	101	105	125	101	105	125
Taiwan	4,135	4,837	4,463	96	113	115	n.a.	n.a.	n.a.
ASEAN									
Indonesia	2,630	3,293	3,978	101	127	149	100	115	127
Malaysia	2,661	3,205	2,961	98	117	134	99	107	113
Philippines	1,721	2,155	2,470	102	128	135	101	112	108
Thailand	1,825	1,909	1,811	101	120	134	102	108	112
Indochina									
Kampuchea	1,429	1,470	1,700	105	85	92	106	97	92
Laos	1,338	1,441	1,639	97	136	153	98	93	122
Vietnam	2,183	2,106	2,483	97	126	139	97	112	113
Burma	1,816	2,774	3,077	101	126	154	101	109	124
South Asia									
Bangladesh	1,853	2,020	2,000	105	119	123	105	103	96
India	1,858	2,000	2,103	105	114	135	105	102	114
Pakistan	2,296	2,424	2,625	99	119	134	99	101	101
Sri Lanka	1,933	2,590	3,133	100	140	131	100	145	120

Source: *Key Indicators of Developing Member Countries of ADB*, 1985.

food importer. The most significant event in the agricultural and rural development of Asia during recent years has been the success of Indonesia and India, Asia's two largest countries after China, in reaching self-sufficiency in food production. Per-capita food production in Indonesia has grown by 27% and in India by 14% over the last few years. In the case of India, it has attained not just food self-sufficiency but also some degree of food security, with its agricultural production becoming less vulnerable to adverse weather changes. This is due to the increased area under irrigation as well as more extensive application of such modern inputs as chemical fertilisers. For such a big and heavily populated country as India, improvement of agricultural productivity and then the overall increase in agricultural surplus will provide a strong and stable base for industrialisation. This is actually the route to development which Meiji Japan took a century ago.

A second promising development has taken place in the industrial sector. Gradually the governments of the Indian Sub-Continent have become aware of the need for more liberalisation of their economies by exposing them to the world economic forces and giving a little more scope to private enterprises. In India, for example, a number of measures has been taken to revitalise the manufacturing sector through simplifying licensing procedures and minimising physical controls. More foreign firms are now allowed to operate in areas where they were formerly barred, so as to create a competitive environment for domestic industries. Import controls have also been liberalised while more export incentives are offered. The overall objective is to quicken the transition from import substitution to export expansion. Measures of liberalisation in different forms have also been introduced in other countries in the region.

VI Indochina

In this group Burma stands apart from the rest of the countries in that it has not been ravaged by war and has been left alone to pursue its own pattern of self-reliant development. For almost three decades, the Burma economy chose to divorce itself from the international economy as a result of its following the 'Burmese way to socialism'. In recent years, Burma (which is essentially a primary producing country) has gradually reoriented its economy outward in order to exploit its natural comparative advantage in the international commodity markets for higher economic growth. The process of liberalising and opening up the Burma economy, though just at its beginning, has already made its impact on the economy, with its steady rate of 5–6% growth. This trend is expected to continue, though it will mean a further dilution of the original socialist ideals once cherished by the country's leaders. Burma's past development experience has amply demonstrated that it is difficult to devise an effective strategy which can maximise growth within a socialist framework.

The lesson of Burma should be instructive for the socialist countries in Indochina, which share a great deal of structural similarity. They are all in urgent need of mobilising sufficient resources for the reconstruction of infrastructure in order to speed up the rehabilitation of their economies. Their export trade has not yet returned to normal, although their agricultural sector, especially rice production, has substantially recovered. Industrial development is still patchy. In the context of Asia's overall industrialisation progress, the Indochina states are destined to be the late late-comers.

EAST ASIA

Taiwan
Hong Kong
North Korea
South Korea
Macao

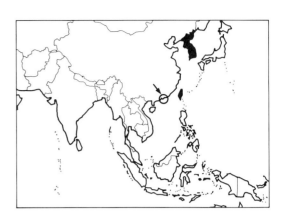

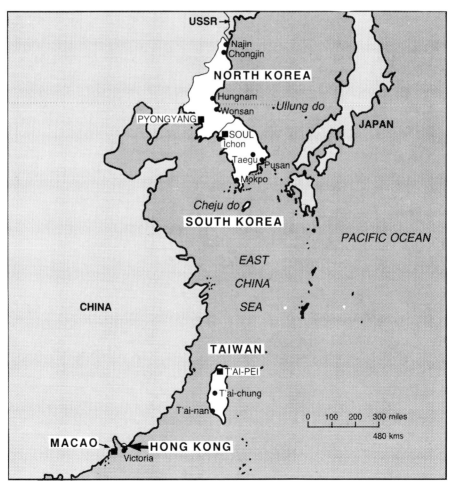

Chapter Three

EAST ASIA

I Overview

Four of the five countries covered in this chapter publish ample national statistics to demonstrate economic growth that is among the fastest on record anywhere in the world today. Continued export-led growth is the main theme apparent in the region, where industrialists have shown an extraordinary ability to adapt new products to cope with changing market conditions overseas. They have sold these at prices that competitors elsewhere have found hard to match. Most currencies are tied to the US dollar, and the weakness of this in 1986 augurs well for continued expansion. Proximity to, and the opening up of, the Chinese market has provided a further spur for growth.

Although the national populations are growing rapidly, living standards are in general at least keeping up, and notable real increases in expenditure on such services as education and health are taking place.

Most governments exhibit stability, and there was a considerable fillip to confidence in 1985 when the Anglo-Chinese settlement was reached over the future of Hong Kong. However, any future political changes in China could have a big impact on the region.

II Population

Although these countries have made great economic progress over the last 25 years, their population characteristics (density and demographic characteristics) place them firmly in the developing country category. Only in North Korea is the population density on a par with that of industrialised Western countries, while Hong Kong and Macao are amongst the most densely populated countries in the world. The populations in each country are increasing rapidly, and a high proportion are under-fives.

33

TABLE 3.1   AREA, POPULATION AND POPULATION DENSITIES

	Year	Area (sq. km.)	Population	Population density per sq. km.
Hong Kong	1984	1,045	5,364,000	5,133.0
Macao	1983	16	350,000*	>20,000
North Korea	1986	120,538	20,543,000†	170.4
South Korea	1984	99,117	41,209,000	415.8
Taiwan	1984	36,000	19,012,512	528.1

Source: National Statistics
Notes: *Due to migration unofficial estimates vary widely
          †Estimate

Hong Kong

The most recent census to be held in Hong Kong took place in 1981, but accurate estimates have been made regularly since, partly because the rate of increase is a source of concern to the authorities, and the number of transient people (excluded in the totals) is monitored closely. Of the 4,986,560 counted in 1981 (377,440 less than 1984) 2,604,168 were males and 2,382,392 were females. The rate of natural increase in 1984 was 9.7/1,000, approximately the same level being maintained since 1975, although in 1979–1981 a much higher rate was recorded due to immigration. Housing 72.9% of the population (1981), Hong Kong Island and Kowloon together constitute one of the densest urban concentrations to be found anywhere in the world. Just under one-quarter of the population are under 15.

A figure of 3% unemployed is considered full employment in Hong Kong, and in 1984 this was very nearly achieved when 3.5% was recorded (4.2% of economically active males and 3.4% females). In 1975 only 2.8% were unemployed. As Table 3.2 shows, a high proportion is employed in the manufacturing industries, particularly textiles, apparel, plastic goods and electrical equipment (the total labour force in 1984 was 2,606,200); other major sectors in 1984 were general services (470,400), construction (205,500), wholesale/retail trade and catering (570,000), transport and communications (206,200) and financial services (135,800). The government workforce in 1984 was 172,390.

The most significant trend in manufacturing employment in the 1980s has been the increase in apparel and electrical equipment employment as the value-added content of industrial output has increased; production of basic items like textiles and fabricated metal structures has been in relative decline. Hong Kong is now one of the world's top fashion centres.

TABLE 3.2   HONG KONG: MANUFACTURING EMPLOYMENT

'000s	1981	1982	1983	1984
Food, beverages and tobacco	22.3	24.1	22.9	22.6
Apparel (excluding footwear)	258.3	251.4	256.4	265.3
Footwear	8.1	7.3	6.6	7.8
Leather products (excluding apparel and footwear)	3.7	2.8	3.1	3.4
Textiles	123.4	111.6	111.8	115.4
Wood and cork products	18.1	16.0	14.6	14.3
Paper and products	12.0	12.3	11.9	13.0
Printing and publishing	28.3	27.9	28.4	29.2
Chemicals, petroleum and products	8.2	8.2	8.5	8.4
Rubber products	4.4	3.5	2.9	3.1
Plastic products	89.1	83.0	82.7	92.3
Minerals	4.9	4.4	4.5	4.2
Basic metals	4.7	4.5	3.5	3.5
Fabricated metal products (excluding machinery and equipment)	82.1	73.5	66.5	67.6
Machinery (excluding electrical)	14.8	14.5	17.8	20.0
Electrical machinery and apparatus	124.1	118.8	131.3	143.9
Transport equipment	15.8	18.1	15.2	13.8
Precision equipment (including photographic)	48.3	44.8	46.7	46.0
Other	33.9	29.3	29.4	30.7
TOTAL	904.6	856.1	865.1	904.7

Source: National Statistics

Macao

The exceptionally high population density recorded for Macao has to be treated with caution because measurement is not as precise as in the

Crown Colony, and there is at any one time a very large number of transients within the territory, mostly Chinese. There is also a large number of Hong Kong citizens temporarily resident within Macao, many of these entering and exiting via China. Unofficial estimates of the population of Macao therefore vary widely; the latest official figures state that 92.5% of the population live in Macao city.

TABLE 3.3 MACAO: MIGRATION BY SOURCE AND DESTINATION

'000s

	1982		1983	
	In	Out	In	Out
People's Republic of China	4,222.4	4,198.6	4,679.3	4,754.0
Portugal	155.6	157.1	169.1	170.6
Other	609.3	602.7	657.2	648.8
TOTAL	4,987.3	4,958.4	5,505.6	5,573.4

Source: National Statistics

Throughout the 1980s the number of births has exceeded deaths by a wide margin; in 1983 6,168 babies were born and 1,514 deaths took place, but these figures only cover registered citizens. Considerable concern is being expressed about the laxity of immigration controls in Macao, because it is believed that many Hong Kong citizens will be able to acquire Portuguese passports, and thereby gain access to the EEC, as 1997 draws nearer.

In view of the uncertainty about Macao's actual population, no unemployment level can be given, but it is certainly low. An estimated 60% of the economically active population work in the service sector, the great majority of the remainder in manufacturing.

North Korea

Very little information is available about the population of North Korea, but it is certainly well in excess of 20 mn. The rate of increase is thought to be in the range 2.4% per annum, approximately equal to that of India and well ahead of that of the ASEAN countries. The overall density is relatively low, but there are large areas sparsely inhabited due to climate and terrain. Also it has to be remembered that there is a 1,260 km² demilitarised zone between the two halves of the peninsula (not counted in the area of either North or South Korea in this review).

According to UN estimates the average annual birth rate in the period 1975–1980 was 32.5 per 1,000, with a death rate of 8.3 per 1,000.

The estimated labour force of North Korea in 1981 was 8,222,000 (1983 estimate 8.7 mn) of which about 49% were engaged in agriculture (43.2% in 1983), 33% in mining, manufacturing and construction, and 18% in services.

South Korea

Of the total population recorded in 1984, 20,798,000 were males and 20,410,000 females. The rate of increase officially recorded for 1984 was 15.3 per 1,000, a fairly steady decline having taken place since the 30.1 per 1,000 recorded in 1961. According to the 1980 census results 45.1% of the population were aged less than 20, and 10.1% were below five. Many more children are undoubtedly surviving the early years, because in 1949 the corresponding figures were 51.6% and 29.1%.

In 1984 the South Korean unemployment level stood at 3.4%, which if sustained will be well within the current Plan target of 4% for 1986. The economically active population is noted for the level of skill it has attained, and for its adaptability. In 1984 the working population was 14,417,000 (35% of the total), and of these 3,909,000 were employed in agriculture, 142,000 in mining, 3,351,000 in manufacturing, 36,000 in utilities supply, 3,148,000 in various forms of trade, 663,000 in transport and communications, 500,000 in the provision of financial services and 1,765,000 in social/personal services. In addition there were 903,000 employees in the construction industry in 1984, and this figure excludes the large workforce employed abroad; South Korea is the home of some of the largest civil engineering firms in the world. The manufacturing workforce has grown through the 1980s; in most other sectors there has been a decline.

Taiwan

The breakdown of Taiwan's latest population figure is 9,875,000 males and 9,137,000 females, increasing at a rate of 1.49% each year. This rate of increase has been falling steadily since the mid-1960s, when it was over 3% per annum, due to higher educational standards and a trend towards rapid urbanisation. Around 50% of the population now live in cities of more than 100,000 people, the population of Taipei having risen from 1,085,000 in 1964 to 2,450,000 in 1984. Over the same period the expectation of life at birth has also increased substantially, from 63.8 years to 70.5 years for males. Females can expect to live five years longer.

Table 3.4 shows the changes in employment by sector that have taken place since 1965, the main features being the huge increase in the manufacturing workforce, and also in the service sectors. Due to mechanisation the agricultural workforce has dropped markedly at the same time as food output has grown substantially.

Estimates of the proportion of the economically active population who are unemployed in Taiwan vary according to the definition applied, but in 1984 it was in the range 2.4–3.4%, the same level as recorded in 1975. In the late 1970s the level of unemployment was well below this, but Taiwan's export industries have subsequently been suffering from increased protectionist trends in world trade.

TABLE 3.4   TAIWAN: EMPLOYMENT BY CATEGORY

'000s	1965	1984
Agriculture, forestry and fishing	1,748	1,286
Mining and quarrying	82	41
Manufacturing	612	2,494
Utilities	15	34
Construction	130	521
Business and commerce	429	1,462
Transport and communications	179	378
Government and social services	568	1,092
TOTAL	3,763	7,308

Source: National Statistics

III   Government policy

Political stability over a long period of time has been an important factor behind the economic success of this grouping of countries. There is no guarantee that this will continue, notably in the cases of South Korea and Taiwan, and doubts persist about the continuation of present economic policies in China; it has been Beijing's liberalisation of trading relations that has allowed so much entrepôt trade development to take place in the region over the last ten years.

Hong Kong

Undoubtedly the key development that has restored confidence to the economy of Hong Kong is the Anglo-Chinese agreement ratified in June 1985; the colony is now in a transition period which will lead to full sovereignty being restored in 1997. A Basic Law Drafting Committee has been set up with representatives from all sides to draft a post-1997 constitution and ensure a smooth transfer of power. From July 1997 Hong Kong will be a Special Administrative Region of China, largely autonomous (except in matters of foreign affairs and defence) with its own legislature to which key appointments will be made by Beijing. It is an essential feature of the agreement that the main features of the economy (freedom of the foreign exchange market, free port status and a separate taxation system) will be retained for a period of 50 years after 1997. The Chinese side is as anxious as the present authorities to retain international confidence so that new industries will be attracted whose exports will maintain the record of recent years. The present Governor is advised by an Executive Council and presides over a Legislative Council; until 1985 all the members of these were nominated or otherwise appointed (businessmen and civil servants predominating).

It is the Hong Kong government's policy to neither protect nor subsidise industry or trade in the territory; essentially a policy of *laissez faire* is applied. Nevertheless there have been some suggestions that the authorities were more active than usual in the run-up to the 1985 agreement, thereby maintaining confidence in the banking and property sectors.

Turnout at the 1985 election was small, and the agreement was widely acclaimed in the colony (most of whose inhabitants will be ideologically ill at ease in the People's Republic) because of the practical good sense that it represented. There had been little pressure for democratic elections before 1985, and China has been keen to discourage the politicisation of Hong Kong. Nevertheless direct elections are a distinct possibility in 1988; political parties (such as the business interest-dominated Progressive Hong Kong Society) are only emerging slowly. 'Business as usual' is the overall theme, but the power of government officials is being steadily diluted ready for the handover. Already most expatriate recruitment has ceased in the public sector.

Macao

Legally there is no reason for change in Macao which has been defined, since 1976, as a special territory of Portugal. However the Portuguese president visited China in 1985 for 'talks about talks', and it is generally believed that the territory's future will closely follow that of Hong Kong, probably with similar timing. Beijing is keen to see recent economic developments maintained so that she inherits an industrially-diversified, tourism-dominated entrepôt to serve Guangdong province. Sovereignty is unlikely to be disputed. In place of the time-honoured annual planning system, three year budgets are now adopted, which allow major developments (such as an international airport on reclaimed land) to take place. Politicisation is low key, and the major issue to be resolved in negotiations is the future of the mixed-blood Macanese who have dominated the political scene until recently.

North Korea

As a centrally planned economy North Korea is officially committed to the re-unification of the peninsula; despite some recent thawing, tension in relations with the South is a primary feature of national life. The current president has been in power for over 35 years, successfully manoeuvring foreign alignment between the USSR and China to maintain a constant if inadequate supply of technical assistance. The country was physically devastated by the 1950–1953 war (it inherited most of the industrial infrastructure put in place by the Japanese), and Seven Year Plan periods (sometimes with intermediate adjustment years), are the basis of economic development. Much criticised, the achievements have nevertheless been notable, such as the recent attainment of self-sufficiency in food.

The current Plan, expiring in 1991, gives priority to export development, using substantially more imported technology than has been available hitherto. The economy is hampered by the fact that observer status only has been granted at the UN, so it seems likely that Third World markets will be the main targets.

North Korea is governed by a Supreme People's Assembly, high level committees and councils and a network of local Assemblies. The principal political organisations are the Democratic Front for the Re-unification of the Fatherland and the Korean Workers' Party.

South Korea

The same degree of stability has not been enjoyed in South Korea where the present regime headed by President Chun, which came to power in 1980, is military-backed. Expansion of the economy via export growth/diversification and the control of inflation are the main objectives of the government. Relations with the United States dominate foreign affairs (defence is a major item of government expenditure) and there is considerable trade friction. The latter seriously threatens the further expansion of the South Korean economy.

The government is involved in most aspects of economic decision-making. In 1985 the economy slowed down, provoking considerable public unrest and anti-US feeling as workers saw the further improvement of their standard of living being threatened. The result has been a loosening up of financial controls in general (money supply increased from around 7.7% in 1984 to near 13% in 1985) and privatisation of the banking system in particular.

The Fifth Plan (1982–86) was substantially revised at the end of 1983. Originally the main objective was to prepare the ground for a 'second industrial take-off', with much more responsibility for growth being placed with industrial heads. World trading conditions have subsequently deteriorated due to the slowdown in growth of the US market and the strength of the dollar in 1985, so the revised Plan is intended to re-adjust policies via structural reforms within the economy—boosting the role of service industries, for example. More reliance is being placed on market forces. The Plan, including its revised form, failed to predict the slump in world oil prices which has come as an unexpected bonus, and should make the target of a current account surplus (targeted for 1986/87) possible.

An annual growth rate of 7.5% is the objective, and the GNP target for 1988 is US$ 107.8 bn (in constant 1980 prices; in that year GNP totalled US$ 61.2 bn).

Several important opposition party leaders were allowed to return from exile in 1984, and the newly formed NKDP party did surprisingly well in the elections held in February of that year (30% of national vote), calling for a non-military presidential system of government with a four-year term of office, renewable only once. The ruling Democratic Justice Party (which gained 35% of votes cast in the election) has promised to relinquish power in 1988, but the present system could hardly be called democratic because opposition parties had insufficient time to organise themselves for the 1985 election.

Taiwan

Taiwan's political and economic situation is similar to South Korea except that the government is not a military one. Relations with the United States dominate foreign affairs and pressure comes from Washington over the question of human rights. A further problem is that Taiwan is technically diplomatically isolated, following the recognition of the People's Republic as the legitimate government of China by the US in 1978. In practical terms most links were restored in 1979, however. In both South Korea and Taiwan trade with China is vital, although officially it is outlawed and has to take place through third countries (most notably Hong Kong).

Key issues being faced under the current Ten Year Economic Development Plan of 1980 are energy conservation, trade growth and the maintenance of full employment. Increased reliance was placed on less energy-intensive industries (i.e. higher value-added ones); the weakness of oil prices was not foreseen. The trade growth target for 1980–1989 is 12.5% per annum in real terms, and by 1989 it is hoped that industrial products will constitute 93.3% of exports. An unemployment level of 1.3% is planned. According to the programme the percentage shares of GDP to be met by different sectors in 1989 (1979 in brackets) are:

all-industry	57.7%	(52.6%)
manufacturing	47.7%	(42.8%)
services	36.8%	(38.5%)
agriculture	5.5%	(8.9%)

The reputation of the ruling Kuomintang party has been adversely affected by recent political and financial scandals in Taiwan, and opposition parties, loosely grouped in *tangwai,* suffer from severe restrictions on their activities.

IV   Economic performance and structure

Measured in real terms, Hong Kong's GDP grew by a remarkable 9.4% in 1984, exactly the same increase as seen in 1981. Three of the other countries in the region have enjoyed similar export-led growth in the 1980s; the North Korean economy also appears to be developing rapidly although insufficient information is available to evaluate the causes.

Hong Kong

Measured at current market prices the development of the Hong Kong economy appears even more impressive—growth of 18.6% in 1984, following 9.8% (1983), 11.3% (1982), and 17.8% in 1981. No figures for GNP are available because of the absence of monitoring of investment income from abroad, a characteristic feature of the colony's economy.

TABLE 3.5   HONG KONG: MAIN COMPONENTS OF EXPENDITURE ON GDP AT CURRENT MARKET PRICES

HK$ bn	1975	1980	1981	1982	1983	1984
Private consumption expenditure	31.2	85.3	102.7	119.3	139.6	160.0
Government consumption expenditure	3.5	8.8	12.4	15.0	16.8	18.4
Gross domestic fixed capital formation	10.5	45.5	55.4	57.8	51.7	55.5
Increase in stocks	0.7	3.7	4.0	1.4	4.3	4.7
Net exports—goods	−3.7	−13.5	−17.1	−16.4	−15.9	−3.4*
—services	4.1	7.3	8.0	9.8	11.8	14.4†
TOTAL EXPENDITURE	46.5	137.2	165.3	186.9	208.4	249.6
(Per capita GDP in HK$	10,570	27,232	32,080	35,710	39,222	46,526)

Source: National Statistics
Notes: *1984 exports of goods HK$ 221.4 bn; imports HK$ 224.8 bn.
　　　　†1984 exports of services HK$ 44.1 bn; imports HK$ 29.7 bn.

Table 3.5 shows the main components of expenditure on Hong Kong's GDP, and the most interesting feature is that net commodity trade has actually been in deficit consistently since 1975 while net exports of services have been in surplus. The rapid growth of private consumption expenditure has been the main impetus behind the GDP increase, a result not only of the expanding population but also of the rising standard of living.

Another noteworthy feature of GDP breakdown is the high proportion of gross domestic fixed capital formation; consistently over 20% of GDP since 1975, and over 30% between 1980–1982 inclusive. Amongst the industrialised countries this rate of increase has been matched only in Japan.

Another exponent of growth over the years has been the development of total turnover of the Hong Kong stock exchange. This reached a peak of HK$ 106 bn in 1981, compared with HK$ 10.3 bn in 1975, but then turned sharply down before the Anglo-Chinese agreement on the future of the colony was ratified in 1985; it has subsequently built up again as confidence has returned. The colony is a significant financial centre having 136 banks and numerous representative offices.

TABLE 3.6   HONG KONG: FINANCE CENTRE INDICATIONS

**(a) Stock Exchange turnover
(HK$ mn)**

	1980	1981	1982	1983	1984
	95,684.3	105,986.8	46,229.9	37,164.7	48,787.0

(b) Banks and finance companies

	1980	1981	1982	1983
Number of banks	115	123	131	136
Representative offices of foreign banks	107	121	118	129
Number of deposit-taking companies	296	350	360	364
Profits from foreign exchange dealing* (HK$ mn)	1,279.2	1,613.9	1,655.9	1,939.8
Net interest receipts (HK$ mn)	6,630.7	9,571.4	10,846.1	11,162.5
Earnings of banking services (HK$ mn)	500	751	806	1,077†

Source: National Statistics
Notes: *excluding representative offices of foreign banks
          †1984 earnings HK$ 1,346 million

In 1983, 22.7% of Hong Kong's GDP was derived from manufacturing industries, consistent with the 1980–1982 level. Agriculture is relatively unimportant as land resources are at a premium to permit anything more than a little intensive vegetable and livestock production. Whole-sale/retail, import/export, hotel/catering, finance/insurance, property and business services contributed a further 37.3% (Hong Kong's financial services suffered a crisis of confidence in 1983 from which they have largely recovered). Gross output of manufacturing industry (in current prices) rose by 44% in 1979, 19% in 1980, 17% in 1981 and 29% in 1983; it actually fell (by 3%) in 1982. In 1983 the main sectors were apparel (HK$ 36.0 bn, up 22%), machinery and equipment (HK$ 31.4 bn, up 29%), electrical and electronic products (HK$ 31.2 bn, up 28%), textiles (HK$ 28.5 bn, up 42%) and general plastic products, notably toys (HK$ 11.9 bn, up 31%). The total output of Hong Kong's manufacturing industries in 1983 was HK$ 170.7 bn according to official sources. Light industry now employs approximately two-fifths of the workforce, most being engaged in the manufacture of consumer goods. For example, Hong Kong now produces approximately one-third (by volume) of global watch output. The real growth is taking place in tourism and financial services; more than 2 mn tourists now visit Hong Kong each year and the colony's excellent strategic position (particularly its proximity to China and the rapidly developing ASEAN economies) coupled with its liberal financial policies, sound currency, well-established stock and commodity exchanges, generous taxation system and modern international communications makes it a first choice for many multi-national companies who want a presence in the Far East.

Macao

Macao has also enjoyed a rapid rate of export-led growth, the official figures showing a 10% increase in GDP in 1983 and 9.5% in 1984; the current level is thought to be in the range of 8–9% per annum. This is a major achievement for an economy almost entirely dependent on imported raw materials, but it is well below the 16% that took place in the 1970s when the textile industry was establishing itself. By the broad M2 definition Macao's money supply increased by 21.9% in 1984; inflation is consequently high with consumer prices increasing by 11% in 1984.

Macao's prosperity in the past has always depended on its proximity to China and the resulting entrepôt trade (particularly in gold).

45

Primarily as a result of the boom in the textile industry manufacturing now provides the greatest proportion of GDP, but tourism is also a major source of wealth (estimated 25% of GDP in 1983, the contribution of gambling being particularly noteworthy). Tourism was up by 7.9% in 1984, most visitors arriving via Hong Kong.

North Korea

North Korea's centrally-planned economy has undergone a process of rapid growth over the last three decades, but it is not possible to measure this precisely due to suspect official data. According to the official figures gross industrial output in 1984 was 220% above the 1978 level, with an annual overall growth rate of 9.6% over the period (output of foodstuffs up 120%, steel 85%, cement 78%, coal 50%, textiles 45%). Observers overseas in general estimate that industrial output has only increased in real terms by 2–4% per annum over the period, however; this is to be compared with the Plan target of 9.6% per annum.

In both parts of the Korean peninsula economic development is hampered by the continuing state of tension that exists between the two countries. Hence the maintenance of armed forces absorbs a high proportion of each nation's wealth; an estimated 20–25% of North Korea's GNP goes to the military. Industrial production constitutes around three-quarters of GNP with most of it mineral-based. When the peninsula was divided the North inherited most of the industrial infrastructure and the mineral wealth on which it was based. Heavy industry prevails with emphasis on steel, cement, chemical fertilisers and synthetic fibres. Agricultural productivity has risen impressively and currently the sector employs an estimated 45% of the country's total workforce. North Korea is the main rice-producing country in the region (14.2 mn tonnes in 1983, compared with nearly 5.7 mn tonnes in South Korea in 1984 and 2.24 mn tonnes in Taiwan in 1984). An estimated 80% of agricultural production in North Korea is organised into about 1 mn co-operatives, leaving less than 6% of the cultivated area in private plots. Total food output increased from 14.4 mn tonnes in 1980 to 17.0 mn tonnes in 1983, making the country self-sufficient in most commodities. Investment in agriculture is high; irrigation is comprehensive, heavy use is made of chemical fertilisers and operations such as rice transplanting are now largely mechanised resulting in yields being higher than ever before.

Very high productivity is also a feature of agriculture in South Korea and Taiwan, where production continues to rise even though the total cropped area is falling. Mechanisation is the key to the process; in South Korea in 1984 there were over 538,000 power tillers in ownership, nearly double the number existing in 1979. Most production units in these countries are small and owner-occupied; in Taiwan a crash programme to create a 'reserve army' of highly trained farmers, initiated in 1982, is nearing completion.

South Korea

Measured in current prices South Korea's GNP has increased fairly steadily recently, from won 37,205 bn in 1980 to won 65,380 bn in 1984. At constant 1980 prices the 1984 GNP total is reduced to won 49,168 bn, giving an annual percentage increase of 6.2% in 1981, 5.6% in 1982, 9.5% in 1983 and 7.6% in 1984. Measured at constant prices GNP actually fell in 1980, by 5.2%.

TABLE 3.7   SOUTH KOREA: SOURCE OF GNP 1974–1984

	1974 %	1984 %
Activity		
Agriculture, forestry and fishing	24.8	14.0
Mining and quarrying	1.2	1.5
Manufacturing	25.4	28.9
Construction	4.5	8.1
Utilities	0.9	2.2
Transport, storage and communications	6.1	8.3
Commerce	20.7	17.5
Business services	3.9	5.8
Other	12.5	13.7
TOTAL	100.0	100.0

Source: National Statistics

Table 3.7 shows the contribution of various sectors to the economy; agriculture is seen to have declined whilst manufacturing has increased over the past ten years. In 1985 GNP growth slowed to 5%; however, projections for 1986 are around 7.5% based on the fall in oil prices combined with lower international interest rates and a high priced yen (Japan is South Korea's major foreign trade competitor).

The inflation rate has been brought down from an annual level of 28% in 1980 to 3% in 1985, mainly through constraints on money supply growth, which fell to 9% in 1984 (although increased to 14% in 1985) from a high of 40% in 1977.

It is the successful development of export markets for South Korean goods and services that is responsible for the growth record; industrialists in this country have been particularly adept at adapting to changing market conditions, particularly in high technology industries such as consumer electronics and automotive components.

TABLE 3.8   SOUTH KOREA: GROSS OUTPUT OF MINING AND MANUFACTURING

won bn	1980	1981	1982	1983
Mining	538.2	764.9	803.1	784.1
of which: coal	349.1	519.9	564.8	560.4
metal ores	71.2	84.3	66.3	61.3
Manufacturing	36,279.1	46,717.5	51,648.9	60,545.7
of which: food, beverages and tobacco	4,979.4	6,164.8	7,220.1	8,162.7
textiles, apparel and leather	6,495.4	8,270.7	8,499.1	9,377.4
wood and wood products	883.8	970.1	1,036.3	1,167.1
paper, paper products, printing and publishing	1,401.6	1,806.3	2,008.2	2,489.3
chemicals, petroleum, coal, rubber and plastic products	10,068.4	12,641.9	13,553.4	15,149.0
other non-metallic mineral products	1,601.6	1,781.1	1,993.7	2,517.1
basic metal industries	3,387.3	4,504.1	4,932.7	5,805.7
fabricated metal products, machinery and equipment	6,960.8	9,816.8	11,616.8	14,948.4
other	500.7	761.5	788.7	929.0
TOTAL	36,817.3	47,482.4	52,452.0	61,329.9

Source: National Statistics

In consumer electronics a recognisable shift away from televisions and radios has occurred, substituted by microwave ovens, computers and VCRs and the Koreans are fast developing their own domestic raw materials (viz. chips) instead of importing extensively from Japan.

The automotive sector has witnessed spectacular growth over the past few years, looking beyond the domestic market. The foundations for expansion are the existence of foreign partners for the main auto-makers and substantial resources available due to the diversified nature of the manufacturers' businesses.

The notable successes associated with the high tech industries have been counterbalanced to some extent by the recent decline in Korea's overseas construction and shipbuilding industries. After a rapidly expanding period in the 1970s the construction and shipping sectors are endeavouring to move up the technological scale by bidding for more advanced projects and investing in new vessels.

In the 1980s the most widely recognised growth commodities within the manufacturing sector have been textiles and apparel. However, fabricated metal and plastic products for both consumer and industrial use have given the sector considerable growth impetus.

Taiwan

Table 3.9 shows that Taiwan's economic growth record in the 1980s has been impressive, with an 11.5% increase in GDP (at current prices) in 1984. At current prices the GNP has risen from NT$ 1,468.1 bn in 1980

TABLE 3.9   TAIWAN: GDP AT CURRENT PRICES

NT$ bn

1975	584
1980	1,470
1981	1,749
1982	1,860
1983	2,041
1984	2,275

Source: National Statistics

to 2,290.5 bn (provisional) in 1984, an average growth rate of 11.8% per annum. At constant prices the mean post-1980 growth rate has been 7.3%, with a particularly impressive performance (11.4%) in 1984. At constant 1981 prices Taiwan's 1984 GNP stood at NT$ 2,190.0 bn compared with NT$ 1,650.2 bn in 1980. Impressive as this is it is below the average yearly increase of 10.5% achieved in 1976–1980.

In both Taiwan and South Korea growth of the domestic economies has been accompanied by a high rate of investment; for 1982 UN figures show a figure for gross capital formation as a percentage of national expenditure of at least 25% (compared with 15–16% in the UK and USA). The export earnings of highly successful industries have been used in large part to found an even more competitive industrial base for the 1990s.

The relative importance of different sectors to the economy of Taiwan is shown in Table 3.10; nearly two-thirds of GDP derived from manufacturing, financial and other business services in 1984. Industry now contributes 43% compared to 29% in 1964; for agriculture and related activities the corresponding figures are 6.4% and 25%.

TABLE 3.10   TAIWAN: GDP IN 1984 BY CATEGORY OF ECONOMIC ACTIVITY

NT$ mn

Agriculture, forestry and fishing	145,371
Mining and quarrying	14,195
Manufacturing	937,904
Utilities	88,644
Construction	99,731
Business and finance	518,655
Transport and communications	135,941
Government services	223,065
Others	147,106
less imported bank service charge	(55,501)
TOTAL	2,255,111

Source: National Statistics

Taiwan's industries are heavily export-orientated. In 1984 overall output (1981=100) stood at 127.46 for mining and manufacturing as a whole (mining 84.46, food 123.69, textiles 114.20, basic metal industries

151.55, electrical/electronic machinery 170.02). There is substantial evidence of dynamism on the industrial scene in Taiwan; three export zones are already in operation, major investment in infrastructure (notably port development, transport and power) is taking place, and the Science Industry Park is the scene of important high-technology developments at Hsinchu.

Total consumption expenditure in Taiwan in 1984 (1975 in brackets, current prices basis) was NT$ 1,506 bn (425 bn) of which NT$ 1,138 bn (334 bn) was private and NT$ 368 bn (91 bn) was government expenditure.

V Energy

With the exception of small-scale oil and natural gas production in Taiwan there has been no hydrocarbon development in the region. Energy demands are met primarily from imported crude oil and LNG, from the development of domestic coal and hydro resources and, in the cases of both Korea and Taiwan, from nuclear sources. There are major opportunities for suppliers of coal, hydro (especially small- to medium-scale) and nuclear technology. Despite this scenario Hong Kong manages to supply a small amount of electric power to China.

Statistics are presented in a form that makes meaningful comparisons within the region impossible, but in terms of gross production Macao's record is typical; gross output of electrical energy was 403.9 mn kWh in 1983 compared with 262.1 mn kWh in 1980. Gross electricity generating plant installed in Taiwan in 1984 stood at 15.36 mn kW, compared with 5.9 mn kW in 1974.

Approximately one-half of North Korea's energy requirements are met by coal. Hydro development has been extensive, and there are several schemes that have been implemented jointly with China. Some nuclear power is already generated, and there is an ambitious scheme to develop tidal energy on the west coast.

The other countries are heavily dependent on imported crude oil. This meets just over one-half of South Korea's energy requirements at present. Of the 53.8 bn kWh generated in 1984, 39.6 bn came from thermal stations (mostly oil-fired, but domestic coal production is important), 11.8 bn from four nuclear plants (two more are planned by 1996) and 2.4 bn from hydro installations. Of total energy production in

Taiwan in 1984 (38.0 mn kilolitres oil equivalent), 62.2% was generated from oil, gas or petroleum products (nearly all imported), 3.6% from domestically-produced coal, 14.1% from imported coal, 3.0% from hydro installations and 16.7% from nuclear plants.

Overall the Middle East is the most important source of hydrocarbons but the ASEAN countries are increasing their market share rapidly.

VI Standard of living

One of the effects of the great economic advances made in the region over the last 25 years is a considerable improvement in the standard of living. Disposable incomes have risen considerably, there is a more equitable distribution of wealth, the proportion spent on food has fallen, and expenditure on welfare/social facilities has risen considerably. There are insufficient data to show that these changes have taken place in North Korea also, but the evidence suggests some improvement.

One indication of the rising standard of living is the number of

TABLE 3.11   HONG KONG: PRIVATE CONSUMPTION EXPENDITURE

	1975 %	1984 %
Food and beverages	31.2	19.6
Clothing and personal effects	15.6	18.5
Rent and water	13.1	12.6
Furniture, furnishings and household equipment	6.1	10.8
Transport and communications	6.8	7.6
Recreation and entertainment	6.1	7.6
Financial and other services	12.0	12.8
Other	9.1	10.5
TOTAL	100.0	100.0
TOTAL private consumption expenditure (HK$ bn)	31.2	159.9

Source: National Statistics

telephones installed per 100 population. In Hong Kong in 1984 there were 30.6 operational; 35.5 was the installed capacity of the system. For South Korea the 1984 figure was 16.7, while in Taiwan it was 27.7 (compared with 5.7 in 1974).

Table 3.11 shows how the pattern of expenditure of Hong Kong residents has changed over the last 10 years, the main feature being the sharp decline in proportional outlay on food. Total private consumption expenditure in 1984 amounted to HK$ 159.9 bn, compared with HK$ 31.2 bn in 1974 (current prices basis). In 1981/82 Macao residents spent 50.7% of their disposable income on food and drink, 24.0% on housing, 5.0% on fuel and utilities, 3.5% on drink and tobacco, 4.5% on apparel/ footwear, 5.5% on miscellaneous services, a mere 1.9% on consumer durables and just 1.5% on transport; the proportional expenditure on food is indicative of the much lower standard of living that is enjoyed in Hong Kong.

A survey of South Korean urban households in 1984 showed that expenditure on food and drink was 37.6%, housing 4.8%, utilities 7.5%, household equipment 4.7%, apparel and footwear 7.8%, transport and communications 6.4%, and other categories 13.4%. A high 17.8% was spent on meeting medical, educational, recreational and cultural needs. In 1977 47.7% was spent on food and drink. The same change has been apparent in Taiwan where spending on food/drink/ tobacco in 1983 was 38.9%, clothing/footwear 6.3%, rent/utilities 24.1%, furniture 4.4%, transport/communications 7.2% and the same 'social' requirements 13.9%.

According to the Hang Seng consumer price index in Hong Kong (1979/80=100), overall 1984 prices stood at 156.8 and most items were close to this, with the exception of alcoholic drink and tobacco (192.3), clothing (137.0), consumer durables (130.5) and transport (179.4). Mean monthly salaries in 1984 were HK$ 2,987, with an average for manufacturing of HK$ 2,868 (lowest in footwear at HK$ 2,271, highest in the photographic industry at HK$ 3,252). In the financial services sector the average monthly salary was HK$ 3,709. Wage rates in Macao are approximately one-half the Hong Kong level.

The progression of South Korean wage rates is shown in Table 3.12; the relatively low level in manufacturing is noteworthy. Working males earn at least double female rates, and the level of unionisation is low at around 25%. Also, the long hours worked warrant particular comment

—an average 53.7 hour week in 1981. Retail prices in Seoul have risen much more rapidly than in other parts of the country, up 67.2% 1980–1984 compared with the 37.6% increase in the general consumer price index.

TABLE 3.12   SOUTH KOREA: MONTHLY EARNINGS BY ACTIVITY

'000 won	1980	1981	1982	1983	1984
Manufacturing	146.7	176.2	202.1	226.8	245.3
Construction	257.7	319.8	366.0	387.1	380.5
Transport and communications	203.5	238.3	271.4	292.2	319.7
Business services	281.6	339.7	388.0	417.3	479.6
Social services	275.3	343.1	409.0	450.4	452.6
ALL-INDUSTRY AVERAGE	176.0	212.5	246.0	273.1	296.9

Source: National Statistics

Manufacturing employees in Taiwan in 1984 earned 34.59% more than in 1981, while for other categories of employment the corresponding figures were: mining 7.43%; utilities 33.14%; construction (domestic) 31.22%; general commerce 21.97%; transport 23.24%; financial services 29.56% and the social services 15.42%. According to the official figures inflation has been negligible since 1981 (a total 5.5% rise to 1984). Officially it is at the same time acknowledged that a 16.3% increase took place in 1981.

The retail trade in Hong Kong employed 160,964 in 1984, compared with 133,953 in 1978. Just over 51% are engaged in the sale of consumer goods, excluding food and apparel. In South Korea in 1982, 945,778 were employed in retail trades (693,459 in 1976); over this period sales rose by a factor of 3.82 to won 12,655.5 bn. In Taiwan there were 176,100 retail employees in 1984 (there was a sharp decline in the 1970s from 233,100 in 1970), but employment has slowly picked up from the 155,000 shopworkers of 1980; wholesale trade employment has however grown consistently. Retail trade sales in 1983 totalled NT$ 476.8 bn, 1.71 times the 1980 level.

Despite the difficulties of measurement, there is no doubt about the great improvement in educational and health standards throughout the region in recent years. Total expenditure on education in Hong Kong stood at HK\$ 1,127 mn in 1974/75, compared with HK\$ 5,568 mn in 1983/84 (at current prices). In 1981 94.4% of children aged 10–14 were in full-time education; the number of teachers at all schools and colleges rose from 36,962 in 1975 to 44,911 in 1984. The government spent HK\$ 2,932 mn on medical services in 1983/84, compared with HK\$ 575 mn in 1974/75. Over this period the number of hospital beds increased from 18,560 to 24,070.

Macao's student population (all levels) was 56,870 in 1982/83, 91% in non-government establishments.

The indications from North Korea are that some 20–25% of annual government expenditure is now directed at social, welfare and cultural activities. The total number of students in 1984 was of the order of 8.5 mn, compared with 2.4–2.5 mn in the mid 1960s.

Just as a middle-class with considerable spending power has arisen in South Korea, so relatively high educational standards have been attained. In 1985 the government planned to spend 16.9% of its total budget on education (and only 1.5% on health). The total student population in 1984 was 11,395,000, almost the same as the 1982 level even though nearly 2,000 schools were opened during this period. The number of hospital beds increased by nearly 28,500 to 93,528 between 1980 and 1984.

The government of Taiwan spent 10.5% of its total budget of NT\$ 275 bn on education in 1984, and 1.25% on health. There were 62,467 hospital beds in 1984, compared with 28,167 in 1974.

VII Foreign trade

Export-led growth has been the cornerstone of economic development in the region. As a result Hong Kong, South Korea and Taiwan are now among the world's leading trading nations, each enjoying a rate of growth of domestic exports far in excess of the overall development of world trade over the last decade. They are consequently very dependent on external circumstances for continuation of this trend. No country in the region belongs to any significant regional trade association like ASEAN (North Korea does not belong to the CMEA) and they compete fiercely with one another (and increasingly with China) for external markets. It has been said of Macao that the colony gets by on orders Hong Kong cannot fulfil. Most are dependent on a few very large markets for the greater part of their export sales. For example, 48.8% of Taiwan's total exports in 1984 were directed at the United States. And it is economic trends in these markets, particularly the protectionist pressures building up in the US, that worry the region's industrialists most. In the case of South Korea, unfair trading practices are alleged by representatives of a wide range of US industries, steel, consumer electronics and footwear among others. It is also feared that a similar mood will develop in the EEC, with the outcome of current talks on textile quotas being critical for the region as a whole.

On the positive side it can be said that these problems are not new,

TABLE 3.13   EXTERNAL DEBT IN 1982

US$ mn Source of funds 1982 (1975 in brackets)	Hong Kong	Macao	South Korea	Taiwan
DAC* countries and capital markets	3,765	46	18,505	5,897
	(424)	(9)	(5,017)	(1,582)
of which:				
Official development assistance	2	–	2,755	46
	(4)	(–)	(1,716)	(130)
Total export credits	3,233	1	6,548	3,521
	(140)	(9)	(1,943)	(1,164)
Total private (including bank loans)	530	45	9,202	2,330
	(280)	(–)	(1,358)	(288)
Multilateral	53	–	3,340	–
	(18)	(–)	(690)	(–)
CMEA countries	– (–)	– (–)	– (–)	– (–)
OPEC countries	– (–)	– (–)	127 (19)	– (–)
Other LDCs	– (–)	– (–)	10 (20)	– (–)
Others and adjustments	– (–)	– (–)	3 (17)	323 (333)
TOTAL DEBT	3,818	46	21,985	6,220
	(442)	(9)	(5,762)	(1,915)

Source: OECD

Note: *Development Assistance Committee of OECD (Australia, Austria, Belgium, Canada, Denmark, Finland, France, West Germany, Italy, Japan, Netherlands, New Zealand, Norway, Sweden, Switzerland, UK, USA, EEC Commission).

and over the last 10 years East Asian industrialists have shown an extraordinary ability rapidly to develop new products to counter external pressures. The move into the high fashion market by Hong Kong apparel manufacturers is a good example, as is the transition from textiles to plastic goods (especially toys) in Macao.

Table 3.13 summarises the region's external debt situation, and from this it is seen that South Korea is the most heavily indebted country in the region, both in terms of aid and trade credits. South Korea's total foreign debt in 1985 reached US$ 46.7 bn with only the Latin American nations in a worse position worldwide. North Korea is also very heavily indebted, to the CMEA countries, China, Japan and West Germany in particular, but it is not possible to put more than an estimated US$ 2 bn figure on this. Nevertheless the great majority of industries in the region is now locally financed from export earnings, even if originally set up, as in the cases of South Korea and Taiwan, by Japanese and later predominantly US AID funding. Macao's debt record is the most impressive, partly because the economy is so small but mainly because earnings from tourism (and especially gambling revenues) are so relatively high.

Already there is a significant trend towards the export of capital from the region; a South Korean vehicle manufacturer is planning a plant in Canada, for example.

Another significant trend is the continued integration of the economies with that of China, even if diplomatic relations do not exist. This trend is most apparent in Hong Kong and Macao. A shift in the domestic or external policies of the People's Republic would have major repercussions on the economies of the countries in this region.

The growth of services also augurs well for the future of the region. Hong Kong's commodity exports totalled HK$ 221.4 mn in 1984 compared with HK$ 29.8 mn in 1975. Over the same period exports of services increased from HK$ 8.7 mn to HK$ 44.1 mn. The 1984 breakdown was: transportation 53.2%, tourism 31.8%, banking and insurance 5.0%, others 10.0%. The tourism and finance sectors are growing rapidly in Macao, South Korea and Taiwan, and South Korea already wins more overseas civil engineering contracts than any other nation.

Despite its massive debt burden South Korea has a good debt service record. Only in North Korea does there appear to be a problem; this country's foreign debt is left over from the mid-1970s when it imported large amounts of capital equipment. Western investors are in consequence cautious of any further financial involvement in this country, and it is desperately short of capital for development projects.

Hong Kong

Tables 3.14 and 3.15 summarise Hong Kong's trading situation since 1975, the 32% increase in domestic exports that took place in 1984 being better than was achieved over the period as a whole. There is heavy reliance on a wide range of consumer goods. Of total exports of HK$ 137.9 bn in 1984, electrical/electronic products contributed HK$ 33.4 bn, apparel HK$ 31.7 bn, textiles HK$ 25.3 bn, plastic products HK$ 11.8 bn and professional/optical equipment HK$ 10.6 bn. There is very heavy reliance on the US market for domestic exports (44.5% of the total) and on China for re-exports (33.6%). The main impetus for Hong Kong's post-1984 export growth has been the boom in trade with China, especially the re-export of goods from South Korea and Taiwan. Other vital markets are West Germany (especially apparel, timepieces, electronic components, radios and travel goods), the UK (apparel, toys, textile fabrics, electronic components, radios and miscellaneous metal manufactures) and Japan (timepieces).

TABLE 3.14   HONG KONG: OVERSEAS MERCHANDISE TRADE

HK$ bn	1975	1980	1981	1982	1983	1984
Domestic exports	22.8	68.2	80.4	83.0	104.4	137.9
(annual change %	−0.2	+22	+18	+3	+26	+32)
Imports	33.5	111.6	138.4	142.9	175.4	223.4
(annual change %	−2	+30	+24	+3	+23	+27)
Re-exports	7.0	30.1	41.7	44.3	56.3	83.5
(annual change %	−2	+50	+39	+6	+27	+48)
TOTAL TRADE	63.3	209.9	260.5	270.3	336.1	444.8
(annual change %	−1	+30	+24	+4	+24	+32)
Merchandise trade balance	−3.6	−13.4	−16.2	−15.5	−14.7	−1.9

Source: National Statistics

TABLE 3.15   HONG KONG: IMPORTS BY END-USE AND MAIN SUPPLIER

HK$ mn	1975	1980	1981	1982	1983	1984
Raw materials and						
semi-manufactures	**13,581**	**46,489**	**57,235**	**56,444**	**75,258**	**99,740**
Japan	4,158	12,790	15,280	15,134	20,660	26,073
People's Republic of China	1,753	6,685	9,315	10,010	14,676	21,150
Taiwan	1,461	5,613	7,728	7,113	8,328	11,729
USA	973	4,196	4,886	4,912	6,650	9,577
South Korea	542	2,865	3,720	3,129	3,592	5,417
Consumer goods	**7,235**	**29,469**	**37,070**	**38,614**	**46,659**	**58,380**
People's Republic of China	1,384	6,883	9,727	11,423	14,971	21,089
Japan	1,347	6,931	9,001	8,603	10,420	12,770
USA	1,040	3,111	3,418	3,827	4,143	4,454
Taiwan	213	1,219	1,650	1,721	2,155	2,746
Singapore	158	807	1,124	895	1,146	1,863
Capital goods	**4,340**	**16,055**	**18,822**	**19,943**	**22,540**	**32,781**
Japan	1,054	4,987	6,733	6,582	7,829	12,230
USA	1,280	4,373	4,229	4,451	5,168	7,220
UK	633	2,344	2,815	3,207	2,851	3,459
Taiwan	137	698	787	850	1,268	2,164
People's Republic of China	156	582	989	1,054	1,336	1,752
Foodstuffs	**6,283**	**12,065**	**14,660**	**16,785**	**19,732**	**20,681**
People's Republic of China	3,240	5,624	7,240	7,941	9,071	9,295
USA	666	1,530	1,909	2,152	2,494	2,667
Japan	348	892	974	1,125	1,377	1,517
Thailand	516	675	799	844	1,064	949
Australia	276	550	663	789	776	882
Fuels	**2,033**	**7,573**	**10,588**	**11,107**	**11,253**	**11,788**
Singapore	1,246	4,901	7,335	6,829	6,100	6,411
People's Republic of China	270	2,175	2,239	2,507	2,767	2,468
Philippines	4	3	10	5	94	694
Australia	*	43	*	180	381	658
South Africa	3	54	154	175	426	555

Source: National Statistics
Note: *Less than HK$ 0.5 mn

The vital importance of re-exports, 37.7% of total exports in 1984, is also highlighted in the above tables. Amongst the reasons for this are the possession of the third largest container terminal in the world, the necessity for South Korean and Taiwanese exporters to employ a third party when trading with China and the absence of adequate handling facilities in Macao and the southern Chinese ports. China and Japan are the most important sources of re-exported commodities (supplying 60% of the textiles, apparel, electrical machinery, sound equipment, road

TABLE 3.16 HONG KONG: TRADE BY MAIN COUNTRY

HK$ mn	1975	1980	1981	1982	1983	1984
Imports						
(main suppliers)	**33,472**	**111,651**	**138,375**	**142,893**	**175,442**	**223,370**
China	6,805	21,948	29,510	32,935	42,821	55,753
Japan	6,991	25,644	32,130	31,540	40,333	52,620
USA	3,961	13,210	14,442	15,459	19,179	24,377
Taiwan	1,943	7,961	10,762	10,198	12,448	17,347
Singapore	1,921	7,384	10,627	10,207	10,482	12,229
Domestic exports						
(main markets)	**22,859**	**68,171**	**80,423**	**83,032**	**104,405**	**137,936**
USA	7,334	22,591	29,200	31,223	43,802	61,374
China	28	1,605	2,924	3,806	6,223	11,283
UK	2,778	6,791	7,710	7,187	8,538	10,497
West Germany	2,860	7,384	7,048	7,031	8,043	9,522
Japan	956	2,329	2,940	3,167	3,910	5,151
Re-exports (main						
countries of destination)	**6,973**	**30,072**	**41,739**	**44,353**	**56,294**	**83,504**
China	137	4,642	8,044	7,992	12,183	28,064
USA	555	3,085	4,785	5,615	8,028	12,109
Taiwan	600	2,229	2,420	2,662	3,454	4,868
Japan	964	2,201	2,792	2,566	3,176	4,633
Singapore	928	2,510	3,243	3,648	4,523	4,511
Re-exports (main						
countries of origin)	**6,973**	**30,072**	**41,739**	**44,353**	**56,294**	**83,504**
China	1,743	8,394	12,834	14,694	19,680	28,107
Japan	1,210	5,884	8,394	9,084	11,629	18,695
USA	969	3,157	4,041	4,940	6,038	8,516
Taiwan	196	2,134	3,379	2,500	2,573	5,111
South Korea	126	877	1,954	1,363	1,360	2,314

Source: National Statistics

vehicles, timepieces and industrial machinery re-exported by Hong Kong in 1984). China is also the main country of destination of re-exports, substantial two-way trade taking place in most of these commodities (of total textile re-exports in 1984, excluding apparel, 51.3% went to China; for industrial machinery the figure was 63.0%).

Table 3.16 shows that nearby Asian countries are easily the most important source of Hong Kong's imports of a wide range of goods.

Macao

Macao's emergence as a significant exporter is largely a post-1976 phenomenon. As the original industrial base is so small, annual growth rates are not very meaningful. Textiles have been the main export (70% of exports in 1984) but restrictive agreements have encouraged rapid diversification, and it is now the toy industry that is growing most rapidly. The country is very dependent on a few large markets; in 1984 30.4% of total exports went to the US and 34.0% to the EEC (mostly West Germany, France and the UK). Textiles and apparel are the main items grouped under 'consumer goods' in Table 3.18. Apart from toys the main growth products are consumer electronics and artificial flowers. Most items are exported through Hong Kong.

TABLE 3.17   MACAO: ENTREPÔT TRADE

MOP mn	1975	1980	1981	1982	1983
Total exports	**782.4**	**3,128.3**	**4,024.3**	**4,533.2**	**5,700.5**
of which:					
Definitive	551.2	2,742.0	3,972.9	4,479.3	5,652.5
Temporary	—	—	9.1	12.1	27.5
Re-exports	650.8	386.3	42.4	41.8	20.5
Total imports	**648.7**	**2,779.9**	**4,156.2**	**4,496.3**	**5,452.2**
of which:					
Definitive	648.7	2,779.9	4,085.1	4,440.8	5,402.2
Temporary	—	—	56.1	34.6	21.1
Re-imports	—	—	15.0	20.9	28.9

Source: National Statistics

TABLE 3.18   MACAO: STRUCTURE OF TRADE

MOP mn

	1983		1984	
	Imports	Exports	Imports	Exports
Food and beverages	637.1	105.4	655.3	115.1
Fuels and lubricants	400.7	0.9	382.5	1.0
Unspecified industrial materials	3,030.9	1,056.7	3,730.7	1,409.4
Capital goods				
(excluding transport equipment)	448.5	100.7	507.0	159.5
Transport equipment	101.6	4.0	120.4	3.6
Consumer goods	769.0	4,381.0	985.7	5,616.2
Other	14.3	3.7	3.9	—
TOTAL	5,402.2*	5,652.5†	6,385.5*	7,304.9†

Source: National Statistics

Notes: *excluding temporary and re-imports   †excluding temporary and re-exports

Imports are principally industrial raw materials and food, China being the main original supplier. Very little trade, in either direction, takes place with Portugal. Entrepôt trade is relatively unimportant.

North Korea

Figures for North Korea's exports (mainly industrial raw materials) and imports (mainly machinery and transport equipment) have been obtained from a West German source (refer Table 3.19). 55.0% of exports in 1981 went to the centrally planned countries (58.2% in 1975). The import pattern is similar. Barter is a significant means of trade. The country earns little hard currency from the West and therefore lacks the funds necessary to import much-needed industrial equipment.

TABLE 3.19   NORTH KOREA: TRADE BY MAIN COUNTRY

US$ mn	1975	1980	1981	1982
Exports:				
USSR	209.9	438.0	347.0	499.5
People's Republic of China	197.8	303.3	200.0*	—

TABLE 3.19   NORTH KOREA: TRADE BY MAIN COUNTRY *(continued)*

US$ mn	1975	1980	1981	1982
West Germany	51.3	189.1	55.4	151.2
Japan	64.8	181.6	139.7	144.4
Saudi Arabia	8.9	201.6	128.0	—
India	5.0	75.0	75.0	—
Czechoslovakia	9.3	21.0	19.5	18.0
Poland	18.1	38.3	19.6	17.7
Romania	15.0	32.5	19.0	—
Hong Kong	6.9	29.1	14.1	14.0
Indonesia	—	34.0	13.0	8.9
Imports:				
USSR	258.9	443.4	385.9	438.8
Japan	179.7	374.3	290.0	328.8
People's Republic of China	284.1	374.2	290.0*	—
France	22.7	5.0	69.0	48.9
West Germany	75.6	33.3	30.0	33.5
Singapore	8.0	33.0	36.0	33.0
Poland	11.4	42.1	30.4	26.8
India	8.0	25.0	25.0	—
Czechoslovakia	11.6	16.2	17.5	21.3
Switzerland	10.0	9.0	7.0	17.1
Romania	22.2	44.6	13.7	—
Hong Kong	2.0	61.0	45.0	6.2

Source: Statistisches Bundesamt Wiesbaden, West Germany
Note: *estimate

South Korea

In real terms South Korea's export growth over the last 15 years has been in excess of 15% per annum. The country is very dependent on the US and Japanese markets, where approximately one-half of export goods is normally sold. There is a large (and friction-generating) surplus with the US (US$ 4.2 bn in 1985), and a large deficit with Japan (US$ 3 bn in 1985). Not all items are sold according to this pattern, however; of the 52,000 cars exported in 1984 approximately one-half

63

went to Canada. There is only a small deficit in commodity trade overall.

TABLE 3.20   SOUTH KOREA: COMMODITY TRADE SUMMARY

US$ mn

	Exports (f.o.b.)	Imports (c.i.f.)
1970	835.2	1,984.0
1980	17,504.9	22,291.7
1981	21,253.8	26,131.4
1982	21,853.4	24,250.8
1983	24,445.1	26,192.2
1984	29,244.9	30,631.4

Source: National Statistics

The magnitude of the trade imbalances with the US and Japan has recently are shipbuilding, office machinery and apparel/footwear, the shipyards being conspicuously so at a time when nearly all competitors have faced a downturn.

The magnitude of the trade inbalances with the US and Japan has prompted South Korea to focus its attention on other trading partners, in particular Europe. In 1985 trade with the EEC totalled US$ 6.1 bn (exports US$ 3.2 bn; imports US$ 2.9 bn) with the main partner being West Germany.

South Korea's major imported items are fuels (valued at US$ 7.3 bn in 1984) and machinery/transport equipment (US$ 9.8 bn). The value of total imports has been closely related to the volume of exports generated, although this relationship is now breaking down as the price of crude oil weakens. In 1984, 24.9% of imports came from Japan, and a further 22.4% from the US. ASEAN and Middle Eastern oil producers accounted for most of the rest, though Australia is also a significant source (3.6% in 1984).

The country has recorded current account deficits for many years peaking at US$ 5.3 bn in 1980 (as a result of the oil price hike in 1979/80) and reducing to just under US$ 1 bn in 1985. The sustained lower oil prices in 1986 and high price of the yen should ensure a current surplus for the year and projections are as much as US$ 1 bn.

TABLE 3.21   SOUTH KOREA: PRINCIPAL EXPORT COMMODITIES

US$ mn Commodity	1980	1981	1982	1983	1984
Chemicals	754.7	644.4	669.6	677.2	845.4
Basic manufactures	6,251.9	7,231.6	6,649.8	6,956.9	7,377.4
of which: textiles	2,210.1	2,458.9	2,250.4	2,423.0	2,614.5
iron and steel	1,651.3	1,843.4	1,901.0	1,832.3	2,044.7
metal structures	147.4	328.4	393.6	581.0	557.5
Machinery and transport equipt.	3,555.4	4,839.1	6,152.7	7,981.3	10,462.0
of which:					
office machinery	88.6	95.3	121.4	235.5	438.8
TV, audio and telecom.					
equipment	1,086.7	1,283.2	1,111.4	1,540.5	1,857.0
road vehicles	362.8	457.5	425.1	334.1	669.0
ships and floating structures	617.6	1,411.4	2,831.7	3,735.0	4,683.6
Miscellaneous manufactures	5,229.1	6,501.2	6,534.4	6,721.1	8,093.1
of which: apparel	2,949.4	3,867.5	3,773.9	3,707.3	4,499.5
footwear	874.5	1,024.1	1,154.4	1,234.8	1,351.6
toys and sports goods	367.8	366.0	434.1	428.7	675.4
TOTAL	17,504.9	21,253.7	21,853.4	24,445.0	29,244.9

Source: National Statistics

TABLE 3.22   SOUTH KOREA: MAJOR EXPORT MARKETS

US$ mn	1980	1981	1982	1983	1984
Japan	3,039.4	3,502.8	3,388.1	3,403.6	4,602.1
People's Republic of China	216.3	262.6	206.8	150.1	258.8
Hong Kong	823.3	1,154.7	903.8	817.7	1,281.2
Singapore	266.3	305.6	380.8	538.8	496.8
Saudi Arabia	946.1	1,136.2	1,125.4	1,436.5	990.9
West Germany	875.5	804.5	757.9	775.3	924.2
UK	572.5	705.0	1,102.6	1,005.2	955.5
Canada	343.4	483.5	442.8	629.2	878.5
USA	4,606.6	5,660.6	6,243.2	8,245.4	10,478.8
Australia	230.4	293.6	307.4	332.5	392.2
TOTAL	17,504.9	21,253.7	21,853.4	24,445.0	29,244.9

Source: National Statistics

Taiwan

Taiwan's trading position is summarised in Tables 3.23–3.25, the rapid development of the visible surplus in the 1980s being noteworthy. The current surplus in 1984 was US$ 6 bn compared to US$ 588 mn in 1975, US$ 630 mn in 1981, US$ 2,347 mn in 1982 and US$ 4,609 mn in 1983. The two most important categories of goods exported are textile products and electrical equipment; of total textile exports in 1984, 41.4% went to the US and 11.3% to Hong Kong, much of the latter for re-export. Japan took 9.1%. The US purchased 58.7% of electrical

TABLE 3.23   TAIWAN: COMMODITY TRADE SUMMARY

NT$ mn	Exports (f.o.b.)	Imports (c.i.f.)	Balance
1970	59,257	61,110	−1,853
1980	712,195	711,433	762
1981	829,756	778,633	51,123
1982	864,248	736,084	128,164
1983	1,005,422	813,904	191,518
1984	1,204,697	870,861	333,836

Source: National Statistics

TABLE 3.24   TAIWAN: PRINCIPAL TRADING PARTNERS IN 1984

	Exports			Imports	
Country	Value (mn NT$)	% of total	Country	Value (mn NT$)	% of total
USA	588,060	48.8	Japan	255,441	29.3
Japan	126,092	10.5	USA	200,003	23.0
Hong Kong	82,523	6.9	Saudi Arabia	78,158	9.0
Canada	36,258	3.0	Australia	30,862	3.6
Singapore	34,431	2.8	West Germany	30,441	3.5
West Germany	34,354	2.8	Kuwait	28,890	3.3

Source: National Statistics

equipment exports, other important destinations being Hong Kong (8.4%), Japan (5.1%) and West Germany (3.5%).

While the composition of imports has changed very little over the last twenty years, the growth of the above-mentioned industries has had a profound effect on the structure of exports. In 1964, 55.7% of exports were food or beverage products, but by the end of 1984 this had fallen to 5.5%.

TABLE 3.25   VALUE OF PRINCIPAL EXPORTS

US$ mn	1970	1980	1981	1982	1983	1984
Textile products	469.8	4,480.1	5,031.4	4,787.6	5,000.3	6,086.8
Wood and wood products (excl. plywood)	50.1	811.6	813.0	776.5	945.0	1,070.6
Refined petroleum products	6.4	289.9	440.0	418.4	455.5	540.2
Plastic products	—	1,459.5	1,616.5	1,499.3	1,781.8	2,413.6
Chemicals	35.6	445.9	540.9	594.0	588.4	704.2
Basic metals	65.2	396.6	504.6	663.9	695.5	737.5
Metal manufactures	28.4	861.8	1,051.9	1,018.7	1,354.3	1,740.6
Machinery (excl. electrical)	48.4	744.7	941.2	844.8	966.2	1,143.8
Electrical machinery and apparatus	182.4	3,598.8	4,170.8	3,910.0	4,853.8	6,578.4
TOTAL	1,481.4	19,810.6	22,611.2	22,204.2	25,122.7	30,456.4

Source: National Statistics

Imports in 1984 were dominated by crude oil (17.1% of the total, approximately one-half from Saudi Arabia). Japan and the US are the principal suppliers of machinery, transport and electrical equipment which constitute 27.1% of Taiwan's total import bill.

VIII   Foreign investment

The Hong Kong authorities publish little information about investment from overseas, but do provide domestic figures for total loans and advances made available to different sectors of the productive economy on a year-by-year basis. Of the HK$ 220.9 bn advanced in 1984 by banks and deposit-taking companies, only HK$ 18.8 bn went to manufacturing (the textile, electrical and electronic industries getting the largest shares). A further HK$ 20.6 bn was advanced to the transport/ transport equipment sector, with HK$ 48.1 bn going to construction. Advances to wholesale and retail trades totalled HK$ 28.2 bn. The main purpose of other loans was the purchase of residential property.

Of the 2,005 companies known to be operating in Hong Kong in 1984 but incorporated outside, 473 were US concerns, 294 from the UK and 238 from Japan. South Korean enterprises active in the colony numbered 22. There is a growing number of companies operating in Hong Kong that are sponsored from China.

Little information is available about investment in Macao, but it is believed to be growing fast now that a political settlement looks likely to be reached shortly.

There is certainly some Soviet investment in North Korean industry, although how much is not known. A recently-introduced law permits joint ventures with foreign partners, but so far there have been few takers.

Foreign investment is encouraged in South Korea, where most basic industries were set up with Japanese or US funding. Only in certain high-technology industries is a 51% joint venture participation by a foreign concern permitted.

Table 3.26 demonstrates that private foreign investment is growing

TABLE 3.26   TAIWAN: PRIVATE FOREIGN INVESTMENT (APPROVALS) BY SOURCE

US$ '000 Year	Total	USA	Japan	Europe
1980	**243,380**	110,093	86,081	14,428
1981	**356,294**	203,213	64,623	12,636
1982	**320,286**	79,606	152,164	46,570
1983	**375,382**	93,294	196,770	20,746
1984	**518,971**	231,175	113,978	92,242

Source: National Statistics

very rapidly in Taiwan. Over the period 1952–1984, 31.0% has been in the electrical/electronic industries, 15.7% in chemicals and 12.3% in services. Nationals resident abroad are a major source; over the same period these provided 25.4% of the funds.

ASEAN Countries

Malaysia
Indonesia
Singapore
Philippines
Thailand

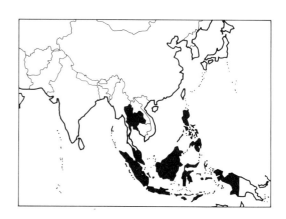

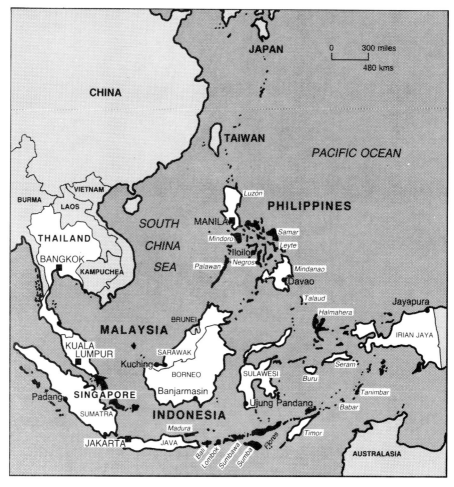

Chapter Four

ASEAN COUNTRIES

I Overview

The five countries examined in this chapter, Indonesia, Malaysia, the Philippines, Singapore and Thailand are all members of ASEAN. Indonesia has been run for 20 years as a virtual one-party state, in which the 'New Order' alliance (*Golkar*), with its military administrators, holds undisputed power. The country has achieved considerable growth during this period, based on its magnificent agricultural potential and its considerable natural resources; but in the mid-1980s its prospects were dimmed by falling oil prices and by foreign protectionism which seemed likely to damage its trading position.

Malaysia, one of the fastest-developing countries in the ASEAN region, has owed its relative prosperity almost exclusively to its dominance of world markets for its principal export commodities. Its most impressive period of growth came during the commodity boom of the late 1970s, but in the mid-1980s the economy has become increasingly bogged down by the slump in international markets and by the worsening financial difficulties which have ensued. Economic growth was halved between 1984 and 1985, and early 1986 brought no indications of an upturn. As a result the government has been forced to review several of its political priorities and to reduce its planned expenditure on industrial and infrastructural development.

The Philippines, with its tropical climate, its fertile soil and its placid, hard-working population, would seem in itself to have ideal prospects for economic growth. Its strategic position between the South China Sea and the Pacific, with its clear sea access to the other ASEAN nations, to Taiwan and Indochina, has attracted substantial financial assistance and patronage from many countries over the years—notably the United States, which has its two largest overseas military bases stationed at Clark Field and Subic Bay, and which maintains close political, social and economic links with the islands.

The mid-1980s brought, however, a serious deterioration of the national economy, and a massive loss of international confidence ensued which had still to be resolved at the start of 1986. The instability was mainly due to the increasing political turmoil in the Philippines, which suddenly worsened in August 1983 with the murder of the opposition leader Benigno Aquino, apparently by government forces, which signalled the end of President Marcos' domination of the political scene. In February 1986 Benigno Aquino's widow, Corazor Aquino, became president, following a general election which the incumbent president Ferdinand Marcos claimed to have won (although the election appeared to be rigged in Marcos' favour). Marcos then fled the country, to take refuge initially in the USA.

The true extent of the economic dislocation under Marcos will not become clear for some years. Many of the country's official figures have long been tampered with, in an effort to conceal the deterioration and thus to preserve the Marcos regime; the government information given in this section, especially the monetary statistics, remains subject to revision.

Singapore, by far the smallest country in the ASEAN group, has nevertheless become one of the most prosperous nations in east Asia, thanks to the intelligent use of its well-placed port facilities and its thriving relations with Western nations. The country has also established a comprehensive manufacturing base, and has attracted substantial investment from abroad; it is, for example, the third largest oil refining centre in the world, after Houston and Rotterdam, and it has the world's second most active port.

The mid-1980s have, however, brought clear signs that the boom may be over for the time being. The slowing of growth in the US and the general depression in commodity markets have made deep inroads into Singapore's traditional export activities; simultaneously the completion of Indonesia's own oil refineries in 1984 has removed some of the country's traditional processing business whilst at the same time sharpening price competition in the local market.

Thailand's economy is almost entirely based on the agricultural sector and on the export of agricultural raw materials. As such it has made remarkable progress since the 1960s, although from a very low base, and it has managed even during the regional recession of the mid–1980s to keep its annual growth comfortably above 5%. The country has had difficulty in restraining monetary forces, however, and in the early 1980s the government had to act against clear indications of overheating. Events since then have been dominated by its efforts to restrain the expansion-led growth of the national debt, and to counter the

72

increasingly difficult conditions in the export commodity markets on which the national economy depends.

Political affairs are heavily dominated by the armed forces, which have traditionally adopted a centralised and indeed dirigiste attitude to the economy. Political differences have arisen among army factions, however, and by the end of 1985 at least three unsuccessful coup d'etats had been staged against the military-dominated government of Prem Tinsulanond.

II Population

Indonesia

Indonesia has the fourth largest population in the world, with 165,153,000 inhabitants in 1985. The rate of growth has slowed somewhat since the 1960s, thanks to a concerted family planning effort, but the economy is still weighed down by the 1,800,000 people joining

TABLE 4.1   INDONESIA: POPULATION

'000s at mid-year excluding East Timor	1980	1981	1982	1983	1984	1985
Sumatra	28,121	29,028	29,962	30,929	31,928	32,960
Java	91,610	93,340	94,103	96,893	98,712	100,560
Nusa Tenggara	8,519	8,676	8,835	8,996	9,160	9,325
Kalimantan	6,748	6,942	7,143	7,350	7,564	7,784
Sulawesi	10,448	10,665	10,887	11,112	11,341	11,575
Maluku and Irian Jaya	2,595	2,663	2,732	2,803	2,875	2,949
TOTAL	148,041	151,314	153,662	158,083	161,580	165,153

Source: Government of Indonesia

Notes: East Timor: 555,350 (1980 census). This is regarded as a low figure by the United Nations, which had put the figure at 720,000 in 1978.
Total area (excluding East Timor): 1,904,569 sq km. East Timor: 14,874 sq km. Population density (1983, excluding East Timor): 82.1 per sq km. East Timor (1980): 37.4 per sq km.

the workforce every year; it has been calculated, for example, that Indonesia would need an annual economic growth in excess of 10% to supply enough new jobs. By the year 2000 the total population is likely to exceed 200,000,000, even at the current growth rate of 2.2% per annum.

As Table 4.1 shows, around 61% of the population live on Java, the central island in the main land chain. Java's rich volcanic soil certainly offers the most scope for agriculture, but it represents only 7% of the country's total land area, and serious overcrowding problems have resulted here. The government has been worried by a continuing drift of unemployed people towards the capital, Jakarta, and it has instituted a resettlement scheme which aims, with state funding and subsidies, to move 750,000 families out to Sumatra, Kalimantan and Irian Jaya by 1988/89; by early 1986, however, the level of take-up by settlers had been highly disappointing for the authorities.

The Indonesian population comprises a rich mixture of races, of which Malays are by far the dominant group; Chinese represent a small proportion by local standards, at about 3%. Over 85% of the population profess the faith of Islam, meaning that Indonesia has by far the largest Muslim population in the world.

Malaysia

Malaysia has a strongly heterogeneous population, with Chinese and Indians forming more than a third of the total. There are recurring tensions between the Chinese, who have historically been the more wealthy and entrepreneurial sector, and the more numerous Malays, who have always been poorer but who currently enjoy greater official favour. A prime aim of the government's long-term policy is to deliver more economic power to the Malays; they already control the political structure.

As Table 4.2 shows, over 80% of the population live on Peninsular Malaysia, which comprises 40% of the country's total 330,434 sq. km. The remainder is located on Sarawak and Sabah, which lie across the South China Sea bordering on Indonesia. In recent years political tensions have sharpened in these territories, and in 1985 the government suffered a major defeat in local elections at Sabah, during which secessionist sentiments were very much in evidence.

74

TABLE 4.2 MALAYSIA: POPULATION

'000s at mid-year

	1984	1985	1986*	Population density, persons per sq. km. 1986*
Peninsular Malaysia	12,651	12,978	16,095	40.64
Malays	7,122	7,344	7,573	
Chinese	4,168	4,244	4,377	
Indians	1,280	1,307	1,347	
Others	81	83	85	
Sarawak	1,442	1,477	1,485	11.98
Sabah	1,177	1,222	1,228	16.66
TOTAL POPULATION	15,270	15,677	16,095	48.88

Source: Ministry of Finance, Government of Malaysia
Note: *Government estimates

TABLE 4.3 MALAYSIA: COMPOSITION OF THE WORKFORCE

	1983	1984	1985	% of total, 1985
Agriculture, livestock, forestry and fishing	1,940,900	1,960,900	1,980,900	35.5
Mining and quarrying	64,900	64,000	63,400	1.1
Manufacturing	800,300	833,300	876,300	15.7
Construction	345,600	369,400	386,800	6.9
Transport, storage and communications	241,800	256,300	272,300	4.9
Commerce, finance and business services	712,800	742,500	773,500	13.9
Government services	837,100	867,800	895,500	16.1
Other services	301,400	312,700	327,200	5.9
TOTAL	5,244,800	5,406,900	5,575,900	100.0

Source:

Philippines

The Philippines has a population estimated in mid-1984 at 53,350,000, and the number has been growing at around 1,250,000 per annum since the mid-1970s. Over 45% are under 15 years old, and although the majority still live in rural areas, there has been a drift since the mid-1970s toward the towns, where 37.3% lived in 1980 (according to the latest available government statistics). Most of the inhabitants are Malays, but there are some Chinese and a few Spanish speakers. US forces are influential in the areas around the two military bases.

Reflecting the country's past as a former Spanish colony, some 85% of the population practise the Roman Catholic faith, with around 2,000,000 Muslims living in the southern islands. Although most people speak the national language, Filipino, the English language is normally used in business, education and even politics.

TABLE 4.4   PHILIPPINES: POPULATION

	Total	Urban	Rural
1950	20,274,800	n.a.	n.a.
1960*	27,087,685	n.a.	n.a.
1970*	36,862,486	11,677,820	25,006,666
1975*	42,070,660	14,046,527	28,024,138
1976	43,406,278	14,872,747	28,533,531
1977	44,584,324	15,619,210	28,391,205
1978	45,794,343	16,403,138	29,391,205
1979	47,037,201	17,226,412	29,810,789
1980*	48,098,460	17,943,897	30,154,563
1981†	49,540,000	n.a.	n.a.
1982†	50,780,000	n.a.	n.a.
1983†	52,060,000	n.a.	n.a.
1984†	53,350,000	n.a.	n.a.

Source: Philippines National Census and Statistics Office

Notes: *Census results   †IMF estimates

TABLE 4.5   PHILIPPINES: COMPOSITION OF THE WORKFORCE IN 1983

'000s

Agriculture, forestry and fisheries	9,880
Mining and quarrying	102

TABLE 4.5   PHILIPPINES: COMPOSITION OF THE WORKFORCE IN 1983

(continued)

'000s

Manufacturing	1,887
Electricity, gas and water	78
Construction	697
Commerce	2,197
Transport, storage and communications	831
Finance and business services	356
Community, social and personal services	3,184
TOTAL	19,212

Source: Philippines National Census and Statistics Office

Singapore

Singapore has one of the highest population densities in the world, with 4,126 persons per sq. km. in 1985. The total 2,558,000 inhabitants of the city state are predominantly of Chinese origin, but they also include about 15% Malays and 6% Indians. The country has achieved a very low birth rate of 1.1%, after years of concerted effort.

The Government of Lee Kwan Yew aims in the long term to achieve

TABLE 4.6   SINGAPORE: POPULATION

'000s

	Total	Male	Female	% Annual increase
1970 census	2,074.5	1,062.1	1,012.4	2.8
1980 census	2,413.9	1,231.7	1,182.2	1.5
1981 estimate	2,443.3	1,246.3	1,197.0	1.2
1982 estimate	2,471.8	1,260.4	1,211.4	1.2
1983 estimate	2,502.0	1,275.5	1,226.5	1.1
1984 estimate	2,529.1	1,288.7	1,240.4	1.1
1985 estimate	2,558.0	1,302.9	1,255.1	1.1

Source: Government of Singapore

TABLE 4.7 SINGAPORE: COMPOSITION OF THE LABOUR FORCE IN 1984

	Total	Employees	Employers	Self-employed	Unpaid family workers
Agriculture and fishing	8,830	3,046	247	3,561	1,976
Quarrying	1,894	1,811	62	21	—
Manufacturing	322,189	301,194	9,942	9,965	1,358
Utilities	9,160	9,160	—	—	—
Construction	99,787	82,209	7,410	9,715	453
Trade and commerce	264,638	173,722	27,252	45,139	18,525
Transport and communications	122,408	99,046	3,129	19,842	391
Financial and business services	100,940	91,945	5,393	3,499	103
Other services	242,182	226,950	5,002	9,365	864
Other activities	2,799	2,120	21	659	—
TOTAL	1,174,827	991,205	58,456	101,496	23,671

Source: Ministry of Labour

Note: Columns may not add up, due to rounding

a complete transition of the economy towards higher added-value activities, and away from the traditional low-skill, low-wage industries. It particularly wants to see Singapore become the centre for intellectual and skilled labour within the ASEAN group, and has invested vast sums over the years in education and vocational training.

Thailand

Thailand has a strongly homogeneous population which in 1984 comprised about 45,000,000 ethnic Thais, some 4,000,000 Chinese and 700,000 Muslims, as well as a scattering of hill people. According to the 1984 census, over 40% of the population were aged under 15, but the trend has evidently slowed; population growth in 1986 was down to around 1.5% per annum—fairly low by regional standards.

Only about 20% of the population are currently living in urban centres, but its number is growing rapidly in the mid-1980s as peasants, attracted by the higher living standards, have moved to the cities; it has been estimated, for example, that the urban middle-class earns nine times as much as the average farmer. The government is seriously worried by this development, and has set out to improve conditions in rural communities so as to rectify the demographic balance.

TABLE 4.8   THAILAND: POPULATION

'000s, at mid–year

	Total	Male	Female	Population density (per sq km)
1960 census	26,258	13,154	13,104	51.1
1970 census	34,397	17,124	22,008	67.0
1980 census	44,825	22,329	22,496	87.2
1982 estimate	48,450	24,339	24,111	94.0
1983 estimate	49,585	24,904	24,681	96.5
1984 estimate	50,588	n.a.	n.a.	98.6

Source: Government of Thailand

III   Government policy

Indonesia

The immense progress made by the Indonesian economy since 1962 is in no small part due to the long-term economic planning conducted by President Sukarno and his successor Dr Suharto. The government operates a system of Five-Year Plans, of which the current Plan (Repelita IV, for 1984/85–1988/89) aims to consolidate the results of earlier Plans, to promote living standards, to spread wealth more evenly and to create the foundations for the next stage of development (Repelita V). The Plan places emphasis on agricultural and rural development, and the improvement of the rural infrastructure—particularly important in view of the population drift toward the cities—and the continuing development of the country's industrial base. This has also involved the modernisation of communications systems throughout this vast country, and notably the launching into orbit of telecommunications satellites.

The first Plan, Repelita I, aimed to establish agricultural self-sufficiency, and was largely successful; the second stressed the start of industrial development, based mainly on the country's abundant raw materials; and the most memorable achievement of the third was the inauguration of Indonesia's own oil refining facilities, enabling Indonesia for the first time to establish itself as a major exporter of petroleum products—much to the chagrin of Singapore, which had until then held a local near-monopoly.

Nonetheless, the prospects for the new Plan have been dampened by the continuing downturn in world commodity markets, notably for oil, and by protectionism in the United States. It appears likely that economic growth in 1986 will be flat, falling far short of the reduced growth target of 5% per annum; the Plan for 1978/79–83/84, by comparison, set a target of 6.5% per annum.

It also appears that the huge and unwieldy bureaucracy in Indonesia will continue to put a brake on future development. The government has made little sincere effort to reform the system, in which up to a third of all central spending is believed to disappear without trace, thanks to the persistence of corruption and favouritism.

Malaysia

The chief achievement of Malaysia's current administration has been the implementation of the New Economic Policy, a 20-year programme first introduced in 1970. The Policy aims at nothing less than a revolution in economic relations, involving the promotion of domestic industry using domestic resources; the diversification of the economic base away from the then dominant rubber and timber businesses; and, most controversially, the changing of the ethnic power balance (meaning in effect the promotion of economic and political power among Malay rather than Chinese groups). This has caused deep discontent not only among the country's Chinese, but also in the Chinese government, which has repeatedly protested over the issue; Malaysia was the only ASEAN member to be doing less business with China in 1985 than it was in 1980. Overall, Malaysians are intended under the New Economic Policy to own at least 70% of every business by 1990, and of this at least 30% is to be held by Malays.

In February 1986 the government unveiled an ambitious development plan for the period to 1995. During this period, it claimed, real GDP would rise by an average 6.4% per annum (compared with the 4.8% recorded at the start of 1986, and the target of 7%). The government said it believed that Malaysia should be able to move directly into a stage of advanced industrialisation, bypassing various intermediate stages, if it could quadruple the number of technicians from the 12,000 it had in 1985. The plan was based, like previous plans, on the optimal use of local natural gas and oil; however, it also envisaged an increase in the use of Malaysian rubber and palm oil.

Philippines

The former Marcos regime spent its last years embroiled in a civil war with the communist guerrillas of the New People's Army, who were rapidly gaining ground in the rural districts of Mindanao by the mid-1980s, and who capitalised on the then growing dissatisfaction with Marcos. The incoming Aquino administration appeared in early 1986 to have reached a temporary truce with them.

On the economic front the Aquino/Laurel government immediately announced its intention to reform the economy, to seize the assets of the former Marcos administration, to clear the bureaucracy of corruption and to ensure a more equitable distribution of wealth. It did not appear to have any scope for an expansion of public-sector spending, particularly in view of the pressing external debt; the President said that she would be seeking a rescheduling of the Philippines' international obligations as soon as possible.

Since June 1984 the country has operated a dual-rate exchange system, in its efforts to obtain the all-important foreign currency. In 1985 the peso remained stable because of the cutbacks on imports, and ended the year at P19=US $1.00—almost certainly too high, and a depressant factor on exports. It has been alleged in early 1986 that the Marcos administration falsified the money supply figures by various means; if this is corroborated, the effects on the exchange rate could be considerable.

Singapore

For many years the government of Singapore has sought to stimulate the domestic sector with massive central spending—notably on construction projects, in the firm Keynesian belief that the benefits would filter down through the entire economy. While this has undoubtedly been true, it has led to a high level of foreign borrowing, to a consistent overvaluation of the Singapore dollar on world money markets, and finally to the recent surplus of buildings in the city. With the recession which set in during 1985, many of its plans have had to be shelved; but, unrepentant, it was still planning in 1986 to proceed with its massively expensive underground railway, the Mass Rapid Transit system.

The steady rise in average wages has severely limited the country's international competitiveness, but by early 1986 the government had still to take restraining action. It conceded, however, in January 1986 that the profitability of the manufacturing sector had fallen by 70% in 1985.

In April 1985 the government established a 12–member economic committee to review the country's development plan for the 1980s, in the light of the continuing recession. It reported later in the year that the country's policy of leading wealth creation through the construction sector had been misguided, and it demanded lower wages, especially changes in the system of centralised pay bargaining. The government nevertheless announced in March 1986 that state spending was once again to increase sharply, in another effort to stimulate growth through centralised funding.

Thailand

Thailand's economic policy has undergone some very marked fluctuations in recent years, due to the changing external conditions on which the export-dependent country relies. Medium-term policy is defined by a series of Five-Year Plans, the last of which (1982–86) stressed that structural reform would soon be needed, even at the expense of slower economic growth. Accordingly, the government introduced a series of austerity budgets in 1983–86, targeted mainly to limit public spending and to restrain consumer demand. This would have happened even without the contraction of world commodity markets, but the task has clearly taken on a new urgency in the mid-1980s.

As has already been noted, rural development is regarded as the most pressing problem facing the government, but there has been increasing emphasis on the reduction of overspending by state agencies. In 1984 and early 1985 the authorities tried, unsuccessfully, to stop nationalised industries from undertaking heavy foreign borrowing, and the government was looking at the possibility of selling off some of the nationalised industries in an attempt to reduce its own level of commitments. It has also disappointed its ASEAN partners by cancelling two major projects, a soda ash plant and a steel complex, which were to have formed part of an ASEAN regional development programme.

The government is committed to the development of roads, transport and infrastructural facilities, and was due by 1986 to have completed two new deep-water docks for the facilitation of international trade.

The government has continued in the mid-1980s to face serious armed opposition from practically all sides, and the role of the army in state affairs seems unlikely to diminish in the foreseeable future. Firstly, Muslim secessionist factions have been active in the south of the country, and have periodically caused disruptions; secondly, the opium warlords of the north have continued to pit their own private armies against the government forces; and thirdly, the army has been engaged in a prolonged and largely successful campaign against the guerrillas of the Communist Party, who have launched frequent and violent attacks over the years—although there were indications by 1985 that their political support was on the wane.

IV Economic performance and structure

Indonesia

Indonesia has achieved steady and impressive growth since the 1960s, thanks to a generally conservative policy of growth based on the country's natural resources—mainly the processing of agricultural raw materials and the export of commodities. In 1985 the country's national debts, at around US $30,000 mn, were regarded as well within its ability to pay, and the country has accumulated a substantial volume of foreign exchange reserves to safeguard its foreign trade position.

Nevertheless, Indonesia has not escaped the impact of a slowing world market for crude oil, the commodity which, together with natural gas, accounted in 1983 for 73% of foreign exchange earnings and 65% of government revenues; in 1982 the growth of GDP slumped from 7.9% to only 2.2%, and in 1983 the government was forced to shelve some of its more ambitious plans for industrial expansion, while at the same time devaluing the national currency, the rupiah, by 27.5%.

TABLE 4.9   INDONESIA: ECONOMIC GROWTH

'000 rupiahs	1979	1980	1981	1982*	1983*
GDP at current prices	223,887	310,502	360,957	389,786	455,418
GDP at constant 1973 prices	71,062	76,312	80,537	80,564	82,126
GNP at current prices	213,509	296,764	348,097	376,991	436,004
GNP at constant 1973 prices	66,523	71,128	76,036	76,298	76,785
National Income at current factor cost†	189,781	265,358	312,928	337,716	391,817
National Income at constant 1973 factor cost	58,419	62,432	66,859	67,118	67,427

Source:

Notes: *Provisional figures

　　　　†National Income is defined as net national product

TABLE 4.10   INDONESIA: COMPOSITION OF GDP

mn rupiahs	1979	1980	1981	1982	1983
Agriculture, forestry and fisheries	3,255.6	3,424.9	3,593.5	3,669.8	3,845.6
Mining and quarrying	1,046.9	1,034.6	1,069.1	939.8	956.5
Manufacturing	1,395.3	1,704.6	1,877.8	1,900.7	1,942.5
Electricity, gas and water	68.6	77.9	89.9	105.5	112.8
Construction	562.8	639.3	720.2	757.8	804.5
Transport and communications	559.8	609.4	676.9	716.6	752.5
Banking and financial services	179.6	207.8	231.4	258.4	276.5
Ownership of dwelling	306.1	335.8	358.7	377.4	400.6
Public administration and defence	805.1	971.7	318.7	326.1	334.3
Services	304.0	311.3	318.7	326.1	334.3
TOTAL GDP	10,164.9	11,169.2	12,054.6	12,325.4	12,842.2

Source: Indonesian Government Statistical Bureau

At first the economy responded well to these measures, and growth was resurrected to a level of 5% by 1984. However, the impact of the oil price falling to below US$ 15 per barrel in late 1985 (compared, for example, with a high of around $36 in 1980), forced the authorities to take corrective planning measures in 1986 which resulted in the unprecedented 7% budget expenditure cut with development spending slashed by 22%.

Agriculture still accounts for nearly a third of Indonesia's GDP and employs 55% of the labour force. The sector has made great strides since the 1960s, when the country was the world's largest importer of rice. It actually became a rice exporter in 1984, when an embarrassingly large surplus was recorded and domestic prices for rice threatened for a while to collapse. It is estimated that 30 mn farmers are involved in rice production. 38% of the total cultivated land area is given up to rice.

TABLE 4.11   INDONESIA: AGRICULTURAL PRODUCTION

'000 tonnes	1979	1980	1981	1982	1983
Rice (paddy)	26,283	29,652	32,774	33,584	35,237
Rice (wet land)	.24,732	27,993	30,989	31,776	33,210
Rice (dry land)	1,551	1,659	1,785	1,808	2,027
Maize	3,606	3,994	4,509	3,235	5,095
Cassava	1,439	1,412	1,388	1,324	1,242
Sweet potatoes	2,194	2,078	2,094	1,676	2,044
Groundnuts	424	470	475	437	476
Soya beans	680	653	704	521	568

Source: Indonesian Government Statistical Bureau

Agricultural reforms have come about through a concerted government policy of subsidies and incentives for the use of improved seed strains and fertilisers. In 1969 farmers used 357,000 tonnes of fertiliser compared to 4.1 mn tonnes in 1984. The country has also invested heavily in the construction of irrigation systems, and has sought to expand its production of other grains—with somewhat variable results. Java is perhaps the most intensively cultivated island in the world, with a natural productivity vastly superior to the other islands; small wonder, then, that the attempts at resettlement onto the less fertile soil of Sumatra or Irian Jaya have met with resistance.

TABLE 4.12   INDONESIA: VEGETABLE PRODUCTION IN 1982

tonnes

Shallots	70,993
Onions	156,443
Potatoes	157,696
Radishes	17,908
Cabbages	316,161
Mustard green	122,915
Carrots	50,471
Dry beans	25,326
Other vegetables	12,417

Source: Indonesian Government Statistical Bureau

TABLE 4.13   INDONESIA: LIVESTOCK IN 1983

Cattle	9,041,500
of which: dairy	179,800
Buffaloes	2,390,600
Horses	527,000
Goats	10,969,300
Sheep	4,789,400
Pigs	4,065,500

Source: Indonesian Government Statistical Bureau

The government has also sought to develop cash crops in its efforts to improve the foreign trade position and diversify the manufacturing base. The country is already the world's second largest producer of Robusta coffee, and although it has yet to become self-sufficient in sugar it has made substantial progress in recent years. Sugar output has quadrupled over the past 10 years. Production of rubber (the traditional agricultural export) has been dulled by poor world prices for the commodity, but a concerted push to expand the palm oil industry has been highly successful.

Indonesia's tropical hardwoods represent a further important source of foreign exchange, and the country controls about two-thirds of the world market for plywood. Since 1985 the export of whole logs has been banned altogether, in line with the government's policy of developing the country's own timber processing industries.

TABLE 4.14   INDONESIA: FORESTRY PRODUCTION

tonnes

	1979	1980	1981	1982
Sawlogs	25,313,638	25,190,143	15,954,426	13,376,513
Sawn wood	1,636,938	1,784,723	1,791,092	3,686,400
Charcoal	28,540	20,654	3,657	n.a.
Fuel wood	356,228	417,385	364,711	n.a.
Rattan	70,476	53,908	28,921	n.a.
Bamboo*	111,134	41,125	n.a.	n.a.
Resins	2,867	2,450	7,179	n.a.
Turpentine	698,822	838,831	813,831	n.a.

Source: Department of Forestry, Indonesian Government
Note: *Stalks

TABLE 4.15   INDONESIA: FISHERY PRODUCTION

tonnes

	Total catch	Offshore	Inland
1970	1,228,512	807,391	421,121
1975	1,390,074	996,856	393,218
1980	1,849,662	1,394,810	454,852
1981	1,914,505	1,408,272	506,233
1982	1,975,300	1,448,300	527,000
1983	2,046,200	1,486,800	559,400

Source: Government of Indonesia

Rubber currently represents the third largest source of foreign exchange for Indonesia, which has been promoting the continued development of the crop as a means of diversifying away from its dependence on the hydrocarbons sector. The industry is already thought to provide employment for up to 10 mn people, but the government wants to see a further expansion by 1990. Other important export crops include tapioca, but here again falling world market prices have dampened interest in the crop.

Indonesia's industrial base has undergone a significant expansion in the past two decades, under the influence of successive economic plans. The sector grew by an average 12.5% during the 1970s, fuelled by cheap domestically-produced energy and the commodities boom of the mid-decade. Particular emphasis was placed on the processing of agricultural raw materials, and a large proportion of output was exported. At the same time the government invested large amounts in the development of heavy industries (iron, steel, fertilisers, cement, and paper and wood processing), and notably in the oil and petrochemical fields whilst the private sector channelled its funds into light manufacturing operations such as textiles, electronics, pharmaceuticals and plastics.

TABLE 4.16   INDONESIA: MANUFACTURING INDUSTRIES

Quarterly index of production (1975=100)	1982	1983	1984/1	1984/2
General manufacturing index	213	221	229	234
Dairy products	239	261	254	248
Malt liquors and malt	170	193	212	209
Clove cigarettes	187	196	205	321
Cigarettes	115	120	118	118
Yarn and thread	121	114	122	127
Weaving, excl. jute	130	121	125	125
Batik	110	105	122	122
Footwear	124	125	126	126
Plywood	424	438	411	374
Paper	151	136	106	102
Fertiliser	495	560	631	700
Other chemicals	130	132	141	159
Paint and varnish	167	147	161	165
Matches	230	291	308	306
Tyres and tubes	293	300	313	305
Glass and glass products	209	227	242	242
Cement	419	460	484	442
Basic iron and steel	970	1,146	1,232	1,123
Structural metal products	196	203	219	200
Dry batteries	267	328	300	341
Electronics	333	351	319	316
Motorcycles and three-wheeled vehicles	187	130	94	115
Other motor vehicles	226	197	177	153

Source: Statistical Bureau, Government of Indonesia

The decline in oil revenues combined with government protectionism and restrictive practices has caused a significant slump in industrial output in the 1980s. The Repelita IV envisaged annual average growth of 9.5% per annum and this will now not be attainable. The worst hit industries at the moment appear to be automobiles (operating at 60% capacity), cement (operating at 50% capacity) and electronics (in some segments at 25% capacity). Conversely, the plywood sector has been holding up well along with fertilisers, plastics and pharmaceuticals.

As has been noted elsewhere, the government has made particular efforts in recent years to encourage a diversification of the country's industrial structure, and to attract direct foreign assistance to this end. In view of the severe cutbacks forced by trade difficulties, this option is likely to appear more and more attractive. In 1985/86 the authorities see particular scope in the food processing industry, which has the advantage of low import requirements.

Indonesia is exceptionally well endowed with natural resources, the most important of which are its oil and gas reserves; until 1984 most of its crude petroleum was exported to Singapore for refining, but since then a number of plants has come onstream—many of them after months of delay caused by poor design or construction. The state oil company, Petramina, has a formal monopoly on every stage of the oil and gas industry, but in practice joint ventures with foreign oil companies have been the norm. Indonesia's total oil reserves were estimated in 1985 at 9,600 mn barrels, and are of particular interest to Japan, which is a very heavy consumer of hydrocarbons and which has relatively few other sources of energy outside the Middle East.

Despite the downturn in prices in 1985/86, oil is still crucial to Indonesia, accounting along with gas for 55% of government revenues with 70% of the country's foreign earnings deriving from the sector. Current capacity is 1.6 mn bpd, but production has been running in 1986 at around 1.4 mn bpd.

Indonesia's natural gas reserves are believed to exceed 2,000,000 mn sq. metres, of which 1,375,000 mn have already been proven. Gas, although also affected by slack world markets, has proved a more resilient export than petroleum, and development plans were going ahead in 1986 regardless of the cutbacks elsewhere in the economy. Indonesia has two major gas fields, at Badak (East Kalimantan) and Arun (North Sumatra), whose total output at the end of 1985 was contracted by Japan, in the form of LNG. The country is the world's largest exporter of LNG at around 15 mn tonnes per year although this could rise to 19 mn tonnes by 1990. A third major gas field has been located near the Natuna islands in the South China Sea, but it had not yet been developed by the start of 1986.

The country is also aiming to develop its extensive hard coal reserves, which are thought to exceed 21,000 mn tonnes. Production is scheduled under the Fourth Development Plan to reach 12 mn tonnes by 1990, compared with only 481,000 tonnes in 1981; but it remained doubtful in 1986 whether the anticipated surge in industrial demand, on which the coal industry depends, will match the government's expectations. However, domestic energy demand is rising at around 10% per annum and the authorities need to divert consumption away from oil.

TABLE 4.17   INDONESIA: MINERAL PRODUCTION

		1981	**1982**	**1983**	**1984**
Crude oil	'000 barrels	584,838	488,189	490,483	476,862
Natural gas	'000 mn cu ft	1,123,720	1,111,928	1,186,362	1,392,595
Tin	mn tonnes	35,394	33,806	26,553	22,547
Coal	mn tonnes	350,350	480,987	485,630	563,118
Bauxite	mn tonnes	1,203,380	700,247	777,869	845,524
Nickel ore	mn tonnes	1,543,219	1,640,922	1,278,031	1,207,976
Gold	kilos	183	223	259	203
Silver	kilos	2,000	3,058	1,794	1,881
Iron sand	mn tonnes	86,626	144,493	132,887	92,174
Asphalt	mn tonnes	276,498	330,842	533,188	597,500
Manganese ore	mn tonnes	2,587	17,894	8,318	9,000
Copper ore	mn tonnes	188,472	233,704	205,015	189,377

Source: Department of Energy and Mining, Government of Indonesia

Although non-oil mining provided only 7.6% of GDP in 1983, it makes a particularly important contribution to the economy since virtually all of its production is sold abroad. Indonesia is an important producer of tin and copper, and has invested large sums in smelting and tinplate installations. Copper is mainly located in Irian Jaya, to the extreme east of the country, while bauxite is found in Kalimantan and nickel deposits are located in Irian Jaya, Sulawesi, Kalimantan and Halmahera.

The sector has suffered in 1985/86 from depressed world markets, however, and the government is seeking further foreign investment in order to facilitate its continued development. Indonesia produces manganese, gold, silver and iron sand, all of which have fared better than its other base metals.

Malaysia

It is clear in the mid-1980s that Malaysia's current difficulties can be traced back to overspending and over-borrowing during the commodity boom of the late 1970s. The continuing depression in world commodity markets seems to have left the economy stranded and battling with a debt servicing burden which practically cancels out the trade surplus. The problem of financial balance became particularly pronounced in late 1985, when the effects of foreign protectionist sentiment were

TABLE 4.18   MALAYSIA: COMPOSITION OF GDP

US$ mn, at constant 1978 prices	1981	1982	1983	1984	1985*
Agriculture, livestock, forestry and fishing	10,375	11,375	11,302	11,623	11,867
Mining and quarrying	4,289	4,617	5,337	6,046	5,944
Manufacturing	9,343	9,694	10,488	11,703	12,464
Construction	2,367	2,598	2,867	2,988	3,157
Electricity, gas and water	689	721	798	890	990
Transport, storage and communications	2,847	2,984	3,138	3,464	3,800
Commerce, hotels and restaurants	5,694	6,104	6,583	7,107	7,668
Finance, insurance and business services	3,953	4,231	4,570	4,892	5,230
Government services	5,649	6,027	6,328	6,817	7,331
Other services	1,065	1,141	1,193	1,249	1,306
less imputed bank charges	877	1,152	1,397	1,595	1,643
plus import duties	2,087	2,116	2,429	2,522	2,615
TOTAL GDP at market prices	47,790	50,456	53,636	57,706	60,729

Source: Ministry of Finance, Government of Malaysia
Note: *Estimate

compounded for Malaysia by the slowing of growth in its manufactured exports, and especially by the failure of the International Tin Council to agree on a formula for reviving the collapsed tin market.

As Table 4.18 indicates, Malaysia differs from many of its neighbours in that mining and quarrying exceed in importance agriculture as a contributor to GDP. The sector grew by some 28% between 1982 and 1985, due mainly to an increase in petroleum production—although the collapse of prices for both oil and tin will have slowed its growth again by mid-1986.

TABLE 4.19   MALAYSIA: MINERAL PRODUCTION

'000 tonnes	1981	1982	1983
Tin concentrates	60	52	41
Iron ore	532	341	114
Copper	120	129	123
Bauxite	701	589	502
Crude petroleum	12,360	14,543	18,287
Liquefied natural gas	—	—	1,690

Source: United Nations

The country ranks as the world's largest producer of tin, but production has been diminishing since 1972, when a peak of 76,800 tonnes was achieved; the decline reflects not only a lack of price incentives but also the depletion of known deposits. Malaysia also produces bauxite, copper and iron ore, but all of these industries are also in steady decline.

Malaysia has an estimated 2,900 mn barrels of petroleum reserves, located mainly offshore Sabah and Sarawak. It has traditionally favoured the conservation of oil stocks in preference to their exploitation for quick rewards, but this policy was reversed in 1982/83, when production was raised by 22% because of the urgent need to increase foreign currency earnings; after a brief relapse in 1984/85 the government determined another major expansion of output in 1986, to approximately 510,000 bpd. Malaysia is not a member of OPEC so the state oil company Petronas has been free of the production constraints formerly imposed by OPEC on its members.

The country is also developing its very promising offshore finds of natural gas, which were estimated in 1985 at 54,000,000 mn cubic feet; new gas liquefaction plants enabled the country in 1984 to double its output of liquefied natural gas to 3,700,000 tonnes, compared with 1,690,000 tonnes in 1983.

The Fourth Malaysia Plan for 1981–85 envisaged that Malaysia's oil and gas industries will play a central role in the development of the country's industrial base—particularly petrochemicals and heavy industries. To this end the Government has offered various incentives and concessions to private enterprise in its search for foreign capital.

TABLE 4.20   MALAYSIA: BASIC PRODUCTION STATISTICS

	Commodities	1980	1983	1984	1985
Rubber	'000 tonnes	1,530	1,564	1,529	1,540
Palm oil	'000 tonnes	2,573	3,017	3,715	3,850
Sawlogs	'000 cu m	27,916	33,723	31,089	30,500
Sawn timber	'000 cu m	6,233	7,138	5,807	5,800
Tin (concentrates)	'000 tonnes	61.4	41.4	41.3	40.1
Crude oil	'000 bpd	275.0	383.0	446.8	430.0
Total industrial	1981=100	104.7	118.6	137.6	131.1
Mining	1981=100	105.4	132.0	165.6	161.4
Electricity	1981=100	103.7	115.6	124.7	133.7
Manufacturing of which:	1981=100	105.6	112.6	125.4	117.0
Food, beverages and tobacco	1981=100	106.8	104.8	115.1	104.0
Textiles, clothing and footwear	1981=100	95.9	95.2	104.4	101.2
Wood products	1981=100	108.4	121.4	99.9	103.3
Rubber products	1981=100	105.7	108.4	119.2	105.7
Chemical and chemical products	1981=100	92.1	95.9	102.7	112.8
Petroleum refineries	1981=100	109.2	139.8	149.0	130.2
Cement and cement products	1981=100	94.8	99.9	111.3	103.1
Basic metal and metal products	1981=100	105.1	103.6	135.1	126.1
Electrical and electronic goods	1981=100	126.7	148.5	201.6	171.3
Transport equipment	1981=100	96.0	111.1	119.7	127.8
Other manufactures	1981=100	93.1	93.4	93.3	97.7

Source: Ministry of Finance, Government of Malaysia

Malaysia has a small-scale but widely diversified industrial structure, manufacturing not only agriculture-based products but also such relatively advanced products as transport equipment and even computers (which are assembled under licence). By the early 1970s it had already moved well beyond the stage of import-substitution, and was seeking external financing for its export-intensive stage of manufacturing. In 1984 the country inaugurated its own car manufacturing plant, which has been seen as a prestige project rather than a genuine export producer. Production of the new car, the Proton, is protected by heavy duties on imported cars, which often exceed 40%.

Agriculture still accounts for more than 20% of Malaysia's GDP, and provides employment for 35.5% of the workforce (1985 figures). The sector has benefited since the 1960s from government incentives, however like the mineral sector it has been adversely affected since the early 1980s by low world market levels, and is constantly seeking new and less vulnerable export crops.

Nevertheless, the rubber industry has experienced a serious slump in recent years, due to world over-production. Malaysia played a key role during 1985 in the international efforts to stabilise the rubber price, but was ultimately unable to procure an agreement—meaning that the pressure on plantations is likely to continue for some years.

Since the 1980s, therefore, the government has turned instead to promoting the production of palm oil, which has the advantage of being

TABLE 4.21   MALAYSIA: PRINCIPAL AGRICULTURAL PRODUCTS

'000 tonnes	1981	1982	1983	1984
Rubber	1,510	1,494	1,562	1,580
Rice	1,301	1,204	1,171	1,134
Palm oil	2,825	3,514	3,020	3,717
Palm kernels	590	911	836	900
Coconut oil	66	70	156	157
Copra	38	39	264	266
Cocoa	51	69	69	90
Pepper	29	26	19	22

Sources: Ministry of Finance, FAO

TABLE 4.22   MALAYSIA: OIL PALM PRODUCTION

'000 tonnes

	1983	1984	1985*	1986*
Crude palm oil	3,017	3,715	3,850	4,040
Palm kernel oil	360.2	423.4	442.8	460
Planted area ('000 hectares)	1,258	1,361	1,400	1,440

Source: Ministry of Finance, Ministry of Primary Industries
Note: *Government projections

less labour-intensive. But even here it has succeeded almost too well; Malaysia now supplies half the world's requirements and has come under pressure to cut its output in order to stabilise world prices— something which it had not managed to do by early 1986. The planted area by 1985 was some 1,420,000 hectares, and this was planned to increase by 75% by 1990.

Another rapidly-growing export crop is cocoa, which like palm oil benefits from government subsidies and incentives. The anticipated yield of 100,000 tonnes in 1985 was virtually double that achieved as recently as 1981, and Malaysia hopes to be the world's largest exporter of cocoa by the year 2000. Staples such as dry beans are widely cultivated, and the various cash crops grown for export include coconuts, pepper and a variety of fruits, including pineapples.

Rice is undoubtedly the most important of Malaysia's crops for domestic consumption, but it is also the most critical. Malaysia is typically able to cover only three-quarters of its own requirements, and its production has been susceptible in recent years to climatic irregularities.

Malaysia is easily the world's largest exporter of natural rubber, supplying more than 40% of world requirements. Rubber plantations are found almost exclusively in peninsular Malaysia, where they are managed mainly by smallholders assisted by the government's Replanting Incentive Scheme.

Forestry accounts in a typical year for more than 9% of Malaysia's exports, most of it in the form of sawlogs. But the government has expressed increasing concern at the depletion of hardwood stands, and has attempted since 1978 to reduce the extent of logging, while phasing out the export of timber logs from peninsular Malaysia. Meanwhile tax concessions are being offered to promote the reafforestation of affected areas.

Fishing is an important activity and provides a useful source of proteins, but as Table 4.23 shows, catches have fallen somewhat in recent years as stocks have become depleted through over-fishing. The table also highlights a pronounced reduction in the number of fishermen and boats over the last few years.

TABLE 4.23 MALAYSIA: FISHERY PRODUCTION

Figures for Peninsular Malaysia only					
	1980	1981	1982	1983	1984
Offshore catches (tonnes)	623,898	649,315	567,323	609,056	545,221
Number of fishermen	88,972	86,925	80,237	75,590	72,303
Licensed fishing boats	32,794	33,052	32,672	30,871	27,071

Source: Fisheries Department, Government of Malaysia

TABLE 4.24 MALAYSIA: LIVESTOCK

'000 head			
	1980	1981	1982
Cattle	529	516	538
Buffaloes	282	188	181
Pigs	1,762	1,921	2,111
Goats	347	330	328
Sheep	63	65	69

Source: FAO

Mention should be made of the financial and equity markets in Malaysia, which are gaining in importance although still unsophisticated by international standards. The banking system is being steadily deregulated in the mid-1980s, and the stock exchange in Kuala Lumpur, the national capital, is nowadays regarded as an important indicator of the state of international commodity markets.

The exchange has trading and stock pricing links with the much bigger market in Singapore, and showed very strong growth throughout the early part of 1985; since then, however, it has experienced something of a crisis of confidence, and trading has periodically been suspended. The banking system for its part was starting in early 1986 to address the implications of a major swindle involving the politically well-connected Bank Bumiputra Malaysia—an issue which seemed likely to cause political controversy, and possibly political instability, for some years to come.

Philippines

The 20-year rule of President Marcos started in 1965, when he was elected on a pledge to restore the economy after the obstructivist political wrangling of his predecessors. Marcos scored many successes in his early years of power, transforming the national economy with agricultural improvements and with the start of the industrialisation process.

Marcos' governing technique, however, soon proved to be less admirable; bureaucracy and corruption masked a system in which the real power lay with a small group of the President's business associates. Meanwhile the government showed itself willing to use force against dissenters, and twice proclaimed martial law in an effort to quell opposition.

Nevertheless, the country expanded vigorously under Marcos in the 1970s, doubling its GNP in real terms and achieving a pinnacle with the discovery in 1978 of petroleum resources offshore Palawan in the South China Sea. But the discoveries came too late to save the country from the oil price explosion of 1979, which greatly increased its fuel import bill, and the economy began to slide; from the 4.4% GNP growth still recorded in 1980, the Philippines was forced to watch its development drop to a mere 1.3% in 1983. It was then that disaster struck. The assassination of Aquino in 1983 reinforced the growing fears of the Philippines' foreign investors, and a massive outflow of funds ensued which was stifled only by a freeze on foreign exchange payments. IMF, moving in to investigate, found irregularities in the country's official reserve figures, and by 1986 it was still virtually impossible to obtain cash payment for any goods or services supplied to the Philippines. (The prevalence of switch-trade and barter since 1983 casts a further confusing light on the country's trading position.) As far as can be ascertained, real GNP fell by 5.3% in 1984, and despite a more modest fall of 3% in 1985 the position remained bleak indeed by early 1986.

TABLE 4.25 PHILIPPINES: COMPOSITION OF GDP

mn pesos, at constant 1972 prices	1975	1980	1981	1982	1983	1984*
Agriculture, forestry and fisheries	18,218	23,732	24,608	25,378	24,845	25,045
Mining and quarrying	1,445	2,236	2,175	2,016	1,966	1,755
Manufacturing	16,537	23,175	23,959	24,535	25,108	23,319
Construction	4,101	7,139	7,830	8,079	7,689	5,866
Electricity, gas and water	607	921	999	1,084	1,192	1,211
Transport and communications	3,277	4,827	5,040	5,165	5,266	5,029
Trade and commerce	15,056	19,345	19,695	13,103	13,930	14,073
Finance and housing	9,120	11,331	11,901	7,252	7,726	7,409
Services	n.a.	n.a.	n.a.	12,387	12,346	11,783
GDP at market prices	68,361	92,706	96,207	98,999	100,068	95,490
GNP	68,530	92,629	96,041	97,539	98,767	93,519

Source: National Accounts Staff, National Economic and Development Authority
Note: *Estimate

Agriculture is still the largest single contributor to the economy, providing 26.8% of GDP in 1984. The sector, which employs more than half of the workforce, has proved more resilient than industry in the face of international recession, and raised its output by an average 2.2% per annum in 1980–85. This was due to an impressive performance in rice cultivation, which almost doubled under the government's Masagana programme; the plan aimed to boost production by organising better irrigation, by improving the supply of fertilisers and the credit with which to buy it, and by promoting improved strains of seed.

About 35% of the population are dependent on growing coconuts, the Philippines' largest export crop, which are thought to supply up to three-quarters of total world demand (exact figures are obscured by their frequent use in barter deals). The coconut business was completely controlled until recently by Eduardo Cojuanco (one of Marcos' business

TABLE 4.26 PHILIPPINES: AGRICULTURAL PRODUCTION

'000 tonnes

	1980	1981	1982	1983	1984*
Total production	29,809.1	29,507.8	29,709.3	27,460.1	27,449.9
Rice	8,376.6	9,304.5	10,924.1	10,721.9	15,311.8
Maize	3,122.8	3,109.7	3,290.2	3,125.9	3,346.2
Bananas	3,977.1	4,072.5	4,077.5	3,885.8	3,887.6
Mangoes	377.2	366.6	426.3	372.6	377.3
Pineapples	1,280.7	1,292.7	1,242.1	1,682.9	1,718.7
Other fruits/nuts	701.4	518.3	578.1	333.7	317.7
Citrus	130.5	129.9	132.6	130.1	124.7
Root crops	3,469.7	3,406.6	3,173.5	2,102.3	2,216.3
Beans and peas	47.3	48.5	50.3	36.9	39.1
Other vegetables	1,247.4	1,411.9	1,506.3	1,258.0	2,078.0
Coffee	125.3	146.7	171.4	146.9	114.3
Groundnuts	49.9	29.6	48.6	35.8	42.3
Other food crops	387.0	397.8	424.9	335.1	352.0
Coconuts	4,570.2	4,312.1	3,785.5	3,381.6	3,042.7
Sugar cane	3,120.8	3,193.0	3,402.7	3,435.6	3,260.2
Abaca	157.2	128.3	119.7	89.3	89.2
Native tobacco	23.5	21.2	22.0	15.7	21.1
Virginia tobacco	18.5	17.9	24.8	29.1	45.1
Rubber	67.7	72.0	78.6	122.9	123.1
Other commercial crops	33.0	38.1	48.0	30.6	46.7

Source: National Economic and Development Authority
Note: *Estimate

TABLE 4.27 PHILIPPINES: LIVESTOCK

'000 head

	1970	1980	1981	1982	1983	1984
Buffaloes	4,432	2,870	2,850	2,908	2,946	3,022
Cattle	1,679	1,883	1,940	1,942	1,938	1,849
Pigs	6,456	7,934	7,758	7,795	7,980	7,613
Goats	772	n.a.	1,696	1,783	1,859	2,362
Chickens	56,999	52,761	57,724	59,710	62,255	59,205
Ducks	2,132	4,725	4,783	4,905	5,419	5,764

Source: Bureau of Agricultural Economics

associates), while the former President's other associates had virtually cornered the sugar cane and banana crops. In 1986, however, the newly-elected Aquino government (led by Salvador Laurel) moved to seize the assets of Cojuanco and several of the other associates who had fled the country with Marcos.

As Table 4.26 shows, there is a wide variety of other export crops available to farmers, most of whom are smallholders, but only rubber and tobacco are making significant progress in the mid-1980s. The Philippines is self-sufficient in pork and poultry, but normally imports a large proportion of its beef requirements.

TABLE 4.28   PHILIPPINES: FISHERY PRODUCTION

'000 tonnes

	1981	1982	1983
Total catch	1,686.6	1,787.7	1,836.9
of which: molluscs	214.1	245.4	270.0
crustaceans	63.0	70.5	76.8

Source: FAO

Fisheries are fairly well developed, with both inland and substantial offshore waters available. The sector is undercapitalised, however, and has ample scope for improvement. Forestry would seem to have great potential, particularly as some 45% of the total surface area is wooded; but the production of hardwood for export has been slowing in recent

TABLE 4.29   PHILIPPINES: FORESTRY PRODUCTION

'000 cu m

	1981	1982	1983
Sawlogs and sleeper timbers	5,400	4,514	4,430
Pulp wood	496	541	732
Other industrial wood	2,038	2,078	2,134
Fuel wood	27,048	27,766	28,491
TOTAL	34,982	34,899	35,787

Source: FAO

years as the country has moved to protect its dwindling stocks of high-quality timber. A ban has been placed on the export of raw logs, and a reafforestation programme is under way, although it is years behind schedule.

Industry, which normally contributes about a quarter of GDP, has been greatly diversified since the early 1970s, and in the mid-1980s the country has a range of heavy industries, including cement, steel, chemicals and fertiliser production. The mainstay of the industrial sector is still the processing of agricultural raw materials, including

TABLE 4.30 PHILIPPINES: INDUSTRIAL PRODUCTION

mn pesos at current prices
expressed in terms of gross value-added

	1980	1981	1982	1983	1984*
Food processing	20,026	23,694	27,189	31,388	49,745
Beverages	2,684	2,818	3,083	3,471	4,544
Tobacco processing	2,544	2,806	2,973	3,277	7,586
Textiles	4,622	5,161	5,261	5,794	7,586
Clothing/footwear	3,657	4,567	4,983	5,852	8,672
Wood and cork products	2,426	2,882	3,042	3,431	3,923
Furniture	327	375	404	435	599
Paper	919	967	920	1,115	1,865
Publishing and printing	632	747	827	936	1,505
Leather products	172	191	201	208	336
Rubber products	780	900	1,029	1,125	1,766
Chemicals and chemical products	5,918	5,983	6,105	7,227	10,334
Petroleum and coal products	9,535	10,651	11,617	13,000	19,184
Non-metallic minerals	1,828	1,978	2,285	2,506	2,956
Basic metal industries	2,237	2,217	2,612	3,126	5,068
Metal products	1,919	1,945	2,283	2,639	2,768
Electrical machinery	2,006	2,844	3,383	4,471	6,405
Other machinery	1,377	1,610	1,824	2,043	1,916
Transport equipment	1,530	1,757	1,841	1,667	462
Other manufactures	854	1,058	1,264	1,461	3,223
TOTAL	65,993	75,151	83,126	95,172	137,251

Source: National Economic and Development Authority
Note: *Government estimates

copra and hardwoods as well as the more usual foodstuffs, beverages and cigarettes.

The former Marcos government laid out a major development scheme for heavy industry, involving the construction of new cement plant, a paper and pulp mill, a steel mill, copper and aluminium smelters, a fertiliser plant and an expanded coconut products industry. The manufacturing scheme was intended to remain in the hands of privately-controlled monopolies, however subsequently proved surplus to the country's actual requirements and therefore had to be shelved or cancelled before completion. Part of the reason was undoubtedly the shortfall in government funds, but equally important was the poor response from foreign investors, particularly since the crisis of 1983.

The country has a fairly strong light manufacturing industry, producing textiles and electronics on behalf of foreign companies, or by way of import substitution. The latter's prospects have been hit, however, by the collapse of domestic purchasing power during the mid-1980s, and the rate of business failures in 1983–85 was alarming. Philippine businesses in general were still afflicted in 1986 with

TABLE 4.31 PHILIPPINES: MINERAL PRODUCTION

		1980	1981	1982	1983
Gold metal	kilograms	20.0	23.6	25.4	26.0
Silver metal	kilograms	60.7	62.9	61.7	56.7
Chromite ore	DMT	496.1	439.2	321.1	n.a.
Copper metal	tonnes	304.5	302.3	292.1	271.4
Iron ore	DMT	n.a.	5.7	5.6	2.6
Lead metal	tonnes	1.8	1.1	n.a.	n.a.
Manganese ore	DMT	2.6	3.1	1.6	2.2
Molybdenum metal	tonnes	0.1	0.1	0.1	40.3
Nickel metal	tonnes	47.1	29.2	19.6	13.9
Pyrite cinders	DMT	75.5	n.a.	n.a.	n.a.
Zinc metal	tonnes	6.8	5.3	3.0	2.3
Coal	tonnes	325.0	373.0	556.7	1,019.6
Sand and gravel	cu m	13,251.0	13,273.0	14,797.3	15,093.3
Salt	tonnes	346.4	355.3	364.4	381.9
Silica sand	tonnes	476.6	484.3	527.3	243.7

Source: Bureau of Mines and Geo-Sciences

unacceptably high levels of corporate foreign debt, and many were completely dependent on an international rescue package for their survival; this applies as much to mining companies, and even to banks, as to the industrial sector. Plans to update the textile industry have meanwhile been cancelled altogether.

The Philippines is a major producer of copper, with a significant output of molybdenum, silver, chromite and gold. Production of virtually all minerals has slowed since 1980, however, due to the decline in world demand.

Coal production has continued since 1983 to make encouraging progress, and output rose by 22% in 1984. The improvement of domestic energy sources is central to the Energy Plan for 1982–87, according to which the Philippines will cover half of its own energy requirements by 1987. Crude oil production, at 3,800,000 barrels in 1984, was down by 15.5% from 1983, as the Nido field was closed in favour of the two other fields, Matinloc and Cadlao. Meanwhile, a nuclear power station has been completed at Bataan, near Manila, and heavy investment continues in geothermal and hydro-electric power.

Singapore

Unlike any of the other ASEAN member states, Singapore makes its living entirely from services and from the processing of imported materials. The island has no significant mineral resources, and scarcely any scope for agriculture because of its tiny land area (620 sq. km.).

Nevertheless, Singapore makes an ideal base for manufacturing and/or distribution. It occupies a strategic position off the southern coast of peninsular Malaysia, where it has easy access to the South China Sea and Java Sea, or alternatively to the Indian Ocean via the Straits of Malacca. Its excellent natural harbour and deep-water ports are also used by its substantial shipbuilding industry and by companies servicing the oil exploration teams in the South China Sea.

For more than a century Singapore has been capitalising on these natural advantages, establishing an excellent communications network and building what is now a range of modern and luxurious hotels. The rapid development of the country's financial services sector has been made possible by this sophisticated infrastructure, and in the mid-1980s

Singapore seems better placed than any of its neighbours to capitalise on the coming internationalisation of securities and money markets.

The country has, however, faced growing problems since the early 1980s due to the fall-off in world trade; these were further exacerbated in 1985 by the slowing of demand in the United States, the sudden slump in world computer and electronics manufacturing, and finally the plummeting price of petroleum and its derivates. The economy shrank

TABLE 4.32   SINGAPORE: GNP, 1975–1984

Singapore $ mn, at current market prices

	1975	1980	1981	1982	1983	1984
GDP	13,373	24,285	28,653	31,783	35,371	38,874
of which:						
Indigenous	10,314	16,748	20,254	22,657	25,696	28,378
Foreign companies	3,059	7,537	8,399	9,126	9,675	10,496
Indigenous GNP	11,061	18,121	21,910	24,558	28,220	31,242
Per capita						
indigenous GNP*	4,889	7,507	8,968	9,935	11,279	12,353

Source: Government of Singapore
Note: *Singapore $

TABLE 4.33   SINGAPORE: COMPOSITION OF GDP

constant 1968 factor cost

	1960 %	1970 %	1983 %	1984 %	1983/4 (% growth)
Manufacturing	13	19	18	18	7.3
Construction	4	7	8	8	13.7
Other goods	5	3	1	1	0.8
Trade, inc. tourism	33	30	22	21	4.3
Transport and communications	14	11	19	19	8.7
Financial and business services	11	14	19	19	9.0
Utilities	2	2	3	2	6.5
Other services	18	14	10	10	2.7
TOTAL GDP	100	100	100	100	

Source: US Embassy, Singapore, based on Singapore's government figures

by 1.7% in 1985—something of a shock for a nation whose economy had expanded by 8.2% the previous year, and whose growth had consistently exceeded 10% per annum in the 1970s.

The growth of manufacturing industry is currently seen as one of Singapore's best safeguards against world recession. The sector, which currently contributes around one-fifth of GDP, began its very rapid growth in the 1960s with the emphasis on its low unit costs. In 1979, however, it moved into a higher gear, with the proclamation of what the government called the second industrial revolution. Basically, this involved the development of higher value-added goods such as electronics, and substantially increased levels of foreign investment. The authorities offered special incentives for 11 special categories of manufacturing (later expanded to 14), many of which were still in force in 1986.

TABLE 4.34 SINGAPORE: SELECTED MANUFACTURING INDUSTRIES

		1980	1981	1982	1983	1984
Vegetable oil	'000 tonnes	95.6	98.2	124.6	77.3	77.9
Animal fodder	'000 tonnes	341.6	268.9	248.2	223.3	238.5
Soft drinks	kilolitres	175.1	189.6	182.0	193.4	159.7
Cement	'000 tonnes	1,952.4	2,224.2	2,794.9	3,126.1	2,821.1
Plywood (plain)	'000 sq m	106.2	98.0	75.2	52.7	20.3
Plywood (printed)	'000 sq m	16.1	16.3	18.5	23.1	27.8
Paints	mn litres	23.8	26.5	27.3	30.5	36.4
Soap	'000 tonnes	28.6	29.9	25.2	26.7	25.4
TV sets	'000 units	1,889.2	2,173.6	1,516.1	1,361.3	1,345.4
Cassette recorders	'000 units	8,060.1	8,551.4	6,591.2	8,520.6	12,167.5
Broken granite	'000 cu m	3,185.0	4,484.4	5,946.9	7,569.3	7,422.1
Bricks	mn	166.5	170.6	188.9	264.0	240.2

Source: Government of Singapore

By far the largest employer among these priority industries is the computer and electronics assembly business, which raised its production by nearly 50% in 1984 alone, and which comprises more than 250 companies. Other priority industries include biotechnology, speciality chemicals, telecommunications, machine tools, car and automotive components and instrumentation, and Singapore is active in the manufacture of rubber goods, optical and precision instruments,

105

chemicals, cigarettes and foodstuffs. There are several special industrial estates, of which the largest, at Jurong, will eventually comprise more than 1,100 factories.

Petroleum products and petrochemicals are still by far the most important element from an export point of view; including the production of offshore platforms and services to the oil exploration industries, the whole sector accounted for 40% of all exports in 1983. But by the same token the industry has proved unusually vulnerable to fluctuations in world demand, and in early 1986 it was doubtful whether the country was using more than half of its 1,100,000 bpd refining capacity.

TABLE 4.35   SINGAPORE: GAS PRODUCTION AND SALES

mn kilowatt-hours

	1980	1981	1982	1983	1984
Production	614.1	625.6	624.8	605.4	609.4
Sales	552.0	560.7	570.0	566.5	573.1
of which:					
Domestic	317.2	315.5	320.1	322.0	327.7
Commercial	186.5	213.5	220.1	225.8	231.2
Industrial	48.3	31.7	29.8	18.7	14.2

Source: Public Utilities Board

TABLE 4.36   SINGAPORE: ELECTRICITY PRODUCTION

mn kilowatt-hours

	1980	1981	1982	1983	1984
Production	6,940.4	7,442.0	7,859.5	8,625.9	9,420.7
Sales	6,198.0	6,660.4	7,000.1	7,697.6	8,398.8
of which:					
Domestic	1,014.3	1,092.8	1,166.9	1,313.0	1,336.2
Public lighting	56.7	60.5	64.5	65.3	69.3
Manufacturing	2,947.2	3,156.2	3,217.6	3,504.9	3,926.7
Other industries	2,087.8	2,277.0	2,499.6	2,759.6	2,994.6
Export	92.0	73.9	51.5	54.8	73.0

Source: Public Utilities Board

Recognising the problem at an early stage, and fearing the worst for its domestic energy requirements, Singapore sought to diversity its own power generation systems away from their heavy dependence on petroleum. The country has arranged to buy natural gas from Indonesia and Malaysia, and the latter alone could fulfil half of Singapore's power requirements by 1990—particularly if a planned pipeline goes ahead to convey the gas directly from Malaysian offshore fields.

Singapore is far from self-sufficient in food crops. Because of the small amount of available land, agricultural production is negligible, and only a few vegetables and fruits are grown domestically. Fishing has perhaps greater scope for expansion, with a special port being built at Jurong; as Table 4.38 highlights, the country's dependence on imported fish is significant.

TABLE 4.37   SINGAPORE: AGRICULTURAL PRODUCE

tonnes	1975	1980	1981	1982	1983	1984
Vegetables	38,285	36,839	42,861	41,388	35,326	32,767
Fruits	14,629	9,055	8,065	8,090	8,070	6,950
Sugar cane	1,820	1,870	1,570	1,460	960	700
Tobacco	311	402	133	88	34	10
Coconuts	7	6	5	5	4	4

Source: Primary Product Division, Government of Singapore

TABLE 4.38   SINGAPORE: FISHERY PRODUCTION

tonnes	1982	1983	1984
Domestic catch	18,830	19,099	25,041
Total domestic supply*	56,939	62,152	71,586
Imports	89,104	99,099	107,784
Exports	50,995	56,046	61,239

Source: Primary Product Division, Government of Singapore
Note: *Including imported supplies

TABLE 4.39   SINGAPORE: LIVESTOCK SLAUGHTERED

	1980	1981	1982	1983	1984
Pigs	968,095	936,751	883,666	926,005	1,026,287
Cattle	1,238	1,214	1,496	1,414	1,471
Buffaloes	185	170	111	138	137
Sheep	73,156	55,707	56,999	59,012	58,045
Goats	475	196	204	249	212

Source: Government of Singapore

The construction industry has long been a beneficiary of the government's somewhat excessive spending on new buildings. In 1985, however, it became obvious that these days were over, as the shrinking national budget coincided with a substantial surplus of office buildings in central Singapore. The steep fall in property prices which ensued was a somewhat disconcerting factor for the country's banking system, and also cast a pall of gloom over such hitherto profitable activities as granite, bricks, cement and paints.

Tourism is an important contributor to the island's economy, and in 1983 there were over 2,800,000 visitors—more than the total population. Tourists are attracted by the high-class hotels, the superb local transport facilities, the climate and the use of the English language. But most visitors stay less than four days, arriving either on tours or on airline stopovers, and the general level of tourism revenues has been declining in recent years.

Singapore's rapidly expanding financial system seems to be among its brightest hopes for the future in the mid-1980s. The island has established itself as one of the largest offshore banking bases in Asia, and occasionally does more business than even Hong Kong. The government has taken steps to increase the scope for adventurous new types of bonds, and is adjusting rapidly to the demands of a changing banking environment; but the sector faces stiff regional competition, particularly from Hong Kong.

The stock exchange is well developed by regional standards, with an emphasis on commodity stocks which reflects its close ties with the Malaysian exchange in Kuala Lumpur. It will be clear from Table 4.40

however, that the Singapore exchange received a sharp setback in 1985, as the worsening external position gave rise to bearish market conditions. The investment climate was further damaged in 1985 by a growing controversy over the role to be played by the Monetary Agency of Singapore (i.e. central bank) in the supervision of the newly deregulating securities market.

TABLE 4.40   SINGAPORE: THE STOCK EXCHANGE INDEX

1975=100

	1980	1981	1982	1983	1984	October 1985
All shares	256.6	355.0	297.0	345.8	335.7	278.2
Industrial	230.5	329.7	252.8	306.5	300.9	242.5
Finance	211.7	302.5	279.0	353.3	338.4	289.3
Hotels	313.6	632.6	518.8	463.4	392.2	290.7
Properties	267.0	425.5	394.6	404.8	378.6	344.1
Mining	440.0	503.0	313.6	316.9	317.7	233.9
Plantations	393.3	412.6	350.8	463.4	507.6	405.8

Source: Stock Exchange of Singapore

Thailand

Thailand achieved an average real economic growth of 7% during the 1970s, peaking at 10.1% in 1978 on the back of a vigorous industrial expansion; it then slowed to 5.5% in 1984 and to approximately 5.3% in

TABLE 4.41   THAILAND: DEVELOPMENT OF GDP

mn baht, at constant 1980 prices

	GDP	GDP deflator (1980=100)	GDP at 1980 prices	GNP
1980	684,930	100.0	684,930	672,440
1981	786,170	108.0	728,010	764,380
1982	846,140	111.6	757,860	819,760
1983	924,250	115.2	802,110	898,880
1984	991,750	116.6	850,310	960,410

Source: IMF

1985—a creditable enough performance by the standards of its neighbours, under the difficult trading conditions of the mid-1980s. On the whole Thailand has no difficulty in attracting foreign investment capital.

The country has a long tradition of free trade and private enterprise, and has been successful in establishing a varied industrial base; in fact, the government's most persistent problem has been that of companies over-importing in their search for growth. In 1981 the baht was devalued by 8.7%, and in November 1984 was further devalued by 14.8%. Meanwhile a tight money policy was introduced, in a renewed effort to stem the growth of borrowing and to boost exports.

TABLE 4.42   THAILAND: COMPOSITION OF GDP

mn baht, at constant 1972 prices

	1980	1984	% of GDP, 1984
Agriculture	72,800	84,100	23.1
Mining and quarrying	4,800	4,600	1.3
Manufacturing	60,600	77,000	21.2
Construction	16,600	16,200	4.4
Electricity and water	5,600	8,400	2.3
Transport and communications	48,200	60,300	16.6
Wholesale and retail trade	17,400	26,200	7.2
Banking, insurance and real estate	4,500	5,300	1.5
Ownership of dwellings	12,400	14,800	4.1
Public administration and defence	31,200	41,800	11.5

Source: Bank of Thailand

Agriculture currently accounts for less than a quarter of GDP, but was still providing 46% of all export revenues in 1984. 71% of the 28 million workforce were engaged in farming in 1983 (compared for example with only 7.8% in manufacturing), but the proportion was scheduled to fall to 67.4% by 1986. Overall, the growth in agricultural output, at around 3% per annum, is keeping well ahead of the population increase, and the cultivated area has nearly trebled since the 1950s; according to the World Bank there is still scope for a further expansion of between 15 and 36%.

Much the most important crop is rice, which as Table 4.43 shows has made progress in recent years, despite severe difficulties. Thailand's rice growing is very inefficient by local standards, due to the inadequate provision of irrigation schemes, and is vulnerable to climatic fluctuations such as the drought of 1982/83 which affected all food crops. Yields per hectare are low, and yet Thailand is able to rank as the world's biggest exporter of rice by virtue of the sheer expanse of land given over to the crop.

TABLE 4.43   THAILAND: PRINCIPAL AGRICULTURAL CROPS

'000 tonnes	1982/83	1983/84	1984/85
Rice (paddy)	16,880	18,780	19,200
Maize	3,350	3,880	4,400
Tapioca roots	19,000	20,000	21,030
Sugar cane	23,920	23,090	22,500
Rubber*	552	576	600

Source: Bangkok Bank
Note: *Calendar years 1982, 1983, 1984

The next most important agricultural product is tapioca, which has made extremely rapid growth in recent years, easily outstripping local demand. Tapioca ranks as Thailand's second largest source of foreign exchange, and most of it is exported to the European Community where it is subject to stringent import quotas; in 1985 Thailand pleaded successfully to be allowed to supply more than hitherto. Nonetheless, its failure to diversify away from this largely unusable surplus crop (derived from cassava) represents one of the more serious problems facing local agriculture.

Rubber is another of Thailand's major crops, catering for over 15% of world requirements and being sold mainly to Japan. The Thai government has strongly encouraged the extension of rubber plantations, offering grants and incentives to the small-scale farmers who dominate the sector, and total production rose by 10% between 1982 and 1984, to 600,000 tonnes. However, the very low prices being offered on world markets have been deeply disappointing during the mid-1980s, and future development appears uncertain; Thailand has repeatedly fallen out with Malaysia over production levels and the pricing structure.

Maize cultivation has also been vigorously encouraged by the government, and in 1984/85 the country achieved its first surplus for export. Sugar cane is gradually losing its attraction with the steady decline in world prices, and as Table 4.43 shows production has been diminishing for some years. Thailand offers a range of tropical fruits for export, and grows jute and kenaf for domestic consumption.

TABLE 4.44   THAILAND: FISHERY PRODUCTION

'000 tonnes	1978	1979	1980	1981	1982
Total catch	2,099	1,946	1,793	1,989	1,980
Marine fish	1,512	1,389	1,302	1,377	1,341
Freshwater fish	138	130	141	161	167
Crustaceans	180	167	172	187	161
Others	205	202	174	235	196

Source: FAO

Fishing provides an important source of proteins for the Thai population, but catches have suffered in the 1980s from the consequences of over-fishing. Forestry continues to flourish despite the efforts of the government, alarmed by deforestation, to limit the export of raw logs and semi-finished wood; the emphasis since 1978 has instead been on the domestic processing of timber.

TABLE 4.45   THAILAND: FORESTRY PRODUCTION

'000 cubic metres	1975	1980	1981	1982
Total production	35,140	38,954	39,024	39,472
Industrial timber	5,001	4,997	4,306	4,009
of which: Teak	176	97	73	58
Yang	922	551	289	341
Fuel wood	30,139	33,937	34,718	35,463

Source: FAO

Manufacturing accounted in 1984 for an uncharacteristically large 21.2% of GDP, and is making considerable progress partly due to foreign investment. In the mid-1980s Thai companies have been moving across from their traditional processing of agricultural raw materials and textiles to new activities, such as artificial fibres, automobiles and even micro-electronics. The government has spent vast sums on developing heavy industries such as cement and steel, although this trend slowed somewhat in 1984/85 as the national debt reduced its room for manoeuvre.

TABLE 4.46   THAILAND: INDUSTRIAL PRODUCTION

		1980	1981	1982	1983
Fuel oil, heavy	'000 cu m	2,794	2,747	n.a.	n.a.
Fuel oil, light	'000 cu m	2,514	2,615	n.a.	n.a.
Cement	'000 tonnes	5,358	6,323	6,664	7,872
Galvanised sheet	'000 tonnes	124	152	127	124
Tin	'000 tonnes	35	31	26	19
Tinplate	'000 tonnes	70	79	62	73
Automobiles*	'000	23	27	25	34
Trucks*	'000	51	61	53	75
Motorcycles	'000	284	305	293	313
Cotton textiles	mn sq yd	761	791	853	889
Synthetic textiles	mn sq yd	672	810	798	851
Plywood	'000 tonnes	4,415	4,193	3,882	3,990
Paper	'000 tonnes	76	71	62	66
Jute bags	mn pieces	179	175	168	158
Sugar	'000 tonnes	856	1,665	2,768	2,035
Beer	mn litres	124	105	122	146
Condensed milk	'000 tonnes	88	89	77	82
Pasteurised milk	'000 tonnes	17	15	14	15
Cigarettes	'000 tonnes	31	33	27	29

Source: West German Government
Note: *Units assembled from imported kits

Despite the raising of interest rates in 1981/83, as part of the government's monetary restraint programme, the industrial sector has continued to expand by up to 5% per annum. This is a result of sustained strong domestic demand, but it also reflects the attraction of Thailand's low labour costs for foreign companies. A further factor in the 1980s is the ready availability of natural gas from the country's offshore fields, and virtually all industry still centres on the capital, Bangkok, where the fuel is piped ashore.

The two major offshore fields located by 1986 are at Platong and Satun, north of the onshore deposits at Erawan. Together they are thought to contain anything up to 16,000,000 mn cubic feet of gas. Meanwhile, limited reserves of petroleum are also being worked in various parts of the country, notably in the Sirkit field in the northern central plain, which started production in 1983, and which was yielding 22,000 bpd by late 1985.

TABLE 4.47   THAILAND: PROJECTED ENERGY REQUIREMENTS

'000 tonnes oil equivalent	1982	1985	1990	1995	1998
Total consumption	13,143	15,993	20,817	28,933	31,175
Oil	10,303	10,313	11,927	13,233	15,374
Hydro-electric power	1,046	1,317	1,487	2,149	2,250
Lignite	519	878	2,294	3,211	3,211
Natural gas	1,172	3,382	5,006	10,237	10,237
Coal	103	103	103	103	103
Domestic production	2,693	6,500	10,264	17,559	16,671
Oil	20	987	1,541	2,027	1,337
Hydro-electric power	982	1,253	1,423	2,084	2,186
Lignite	519	878	2,294	3,211	3,211
Natural gas	1,172	3,382	5,006	10,327	10,237
Imports	10,450	9,493	10,553	11,373	14,204
Oil	10,283	9,326	10,386	11,206	14,037
Hydro-electric power	64	64	64	64	64
Coal	103	103	103	103	103
Imports as a percentage of consumption	79.7	59.4	50.7	39.3	45.6

Source: World Bank estimates

Thailand's oil appears to have only limited potential because of the high wax content (18%), and because the deposits are fragmented, meaning that individual finds are quickly exhausted. Nonetheless, as Table 4.47 shows, the country's overall dependence on energy imports is likely to fall below 50% of requirements by the end of the century, thanks to supplies of oil and gas, together with domestic lignite mining and hydro-electric energy generation. The Thai authorities have been quick to recognise the enormous potential which these energy sources offer for the country's industrial development, and some 53% of all capital investment under the 1982/86 plan was devoted to the energy sector, notably to gas and petroleum processing facilities.

Thailand is well endowed with minerals, particularly potash and tin, and numbers among the world's largest exporters of both commodities. There are also workable deposits of lead, zinc, tungsten, barites, manganese, antimony, gypsum and iron ore. With the notable exception of gypsum, however, production of all these minerals has been falling during the early and mid-1980s, due to the decline in world commodity markets.

TABLE 4.48   THAILAND: MINERAL PRODUCTION

tonnes

	1980	1981	1982	1983
Tin concentrates	45,986	42,968	35,644	27,208
of which: Tin metal exports	33,445	32,007	26,013	17,656
Tungsten concentrates	3,134	2,348	1,661	1,092
Fluorite (metallurgical)	172,784	157,311	176,084	159,959
Antimony ore	6,862	2,820	1,567	2,808
Barite ore	305,057	307,046	318,348	187,437
Gypsum	411,977	540,383	753,433	760,361
Iron ore	84,966	62,472	26,750	40,304
Lead concentrates	24,847	40,667	43,718	49,446
Manganese (battery grade)	2,716	5,205	3,398	4,804
Manganese (metallurgical)	51,583	5,707	4,348	1,906

Source: Industry sources

IV   Standards of living

Indonesia

As elsewhere in the ASEAN region, a significant proportion of the population in Indonesia lives on a subsistence basis in a cashless economy. For those with work, real incomes rose by under ½% per annum between 1982 and 1985, and in 1986 started to decline. The contrast is particularly marked with the expansive 1970s, when an annual average increase of 7% in real wages was achieved. The number of unemployed is difficult to ascertain because of the sheer size of the population and the prevalence of under-employment, but it is unlikely to be less than 20% of the workforce.

As a consequence of this tightening in real incomes, consumer demand has virtually ground to a half during the mid-1980s. Per capita GDP was about US$600 in 1985, rather below the average for the region, and inflation, which peaked at 21% in 1979, was on the way back up in 1985, following a brief drop to only 9.5% in 1982. The upward pressure has come from external rather than domestic factors, and it had yet to respond in 1985 to the restrictive monetary policies imposed by the government.

Malaysia

Malaysia ranks among the most well off of the ASEAN nations, with a per capita GNP of more than US$2,000 in 1985. With a real economic growth of more than 5% (in dollar terms), it has also shown a better equilibrium in the mid-1980s than its smaller but more powerful neighbour Singapore, whose GDP shrank during 1985.

Malaysians have been well able by regional standards to afford consumer manufactured goods. Again by regional standards, domestic price increases have been very modest; they peaked at 9.7% in 1981, but by 1984 the level was back down to 4.0%. Unemployment, although a growing problem, had yet to make any serious impact on the economy by mid-1985.

These figures ignore, however, the impending effects of the economic slowdown which started at the end of 1985. It was already clear by early 1986 that the government's policy of centrally-funded growth would be impracticable under these circumstances, and ultimately some slowing of domestic demand appeared inevitable.

Philippines

The decline of living standards among the Philippine population has been a major factor behind the removal of President Marcos; as already noted, it also caused the dissatisfaction on which the communist rebellion in rural areas fed. Per capita GDP continued to rise in peso terms between 1980 and 1983, from P5,530 to P10,281, but in dollar terms it fell from US$736 to US$616. By 1985 the impact of rising unemployment had added to the general discontent. Filipinos have been unable in the mid-1980s to purchase domestically-manufactured luxury goods or even, in some cases, necessities. Since 1983 they have also been barred from paying in foreign currency for imported goods.

The consumer price index moderated in the early 1980s from the 18.2% increase recorded in 1980 to reach a low of 10% in 1983; the following year, however, it soared to 50.3%, and was believed to have hardly improved in 1985. Clearly, the success of the Aquino administration in containing inflation will become a key issue in its ability to retain the goodwill which has greeted its arrival.

Singapore

Wages in Singapore are generally fixed by centralised bargaining involving the National Wages Council. Settlements were high during the early 1980s, in accordance with the government's commitment to industrial specialisation and mechanisation, and have been hitherto boosted by the scarcity of local manpower.

Rapid increase in productivity enabled Singapore to achieve its industrial expansion while maintaining a remarkably low level of inflation by regional standards. Consumer price rises peaked at only 8.5% in 1980 before settling to a mere 1.2% in 1983; by the end of 1985 the rate was back up to a manageable 4%.

It is evident that real incomes rose very fast during the early 1980s, and that a massive expansion of consumer demand resulted. But the sudden downturn in 1985 represented a considerable shock causing a sharp increase in unemployment which threatened to become a major political problem for the government; over 96,000 jobs were lost during 1985, of which 37,000 had been held by Singapore citizens (equivalent to more than 3% of the workforce) and the remainder by foreigners. (It should be added in this context that the government aims in principle to phase out the use of foreign labour altogether by 1991.)

Thailand

Thai workers' incomes are guaranteed by the statutory minimum levels which the government fixes each year, and have generally kept pace with inflation in recent years; in 1985, for example, the official increase of 6.1% (for the capital Bangkok) was well ahead of the 1% inflation for the previous year. As has already been noted, living standards in cities such as Bangkok are considerably higher than in country districts.

The population has not always fared so well, however. Real earnings were eroded by the high inflation which gripped the country in the late 1970s, and which peaked at 19.7% in 1980; the low inflation since then has been largely due to the extremely tight monetary policies and high interest rates pursued by the government. Consumption expenditure levels have tended to be stable with individuals more inclined to place capital with the numerous and often somewhat dubious private banks. Many of these savings institutions offer improbably high returns, often approaching 100%, and some have been dismantled in the mid-1980s in an effort to head off a possible collapse of confidence.

V Foreign trade and investment

Indonesia

In the mid-1980s, after nearly two decades of relatively low-key foreign policies, Indonesia is once again seeking an active role in international affairs, and has become much more deeply involved in such ASEAN issues as the development of mutual trade, the ASEAN campaigns for reforms at GATT or the calls for Vietnamese withdrawal from Kampuchea.

Since 1984 Indonesia has been attempting to improve the state of its trade relations with the People's Republic of China; diplomatic relations are consistently strained. However, as a potential market, Indonesia cannot afford any longer to ignore China, and it may be that China's support for the Kampuchean rebels will at last prove a topic of agreement.

As Table 4.49 shows, there are considerable discrepancies between the Indonesian Government's official trade figures and those presented by the IMF. Both agree, however, that on the whole Indonesia has managed to hold on to its trade surplus—although the services balance, the international debt burden and other factors have kept the current account in deficit.

118

TABLE 4.49 INDONESIA: TRADE AND THE BALANCE OF PAYMENTS

US$ mn	1980	1981	1982	1983	1984
(a) Indonesian Government figures					
Exports	23,950.4	25,164.5	22,328.3	21,145.9	22,000.0*
of which:					
Oil and gas	17,781.6	20,563.2	18,399.1	17,140.6	n.a.
Imports	10,834.4	13,272.1	16,858.9	16,351.8	17,000.0*
Trade balance	13,116.0	11,892.4	5,469.4	4,794.1	5,000.0*
(b) IMF figures					
Exports	21,800	23,300	19,700	18,700	20,800
Imports	12,600	16,500	17,900	17,700	15,300
Trade balance	9,200	6,800	1,800	1,000	5,500
Current account	2,900	−600	−5,300	−6,300	−2,100
Long-term public debt	15,000	16,000	18,600	21,800	23,500
Official currency reserves	5,400	5,000	3,100	3,700	4,800

Source:
Note: *Estimates

Table 4.50 shows clearly the decline of Indonesia's export markets; foreign sales particularly to Japan, Australia and the European Community fell sharply between 1981 and 1984, while those to other ASEAN members remained reasonably stable.

Indonesia's principal sources of imports, as Table 4.50 shows, remained basically unchanged between 1981 and 1983, except that purchases from Singapore increased (a trend that has since been reversed, with the inauguration of Indonesia's own petrochemical plants).

As Table 4.51 shows, foreign investment has been in decline since 1983, and no upturn was in sight by the start of 1986. The fall is due partly to nervousness about the prospects for the ASEAN area in general, but also to concern over the high degree of monopolisation of certain key industries (notably palm oil and flour), and over the persistence of corruption in the bureaucracy. The government found it necessary in late 1985 to reassure foreign partners of its commitment to the co-development of Indonesia's oil and gas reserves.

TABLE 4.50   INDONESIA: PRINCIPAL TRADE PARTNERS

US$ mn	1981	1982	1983	1984*
Exports				
ASEAN	3,414.8	3,499.1	3,476.3	1,251.9
of which:				
Singapore	2,894.1	3,120.9	3,127.8	1,057.4
Philippines	410.8	292.8	241.9	105.6
Japan	11,949.6	11,192.6	9,678.2	5,116.9
USA	4,852.2	3,546.0	4,266.7	2,413.5
Latin America	1,960.4	928.9	1,014.9	412.4
Australia	447.3	674.2	208.4	128.3
EEC	1,062.7	893.7	952.7	509.9
of which:				
Netherlands	347.2	265.2	289.2	140.0
West Germany	239.1	252.7	252.4	131.9
United Kingdom	131.0	126.4	199.0	85.0
Italy	167.6	141.5	119.5	77.8
TOTAL, including others	25,164.5	22,328.3	21,145.9	10,885.4
Imports				
Japan	3,989.0	4,278.5	3,793.1	3,407.7
Singapore	1,243.4	2,819.0	3,464.5	1,791.4
USA	1,794.7	2,417.2	2,533.7	2,559.9
Saudi Arabia	671.8	1,133.7	905.4	1,344.6
West Germany	904.9	1,192.7	741.4	820.1
France	344.4	571.0	591.1	431.9
South Korea	488.4	303.9	587.5	n.a.
Taiwan	404.2	459.5	510.5	n.a.
Australia	362.1	364.6	402.3	450.1
United Kingdom	546.7	445.3	364.4	297.2
TOTAL, including others	13,272.1	16,858.9	16,351.7	13,882.1

Source: Statistical Bureau, Government of Indonesia
Note: *Estimate

TABLE 4.51   INDONESIA: INVESTMENT PATTERNS

US$ mn	1982	1983	1984	1985
Domestic investment	3,263	6,287	1,875	3,348
Foreign investment	1,259	2,882	1,107	859
Total investment	**4,522**	**9,169**	**2,982**	**4,207**

Sources: Government of Indonesia, foreign business estimates

Malaysia

With the decline of commodity markets during the 1980s, Malaysia found itself faced in 1981 and 1982 with its first trade deficits in more than 20 years. Since 1983 the trade balance returned to surplus and has been comfortable to date, however clearly continues to be vulnerable to external factors and it is necessary for Malaysia to maintain volume levels of exports to sustain a positive balance. The negative impact of invisible trade over the past few years has caused substantial deficits on the current account which in 1985 was running at around US$ 5 bn.

TABLE 4.52   MALAYSIA: FOREIGN TRADE AND THE BALANCE OF PAYMENTS

US$ mn	1981	1982	1983	1984	1985*
Merchandise exports (fob)	26,900	27,946	31,853	38,452	37,817
Merchandise imports (fob)	27,143	29,704	30,760	31,539	32,029
Trade balance	−243	−1,758	1,093	6,913	5,788
Services balance	−5,312	−6,576	−9,098	−10,566	−10,973
Goods and services balance	−5,555	−8,334	−8,005	−3,653	−5,185
Current account balance	−5,633	−8,409	−8,026	−3,743	−5,315
Capital balance	5,931	8,432	9,210	6,502	6,368
Changes in official reserves	510	462	−111	−187	1,340
Net international reserves	8,293	8,375	8,000	7,003	7,856†

Source: Ministry of Finance, Government of Malaysia
Notes: *Provisional figures   †Position at July 1985
Minor discrepancies occur between these trade figures and those calculated by the same Ministry in Table 4.53. These are due to variations in the accounting methods used by the Ministry.

121

Japan is the largest single source of foreign revenue for Malaysia in the mid-1980s, with Singapore a close second. Both are heavy purchasers of raw commodities, with Singapore re-exporting a large proportion of them. The United States purchased around 12% of Malaysian exports in 1985, but this proportion was expected to fall as American resistance to ASEAN countries' products hardened. In

TABLE 4.53 MALAYSIA: PRINCIPAL TRADING PARTNERS

US$ mn	1980	1981	1982	1983	1984	1985*
Exports						
Singapore	5,385	6,178	7,021	7,369	7,913	7,794
Other ASEAN	913	1,082	1,518	1,956	2,410	2,549
Japan	6,429	5,728	5,726	6,429	8,629	8,663
USA	4,609	3,539	3,224	4,335	5,233	4,819
European Community	4,724	4,129	4,217	4,785	4,877	5,491
of which: UK	779	804	772	895	988	986
West Germany/Netherlands	2,709	2,401	2,515	2,847	2,755	3,365
Australia	403	470	523	463	600	621
China	471	204	258	364	387	321
West Asia†	569	575	601	705	833	690
TOTAL	28,172	27,109	28,108	32,771	38,654	38,007
Imports						
USA	3,528	3,875	5,079	4,989	5,402	5,384
Singapore	2,753	3,487	4,165	4,270	4,312	5,247
Other ASEAN	1,105	1,292	1,588	1,514	2,103	2,216
European Community	3,621	3,702	3,534	4,298	4,442	4,538
of which: UK	1,271	1,214	1,185	1,088	1,187	1,284
West Germany/Netherlands	1,403	1,425	1,431	1,833	1,723	1,801
Australia	1,289	1,474	1,371	1,305	1,325	1,380
West Asia†	2,003	2,183	1,498	1,715	1,335	1,326
China	551	632	649	626	670	654
TOTAL	23,451	26,604	29,023	30,795	32,967	33,250

Source: Ministry of Finance, Government of Malaysia

Notes: *Official projections
   †Bahrain, Iran, Iraq, Kuwait, Saudi Arabia, Egypt and the UAE

Europe, the Netherlands is by far the biggest customer because of its heavy purchases of tin and semi-finished timber, and sales to the European Community have been generally holding steady at around 14% in 1985.

TABLE 4.54 MALAYSIA: PRINCIPAL EXPORTS

US$ mn	1980	1981	1982	1983	1984	1985*
Commodities						
Rubber	4,617	3,712	2,655	3,664	3,668	3,003
Palm oil	2,515	2,710	2,656	2,977	4,528	3,978
Sawlogs	2,621	2,473	3,378	2,792	2,760	2,583
Sawn timber	1,178	971	1,035	1,221	994	1,008
Tin	2,505	2,138	1,484	1,718	2,698	1,300
Crude oil	6,709	6,918	7,694	7,871	8,738	8,206
Manufactures						
Food, beverages and tobacco	475	600	524	568	661	601
Textiles, clothing and footwear	806	785	818	943	1,141	1,339
Wood products	467	473	424	492	424	413
Rubber products	84	83	89	99	107	122
Chemical and petroleum products	361	417	522	896	1,375	1,490
Non-metallic minerals	61	51	72	103	131	162
Iron and steel and metal products	161	170	176	194	268	349
Electrical and electronic goods	2,832	3,017	3,868	4,989	6,333	6,963
Other machinery and transport	407	308	467	689	997	909
Other manufactures	447	398	457	581	764	890

Sources: Ministry of France, Government of Malaysia

Notes: *Government estimates

Manufactures figures are based on the export performance for January to June 1985

It is evident that the government's New Economic Policy is based on Malay nationalistic principles, and it is not surprising that state monopolies or pseudo-monopolies receive official favour. But some dilution of this stance has been forced on the government by the expanding public debt, and by the clear inability of the country to meet its own future financing needs. Foreign participation is being sought,

and in late 1985 the authorities were even considering a partial privatisation of certain state interests. Given the uncertainties surrounding
the prospects for development in the mid-1980s, the government may
well need to take a more pragmatic view in future if it wishes to ensure a
continuation of its national development.

TABLE 4.55   MALAYSIA: FOREIGN DEBT

ringgits mn

	1981	1982	1983	1984	% change, 1983/84
Debts					
Federal government	8,280	13,160	17,730	20,680	16.66
Guaranteed loans	3,070	3,710	5,490	7,140	30.05
Private sector	4,020	7,410	8,600	9,220	7.21
Total debts	15,370	24,280	31,820	37,050	16.44
Debt servicing					
Capital repayment	1,080	1,510	1,530	2,430	58.82
Interest payments	1,200	1,590	2,140	2,870	34.11
Total servicing cost	2,280	3,100	3,670	5,300	44.41

Source: Central Bank

Philippines

As has already been noted, the Philippines' foreign currency position
has deteriorated so sharply since 1983 that for many suppliers the
country was still° an unacceptable risk in 1986—unless they were
prepared to accept countertrade, which obviates the need for foreign
currency transactions altogether.

TABLE 4.56   PHILIPPINES: PRINCIPAL EXPORTS

US$ mn fob

	1980	1981	1982	1983	1984
Coconut products	811	750	590	680	727
Sugar and sugar products	657	609	445	321	327
Logs	92	76	78	74	88
Lumber	181	126	124	149	107
Plywood	111	111	67	76	56
Other forestry products	84	156	93	32	72

TABLE 4.56   PHILIPPINES: PRINCIPAL EXPORTS *(continued)*

US$ mn fob	1980	1981	1982	1983	1984
Copper concentrates	545	429	312	249	115
Gold	239	215	169	154	104
Chromite ore	33	25	15	10	19
Other mineral products	214	89	36	27	28
Pineapple products	97	101	107	102	115
Bananas	114	124	146	105	122
Other fruits/vegetables	154	153	121	120	155
Abaca (inc. rope)	31	25	26	25	37
Tobacco and products	30	50	49	35	31
Mineral fuel and lubricants	38	42	33	115	87
Chemicals	89	107	96	87	104
Textiles	33	69	56	25	38
Others	2,198	2,453	2,449	2,586	2,934
Re-exports	37	10	9	33	125
TOTAL	5,788	5,720	5,021	5,005	5,391

Source: National Census and Statistics Office

TABLE 4.57   PHILIPPINES: FOREIGN TRADE AND THE BALANCE OF PAYMENTS

US$ mn	1980	1981	1982	1983	1984
Merchandise exports	5,787.8	5,720.4	5,020.6	5,005.3	5,390.7
Merchandise imports	7,726.9	7,945.7	7,666.9	7,486.6	6,069.6
Trade balance	−1,939.1	−2,225.3	−2,646.3	−2,481.3	−679.0
Capital balance	2,736.0	2,219.0	2,846.0	1,061.0	1,397.0
Total change in reserves*	−1,134.0	1,177.0	−203.0	2,750.0	−391.0
Official reserves, excl. gold	2,846.0	2,064.0	885.0	746.0	602.0
Gold (national valuation)	294.0	508.0	823.0	117.0	288.0
IMF reserves and SDRs	0.0	2.0	3.0	1.0	27.0
Long-term external debt*	9,700.0	11,200.0	13,000.0	15,400.0	15,900.0

Sources: National Census and Statistics Office, International Monetary Fund, external estimates.

Notes: *Estimate

Official figures for currency reserves in the period to 1983 have been queried by the IMF.

Oil is the country's major import, accounting for over 15% of total imports and mainly sourced from the Middle East. Although a significant portion of imports derives from ASEAN countries, Japan and the USA are the largest single exporters to the Philippines. These are principally manufactured items.

The country's leading export is coconuts followed by sugar products. However, these two commodities alone only account for around 20% of total exports. Although the Philippines export base is diverse it is primary product orientated, which has tended to expose larger trade deficits in recent years (due to lower commodity prices). However, the level of imports has been curtailed over the past two years with a steep reduction recorded in 1985 and trade deficits are likely to contract in the immediate future.

TABLE 4.58   PHILIPPINES: PRINCIPAL TRADE PARTNERS

US$ mn	1980	1981	1982	1983	1984
Exports					
USA	1,588.4	1,765.8	1,586.3	1,799.6	1,630.4
Japan	1,533.3	1,250.5	1,145.5	1,015.0	1,042.7
ASEAN countries	377.0	412.2	358.7	352.8	516.8
of which:					
Singapore	112.6	129.2	111.6	140.3	320.5
Malaysia	94.3	104.1	118.7	154.7	363.1
Hong Kong	191.7	221.7	197.9	170.7	232.4
European Community	980.8	924.3	726.3	816.0	680.5
of which:					
United Kingdom	146.6	193.1	190.0	234.7	224.7
West Germany	255.1	240.3	202.8	199.2	182.5
Netherlands	365.8	319.6	189.9	234.7	224.7
TOTAL, including others	5,787.8	5,720.4	7,486.6	6,069.6	5,390.6
Imports					
USA	1,785.7	1,787.2	1,702.7	1,739.1	1,630.5
Japan	1,531.2	1,494.1	1,532.0	1,266.0	814.5
ASEAN countries	483.2	538.3	509.7	671.1	833.9
of which:					
Malaysia	157.8	177.6	118.7	154.7	363.1

TABLE 4.58   PHILIPPINES: PRINCIPAL TRADE PARTNERS *(continued)*

US$ mn	1980	1981	1982	1983	1984
Indonesia	178.0	224.4	142.9	171.4	201.6
China	205.7	194.5	206.3	122.2	220.3
European Community	827.5	819.0	813.8	879.9	674.1
of which:					
West Germany	323.4	315.7	331.9	354.9	192.8
France	88.8	130.9	100.4	88.5	184.2
Middle East	1,975.0	1,694.3	1,455.0	1,451.5	977.0
of which:					
Saudi Arabia	796.6	1,038.1	912.7	812.5	420.1
Hong Kong	194.2	215.6	210.7	256.7	234.3
TOTAL, including others	7,726.9	7,945.7	7,666.9	7,486.6	6,069.6

Source: National Census and Statistics Office

Singapore

Trade statistics are a particularly important barometer of Singapore's economy, in view of the country's major role as an entrepôt and re-

TABLE 4.59   SINGAPORE: FOREIGN TRADE AND THE BALANCE OF PAYMENTS

US$ mn, at current prices	1982	1983	1984	% change, 1983/84
Merchandise exports (fob)*	20,782	21,837	24,068	10.2
Merchandise imports (cif)*	28,152	28,153	28,660	1.8
Trade balance	−7,370	−6,316	−4,591	27.3
Current account balance	−1,300	−990	−1,001	24.7
Capital account balance	2,214	2,709	2,122	−21.6
Official reserves	8,498	9,288	10,444	9.3
External public debt	409	318	294	−22.2

Source: US Trade Department, based on Singapore Government figures
Note: *Excluding Indonesia

TABLE 4.60   SINGAPORE: PRINCIPAL IMPORT AND EXPORT COMMODITIES

Singapore $ mn	1980	1981	1982	1983	1984
Imports					
Foodstuffs	2,915.5	3,270.5	3,601.9	3,503.9	4,157.5
Beverages and tobacco	276.0	282.2	339.5	416.2	460.6
Crude materials	3,416.9	2,775.5	2,306.1	2,624.8	2,510.2
Mineral fuels	14,889.2	19,831.1	20,479.6	18,611.7	16,961.4
Animal and vegetable oils	1,001.0	721.8	671.5	632.1	1,435.9
Chemicals and chemical products	2,686.7	1,756.1	2,790.7	2,981.6	3,096.2
Manufactured goods	7,237.2	8,079.7	8,407.4	8,089.5	8,045.3
Machinery and transport	15,303.8	16,475.1	17,219.3	18,046.1	19,419.6
Miscellaneous manufactures	2,951.1	3,413.0	3,852.3	3,947.2	4,196.7
Miscellaneous transactions	667.4	643.2	576.3	651.1	850.2
Exports					
Foodstuffs	2,008.2	2,124.8	2,388.0	2,025.1	2,895.4
Beverages and tobacco	157.2	174.3	217.0	210.0	209.8
Crude materials	4,700.0	3,665.3	2,781.1	3,388.5	3,410.4
Mineral fuels	11,965.7	14,175.6	14,616.5	12,969.5	13,185.0
Animal and vegetable oils	1,095.5	820.0	780.3	628.2	1,540.5
Chemicals and chemical products	1,418.5	1,556.3	1,722.4	1,956.3	2,463.7
Manufactured goods	3,441.7	3,667.8	3,838.7	3,683.1	3,624.6
Machinery and transport	11,089.4	11,779.4	11,546.2	14,677.9	16,865.0
Miscellaneous manufactures	2,572.4	2,919.1	2,831.7	3,083.7	3,408.0
Miscellaneous transactions	3,003.7	3,406.2	3,751.1	3,532.6	3,737.6

Source: Government of Singapore

export base for the other ASEAN countries. Discrepancies in the figures always arise, however, because Singapore does not record details of its trade with Indonesia, one of its biggest partners. This is partly because of political differences, but it also reflects the extent of smuggling between the two countries—a particularly sensitive issue which Singapore is keen to play down.

Trade figures are also distorted by the national system of accounting, which classifies as imports and exports many transactions which really only amount to the purchase and temporary storage of local goods for re-export in unaltered form.

TABLE 4.61   SINGAPORE: PRINCIPAL TRADE PARTNERS

Singapore $ mn	1980	1981	1982	1983	1984
Exports					
Peninsular Malaysia	4,739.5	5,346.5	6,355.1	6,886.4	7,269.2
Sabah-Sarawak	1,478.5	1,560.1	1,503.7	1,234.9	1,055.0
Thailand	1,809.3	1,864.6	1,708.0	1,994.7	2,458.2
Japan	3,338.3	4,487.6	4,483.9	4,244.4	4,806.7
Hong Kong	3,195.9	3,881.4	3,741.0	3,132.0	3,176.2
Taiwan	702.0	606.6	575.8	687.5	829.6
China	657.9	377.3	516.7	449.8	519.3
Saudi Arabia	824.6	1,064.6	1,275.5	974.7	1,363.5
Kuwait	187.7	253.5	220.0	142.0	309.8
United Kingdom	1,069.2	1,050.6	904.7	1,053.7	1,372.9
West Germany	1,247.0	1,126.2	974.6	1,071.7	1,227.5
USA	5,272.0	5,848.7	5,593.3	8,373.7	10,291.7
Australia	1,670.8	1,770.5	1,772.1	1,355.4	1,751.4
Others	14,353.5	14,256.2	13,816.5	13,892.0	14,271.9
TOTAL	51,344.8	58,248.0	60,244.6	59,504.2	61,133.6
Imports					
Peninsular Malaysia	6,179.1	6,164.5	6,343.7	6,745.9	7,540.7
Sabah-Sarawak	936.6	1,045.0	1,722.0	1,892.8	1,639.0
Thailand	1,019.0	997.6	1,131.8	1,068.2	1,350.9
Japan	9,162.4	10,957.4	10,791.0	10,724.0	11,217.9
Hong Kong	1,055.1	1,093.0	1,261.3	1,268.9	1,281.3
Taiwan	1,216.3	1,275.1	1,309.9	1,601.5	1,997.8
China	1,332.1	1,629.8	1,881.0	1,747.2	2,881.1
Saudi Arabia	6,412.3	10,771.5	9,408.3	6,507.6	5,687.5
Kuwait	2,838.6	1,995.4	948.3	1,545.5	1,882.7
United Kingdom	1,771.2	1,742.9	1,708.4	1,644.2	1,596.0
West Germany	1,677.1	1,610.4	1,912.4	1,619.7	1,667.1
France	699.0	967.6	1,124.6	1,050.1	1,227.5
USA	7,237.2	7,356.4	7,775.4	9,005.5	8,922.9
Australia	1,162.3	1,207.5	1,772.1	1,355.4	1,751.4
Others	8,646.5	9,433.9	11,526.2	11,959.7	10,944.4
TOTAL	41,452.3	44,290.8	44,472.8	46,154.9	51,340.0

Source: Government of Singapore

The ASEAN partners account for about a sixth of all Singapore's foreign trade (if trade for Indonesia, not shown in Table 4.61, is discounted). The next most important client, and certainly the principal genuine export market, is the USA, which virtually doubled its purchases between 1982 and 1984—although a sharp reduction followed in 1985, amid a wave of American disquiet at the extent of import penetration.

Japan remains the next largest purchaser of Singapore's exports and is the largest source of imports. Many of these, however, are electronic components and engineering parts which are then re-exported after assembly in Singapore. Trade with China has been rising slowly, mainly on the import side, while purchases of crude oil from the Middle East have fallen off since the early 1980s with the inauguration of Saudi Arabia's own petrochemical plants in the Gulf.

Singapore remains, as ever, open to foreign investment in local industries of all kinds, but particularly in the high-technology activities where the country sees its future developing. There are few restrictions on the repatriation of profits, and six free trade zones are in existence for the local processing of re-exports.

The country benefits at present from its developing-country status under the Generalised System of Preferences, but it has come under increasing pressure in recent years from trade competitors, notably the United States and New Zealand, for the withdrawal of this status in view of its rapidly rising per capita GDP.

Overall, the recession of the mid-1980s has not dimmed the long-term prospects for Singapore, which managed to maintain a $3,600 mn current account surplus in 1985 (compared with $4,800 mn in 1984); in the short term the picture is less attractive, and it was certainly clear by 1986 that a thorough review of government priorities would be required. Despite the findings of its own commissions however, there had been no sign whatever of any serious change of heart from the government.

Thailand

Thailand's annual trade deficits have remained relatively static in the 1980s, at around US$ 2 bn, despite a temporary dip to US$ 731 mn in 1982 due to a 15% reduction in imports.

TABLE 4.62   THAILAND: FOREIGN TRADE AND THE BALANCE OF PAYMENTS

US$ mn	1980	1981	1982	1983	1984
Merchandise exports (fob)	6,449	6,902	6,835	6,308	7,340
Merchandise imports (fob)	8,352	8,931	7,565	9,169	9,270
Trade balance	−1,902	−2,029	−731	−2,861	−1,930
Current account balance	−2,070	−2,569	−1,003	−2,874	−2,100
Change in official reserves	170	46	120	188	−433

Source: IMF

Thailand normally exports about 20% of its GDP, almost entirely in the form of agricultural products. The country is a heavy importer of manufactured goods and capital equipment, and the government has been generally unsuccessful in its attempts to limit new demand. Abroad, the country has faced considerable difficulties from import barriers erected by its trade partners and is seeking new sources of foreign exchange.

TABLE 4.63   THAILAND: PRINCIPAL EXPORT COMMODITIES

baht mn	1980	1981	1982	1983	1984
Rice	19,508	26,366	22,510	20,150	25,932
Rubber	12,351	10,841	9,490	12,083	13,004
Maize	7,300	8,349	8,330	8,485	10,147
Tin	11,347	9,091	7,773	5,265	5,280
Tapioca products	14,887	16,446	19,752	15,387	16,600
Sugar	2,975	9,572	12,932	6,332	5,221
TOTAL EXPORTS, incl. others	133,197	153,001	159,728	146,472	175,237

Source: IMF

For this reason foreign investment is warmly encouraged, and attractive tax concessions are offered particularly for export-oriented industries, while the rules governing minimum local ownership have been relaxed in such cases. Japan is by far the largest foreign investor,

TABLE 4.64   THAILAND: PRINCIPAL IMPORT REQUIREMENTS

baht mn	1983	1984	% change 1983/84
Fuel and lubricants	57,065	58,284	2.1
of which: Crude oil	39,975	35,035	−12.4
Refined products	17,090	23,249	36.0
Consumer goods	29,699	31,470	4.4
Raw materials and intermediate goods	59,539	61,601	3.5
Capital goods	69,358	72,609	4.7
Others	20,948	21,805	4.1
Total imports (customs cleared)	236,609	245,769	3.9
less goods with no payments	2,296	2,496	−8.0
Total merchandise imports, c.i.f.	234,313	243,273	3.8

Source: Thailand Government Customs Department

holding 24% of the foreign-owned sector in 1985, while the United States has a 10.8% share. The overall levels of foreign investment remain low, however, and growth has been slowing during the mid-1980s, due to external reservations about the economy's resilience in times of international recession.

TABLE 4.65   THAILAND: PRINCIPAL TRADING PARTNERS

baht mn, cif	1981	1982	1983
Exports			
Japan	21,704	21,947	22,087
USA	19,794	20,257	21,895
Netherlands	18,674	21,013	15,883
Singapore	11,991	11,654	11,913
Hong Kong	7,350	7,934	1,281
Malaysia	6,950	8,341	6,561
West Germany	4,934	5,355	5,105
Saudi Arabia	3,107	4,261	4,245
United Kingdom	2,445	3,018	2,990
Nigeria	2,000	1,561	2,907
TOTAL EXPORTS	153,001	159,728	146,472

TABLE 4.65   THAILAND: PRINCIPAL TRADING PARTNERS *(continued)*

baht mn, cif	1981	1982	1983
Imports			
Japan	52,521	46,086	64,757
USA	29,437	26,220	29,708
Saudi Arabia	29,395	29,819	24,430
Singapore	14,949	12,455	14,623
Malaysia	5,890	10,214	12,737
West Germany	9,336	7,624	11,065
Taiwan	4,589	5,501	6,762
China	6,983	5,374	6,099
South Korea	3,017	3,589	5,602
United Kingdom	5,851	5,023	5,390

Source: Thailand Government Foreign Trade Statistics

INDO-CHINA

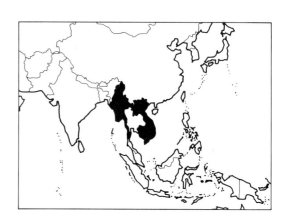

Vietnam
Laos
Burma
Kampuchea

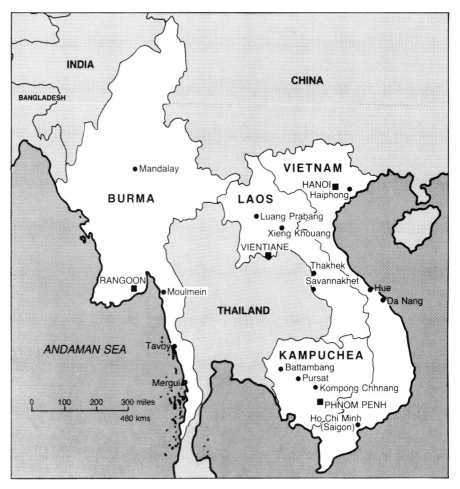

Chapter Five

INDOCHINA

I Overview

Burma

Burma, the most western country on the Indochinese peninsula, may also be regarded as the most westernised in the region. Unlike its eastern neighbours, Laos, Kampuchea and Vietnam, it is both politically and economically independent of the Soviet Union, and it conducts most of its trade with non-socialist countries. It is, however, a collectivist, socialist state in which ultimate power rests with the Socialist Programme Party. The economy is organised on the lines of four-year plans which themselves form part of a 20-year development programme.

Burma is self-sufficient in most commodities, and its economy has a high degree of sophistication by local standards. Nonetheless, the country remains very poor in the mid-1980s, and is in the mood for a relaxation of its rigorous policies for the sake of growth. Change is expected when General Ne Win, the party's somewhat autocratic 75-year-old chairman, finally leaves office after having run the country since 1962.

Burma also differs from its socialist neighbours in that it issues economic statistics of reasonable accuracy and detail. But it should be noted that the country has an enormous black economy, which may well equal the official economy in size and which places most of the trade figures in doubt. Smuggling and drug-running are large-scale activities, and the government's hold over border districts is best described as tenuous. Relations with neighbouring Thailand are permanently strained, and those with South Korea are still recovering from the bomb attack in 1983 which killed four Korean ministers during a visit to Rangoon, the Burmese capital.

Kampuchea

Kampuchea, lying between communist Vietnam in the east and

monarchist Thailand in the north-west, has been embroiled for more than a decade in a ruinous battle of political and military wills which has been exacerbated by drastic changes of policy. Formerly designated as the Kingdom of Cambodia, the country was seized first in 1970 by right-wingers and then in 1975 by the pro-Chinese Khmer Rouge of Pol Pot.

The Khmer Rouge thereupon instigated a notoriously rigorous programme of communist reform, involving the abolition of money and the forced removal of virtually all city-dwellers to the land. This period came to an abrupt end, however, in 1978/9 when the Soviet-backed Vietnamese army invaded, installing a new communist government under Heng Samrin.

Heng Samrin has ever since been engaged in an economically ruinous war against the guerrillas of the former regime. For their part the Khmer Rouge have forged an alliance with the Khmer People's National Liberation Front, and with the deposed Prince Sihanouk (the *Moulinaka*—which are still recognised by most Western countries as being the legitimate rulers of Kampuchea). By the mid-1980s, however, the rebels had been virtually driven out of the country and were continuing their resistance from across the border in Thailand.

In the process a large proportion of the Kampuchean population has been forced to flee the country for Thailand. Vietnam has attracted widespread international condemnation for its aggression against Kampuchea, and has undertaken to leave Kampuchea by 1990; but in 1986 it was steadily reinforcing the country's political and economic dependence on itself.

Laos

The People's Democratic Republic of Laos, comprising the three former principalities of Vientiane, Champassac and Luang Prabang, has been run as a communist state since 1975, when pro-Vietnamese elements were elected to power after more than a decade of growing popular disenchantment with the monarchy. The King thereupon abdicated, and the monarchy was abolished as Prince Souphanouphong became President. The country is heavily dominated by the Lao People's Revolutionary Party, and the economy is run on highly centralised lines.

Laos has been drawn into the military struggles in Indochina by its heavy dependence on Vietnam, with which it signed a 25-year treaty of friendship in 1977. Thailand has frequently accused Laotian troops of border violations, and trade across the long mutual border has been hampered by political tensions even though both sides would like to see an improvement.

Vietnam

Vietnam's economy has made some degree of progress during the early 1980s, as it has slowly recovered from the effects of more than 15 years of civil war. A fully communist state, Vietnam is a full member of the Council for Mutual Economic Assistance (CMEA, or Comecon), and is heavily reliant on both economic and military assistance from the Soviet Union. It remains highly centralised in character, and real power rests not with parliament but with the leadership of the Communist Party.

Since 1979 the country has been undergoing a rapid change of direction, as the government has moved to liberalise the economy in the hope of stimulating the private sector. The results were already becoming evident by 1986; the country has achieved a basic self-sufficiency in food crops, it is an exporter of minerals, with considerable untapped potential, but is still dependent on foreign assistance for the growth of its very small manufacturing sector.

II Population

Burma

Burma has a diversified population structure, in which non-Burmese tribes account for about a fifth of the total; these groups have never fully accepted the authority of the state, and for more than 35 years a civil war has been raging in the remote south of the country, financed largely by smuggling and the black market. Nonetheless, there has been evidence in the mid-1980s that the rebels are being driven back towards the Thai border.

Burma has a high population density and the number of inhabitants is growing at just over 2% a year. Some 70% live in rural districts, particularly in the river valleys; Rangoon, despite being the country's

TABLE 5.1   BURMA: POPULATION

Official estimates

1982	34,976,000
1983	35,680,000
1984	36,392,000

Land area   676,552 sq km

Population density (1984)   53.8 per sq km

Source: Government of Burma

only contact with the outside world, accounts for only 2.4 mn of the country's 36–37 mn people.

Unemployment represents a particular problem for the Burmese government at present, and the situation has worsened since 1984 with the economic slide brought about mainly by falling commodity values. Without further investment there seems little prospect of change, but

TABLE 5.2   BURMA: COMPOSITION OF THE WORKFORCE, 1984/85

'000s

	State sector	Co-operative and private sector	Total
Agriculture	80	9,312	9,392
Livestock and fisheries	16	182	198
Forestry	93	89	182
Mining	72	13	85
Processing and manufacturing	178	1,056	1,234
Electricity	16	—	16
Construction	162	78	240
Transport and communications	114	374	488
Social services	231	84	315
Administration	541	29	570
Trade and commerce	68	1,376	1,444
Others	—	628	628
TOTAL	1,571	13,221	14,792

Source: Government of Burma

the government has actually been forced by declining revenues to cut back on its public spending programmes.

Kampuchea

The last official census was taken in 1962 when the population amounted to 5.73 mn. Since then various estimates of the size of the population have been made, as seen in Table 5.3, and a growth of nearly 25% has been estimated.

TABLE 5.3   KAMPUCHEA: POPULATION

| Mid-year figures | | |
Year	Population	Source
1962	5,728,771	Official census
1975	7,098,000	United Nations estimate
1980	6,747,000	United Nations estimate
1984	7,149,000	West German Government estimate

Area: 181,035 sq km (69,898 sq miles).
Population density: 39.5 per sq km (1984).
Population growth (1962–84): 24.8%.

TABLE 5.4   KAMPUCHEA: COMPOSITION OF THE WORKFORCE

'000s	Total	Male	Female
Agriculture, forestry and fisheries	2,008.1	1,095.0	913.1
Manufacturing industry	68.5	47.7	20.8
Construction	21.8	20.5	1.3
Mining and quarrying	2.4	1.7	0.7
Energy and water	1.6	1.6	0.0
Trade, banking, insurance	143.8	80.1	63.7
Transport and communications	28.8	28.1	0.7
Other services	187.2	152.2	35.0
Others	37.6	22.2	15.3
TOTAL	2,499.0	1,449.0	1,050.7

Source: 1962 census

As in most of the other countries in this region, agriculture is the main source of employment for the majority of the workforce, accounting for 80% of the total in 1962, the last official census.

Most of the Kampuchean population still live in a completely cashless economy, much of it on a subsistence basis. As already noted, Pol Pot removed all money from circulation during the mid-1970s, although it was restored in 1980 by the Heng Samrin administration, together with the National Bank of Kampuchea. The forced exodus of the 1970s has been formally ended by the new administration, but the absence of manufacturing and commerce still makes it most unlikely that any significant re-urbanisation will occur in the foreseeable future. In 1979 the government introduced a new educational programme which it claims has enrolled 1,750,000 pupils, about a quarter of the population.

It was reported in 1978 that Kampuchea had small hospitals and clinics in every region, but it remains uncertain how many have survived the upheavals of the 1980s. Training of medical personnel has, however, been resumed.

Laos

Laos remains essentially a nation of two cultures, the French-speaking and pro-Thai elements of the west and the Lao-speaking pro-Vietnamese of the east who eventually gained the upper hand. The widely scattered population and the remote rural settlements combine to make the collection of all economic or demographic data a particularly difficult task, and many of the official statistics present

TABLE 5.5   LAOS: POPULATION

March 1985		
	Total population	3,584,803
	Males	1,757,115
	Females	1,827,688
	Area	236,800 sq km
	Population density	15.2 per sq km

Source: 1985 census

striking anomalies; as Table 5.5 indicates, the results of the 1985 census fell far short of even the government's own population estimates.

TABLE 5.6   LAOS: POPULATION STRUCTURE

Previous government estimates

	1980	**1981**	**1982**	**1983**
Total	3,756,000	3,846,000	3,938,000	4,033,000
Male	1,870,000	1,915,000	1,961,000	2,008,000
Female	1,886,000	1,931,000	1,977,000	2,025,000
Urban	563,000	585,000	606,000	628,000
Rural	3,193,000	3,261,000	3,332,000	3,405,000

Source: Laotian State Planning Committee

TABLE 5.7   LAOS: COMPOSITION OF THE WORKFORCE

	1980	**1983**	**% of active workforce, 1983**
Productive sector	1,260,000	1,364,000	88.9
Non-productive sector	159,000	169,000	11.1
TOTAL	1,419,000	1,533,000	100.0

Source: Laotian State Planning Committee

Vietnam

Vietnam has a total population of nearly 60 mn, which is increasing at an annual average rate of approximately 1.9%. On the whole the country's inhabitants are racially homogeneous, but severe tensions persist between those in the north and those in the south, who were finally overrun by the north in 1975, after some 30 years of armed struggle against the communists. These differences erupt from time to time into political wrangling between Hanoi in the north, the national capital, and Ho-Chi-Minh City (formerly Saigon, the capital of the defeated south).

TABLE 5.8   VIETNAM: POPULATION

Official mid-year estimates

1979	52,741,766*
1981	54,928,000
1982	55,990,000
1983	57,020,000
1984	58,307,000
Area	329,566 sq km
Population density	179.9 per sq km

Source: Statistical Office
Note: *Census result

TABLE 5.9   VIETNAM: ECONOMICALLY ACTIVE POPULATION

Mid-year estimates

	1970	1985
Total	18,770,000	24,240,000
Males	10,855,000	14,137,000
Females	7,915,000	10,104,000

Sources: International Labour Organisation, West German Government

III   Government policy

Burma

The Burmese economy is organised on the lines of five-year plans, of which the fourth, for 1982/83–1985/86, originally envisaged an annual average growth of 6.2%—slightly less than in the previous plan. It was already clear by 1983, however, that even this would prove impossible under the conditions of depressed world commodity markets, and the annual target was reduced to 5%.

Progress in the agricultural sector is crucially important to the success of all economic planning in the 1980s, since it will continue to form the backbone of industrial development. The government is committed in the long term to the gradual elimination of private enterprise, although it has had to modify its position to a certain degree in its search for faster growth, and is expected to adopt more adventurous policies under future administrations.

Laos

The Laotian economy is organised on the basis of five-year plans. The main priorities set out by the plan for 1981–85 included the progressive collectivisation of agriculture, and also the development of industrial activity—particularly in the south of the country, where the limited transport facilities are most favourable. The government also aims in the long term to develop its trade with Thailand, and to achieve full economic self-sufficiency. Recently it has also signed an agreement for the supply of oil from Vietnam.

Table 5.10 appears to show a gradual increase in the proportion of private industrial enterprise—a somewhat unexpected trend in a communist country dominated by the Vietnamese. The reason is indeed partly that the government has relaxed its policy on private ownership, in the light of slow national development, but it almost certainly also reflects the greater efficiency and profitability of existing private enterprise *vis-à-vis* the less flexible state sector.

TABLE 5.10 LAOS: PRIVATE AND STATE-OWNED ENTERPRISE

Expressed as % of gross industrial production				
	1980	**1981**	**1982**	**1983**
State industry	92.6	93.1	87.8	89.1
Private industry	4.1	4.5	9.3	8.3
Joint state/private	3.3	2.4	2.9	2.6
TOTAL	100.0	100.0	100.0	100.0

Source: Government of Laos

The government claimed that in 1983 only 29.3% of all industry was centrally managed, with the remaining 80.7% under local management.

Vietnam

Vietnam's national economy is organised on the lines of five-year plans as well as annual development plans; these are drawn up by the leadership of the Communist Party for approval by the membership, and are finally rubber-stamped by parliament.

Fundamental changes have been occurring since 1979, as liberal but often controversial measures have been introduced to stimulate production. In particular, the relaxation of constraints on private enterprise has produced a flourishing free market, which by 1983 already accounted for up to 70% of all goods in circulation. In the same year a new tax regime was introduced, which for the first time assessed industrial taxation according to turnover and profit, instead of production volume as previously. In agriculture, taxes are now levied on the area and fertility of farms instead of on the number of persons in a household.

Communist Party hard-liners have complained that the new system provides scope for corruption and the diversion of state funds into private hands; they have also alleged that the sudden expansion of private trading has generated profiteering and boosted inflation. (Consumer price rises are believed to have exceeded 20% in 1983.) Criticism has been particularly strong in Ho Chi Minh City, where much of the country's foreign trade is conducted through private export-import companies.

In June 1985, however, the Party approved another liberalisation of the economic regime. It declared that food subsidies for party members, pensioners and soldiers were to be abolished; that a new and more flexible pricing and wage structure was to be introduced; and, most important, that the focal point of future economic planning was to be the so-called 'socialist economic accounting system'—or, in other words, the profit and loss principle.

Trading regulations have now been tightened up somewhat after the excesses of the early 1980s, and the state has moved again to take control of the monetary system—but with little success. In fact, the sheer scale of the unofficial economy was the main reason for the decision in 1985 to revise the national currency, the dong. The old US dollar rate of 11.7 dong moved on 22 April to 100 dong—although even this fell short of the 375 dong being offered on the black market. On 15 September 1985, a new currency was introduced, with each new dong equivalent to 10 old dong.

IV   Economic performance and structure

Burma

Burma's strategy of self-sufficiency helped to shield the economy in the 1970s and early 1980s from the effects of world recession. During this period the country concentrated on developing its natural resources for export, and achieved an average 6.7% increase in GDP between 1978/79 and 1981/82; in 1982/83 the rate rose to 7.1% but then started to level off, and the growth targets set out in the fourth development plan (1982/83–1985/86) had to be reduced to 5%.

TABLE 5.11   BURMA: COMPOSITION OF GDP

Kyat '000 at constant 1969/70 prices					
	1975/76	1980/81	1981/82	1982/83	1983/84*	1984/85*
Agriculture	37,288	50,597	55,003	58,052	60,898	63,531
Livestock and fisheries	10,708	14,146	15,061	15,505	16,575	18,413
Forestry	4,053	5,309	5,603	5,825	6,115	6,426
Mining	2,146	3,224	3,422	3,634	3,770	5,030
Processing and manufacturing	55,835	73,312	78,707	82,207	85,332	92,958
Power	1,261	2,144	2,644	3,134	3,377	3,896
Construction	6,274	12,824	13,030	14,664	15,324	16,581
Total goods	**117,565**	**161,556**	**173,470**	**183,021**	**191,391**	**206,835**
Transport	10,457	13,336	14,553	16,174	16,601	17,305
Communications	470	837	1,144	1,440	1,633	1,649
Finance	2,150	8,708	9,996	11,156	11,852	12,332
Social and administrative services	20,452	27,440	29,777	31,526	33,045	36,134
Rentals and other services	10,141	11,713	12,092	12,334	12,931	13,416
Total services	**43,670**	**62,034**	**67,562**	**72,630**	**76,062**	**80,836**
Trade	34,940	43,630	46,567	47,744	49,475	52,422
Total output	**196,175**	**267,220**	**287,599**	**303,395**	**316,928**	**340,093**
Less: inter-industry use	80,558	110,044	120,429	126,779	131,879	142,743
Net output	**115,617**	**157,176**	**167,170**	**176,616**	**185,049**	**197,350**

Source: Government of Burma

Note: *Provisional figures

Agriculture has traditionally dominated the economy, accounting for 42.7% of goods production in 1984/85 and providing half of all exports.

Although it has been increasingly challenged by industry in recent years, the government continues to regard it as the key to the future, and it has been intensively promoting new types of export crops, advanced strains of seeds and, where possible, improved cultivation with the use of irrigation schemes and mechanisation.

TABLE 5.12   BURMA: AGRICULTURAL PRODUCTION

'000 tonnes

	1981	1982	1983
Wheat	117	124	183
Rice (paddy)	14,147	14,758	14,500
Maize	166	206	301
Millet	80	85	119
Potatoes	139	119	139
Sugar cane	2,040	2,507	3,135
Groundnuts	439	568	691
Pulses	343	438	552
Sesame seed	157	170	204
Cotton seed	51	73	74
Cotton (lint)	25	36	37
Tobacco	55	55	51
Jute and substitutes	25	21	45
Natural rubber	16	16	16
Fruit	1,032	1,035	1,044
Vegetables and melons	1,887	1,916	1,933

Source: FAO

TABLE 5.13   BURMA: LIVESTOCK

'000 head

	1981	1982	1983
Cattle	8,857	9,182	9,400
Buffaloes	1,969	2,061	2,150
Pigs	2,631	2,883	2,900
Sheep	250	255	260
Goats	769	770	770

Source: FAO

Most Burmese farming is still conducted on small plots of land, however, and agriculture is mainly private in character. Thus the authorities have faced serious obstacles in encouraging the use of modern methods, and as Table 5.12 clearly shows, advances in production have been practically negligible except for maize, millet and pulses. Forestry and fisheries hardly present a more hopeful picture at present, and the whole sector is under-capitalised.

TABLE 5.14 BURMA: TIMBER PRODUCTION

'000 cubic metres	1981	1982	1983
Sawlogs (for sleepers, etc.)	1,909	1,909	1,909
Other industrial woods	1,081	1,110	1,139
Fuel wood	15,431	15,815	16,206
TOTAL PRODUCTION	18,421	18,834	19,254
TOTAL SAWNWOOD	407	335	415

Source: FAO

TABLE 5.15 BURMA: FISHERY PRODUCTION

'000 tonnes	1981	1982	1983
Offshore catches	445.5	450.6	442.9
Inland catches	149.1	133.8	142.9
TOTAL CATCH	594.6	584.4	585.8

Source: FAO

Manufacturing industry has also made disappointing progress in recent years, following a period in the early 1980s when its output grew by 9% per annum. The slowdown has been partially caused by the fall in real export revenues between 1981/82 and 1983/84, partly by difficult investment conditions, and partly by periodic shortages of electric power, At present manufacturing (excluding mineral extraction) provides 10% of GDP.

Traditional industrial activities revolve around the processing of agricultural raw materials (jute, textiles, timber, rice milling and mineral processing), but the country has been seeking to diversify the manufacturing base, and has developed the assembly of machinery, electrical and electronic appliances, and rubber tyre manufacture, often with foreign assistance. But shortages of energy and, most of all, investment capital have presented almost insurmountable difficulties for local producers.

TABLE 5.16 BURMA: MANUFACTURING INDUSTRY

		1979/80	1980/81	1981/82	1982/83	1983/84	1984/85
Cement	'000 tonnes	388	377	307	335	324	308
Bricks	mn	41	43	45	41	44	41
Plywood	mn sq ft	27	39	35	29	19	31
Wire nails	'000 tonnes	6	6	7	6	4	4
Paints	'000 gallons	249	280	430	607	321	325
Fluorescent lamps	'000	52	150	341	307	498	n.a.
Incandescent lamps	mn	1.8	2.3	3.0	3.5	3.6	n.a.
Dry batteries	mn	19	17	19	21	21	n.a.
Soap	'000 tonnes	34	44	48	48	32	41
Paper	'000 tonnes	13	14	18	18	18	18
Aluminium goods	mn	1.3	0.9	2.0	2.4	1.7	1.2
Cotton yarn	mn	29	36	36	45	31	50
Silk yarn	mn	3.2	4.6	5.3	4.6	3.4	0.9
Cotton fabrics	mn	87	104	96	102	99	86
Gunny bags	mn	19	29	26	27	32	38
Fertiliser	'000 tonnes	132	132	125	102	124	157
Beer	'000 gallons	770	749	739	735	748	1,005
Alcohol	mn gallons	3.5	4.1	4.4	3.9	3.1	3.6
Cigarettes	bn	2.3	2.7	3.0	3.2	2.9	2.4
Salt	'000 tonnes	161	94	72	63	92	76
Sugar	'000 tonnes	39	46	43	39	56	65

Source: Central Statistical Office, Government of Burma

Small wonder, then, that the country has focused its attention on its mineral resources, which are in plentiful supply. Deposits such as those at the Bawdwin lead/zinc/silver site in Shan state, or at the Monwya copper complex are being worked at full capacity while a new tin smelter has been built at Syriam, near Rangoon. The fact remains, however, that international interest in metals has also been weak throughout the mid-1980s, and this has depressed sales potential.

TABLE 5.17   BURMA: MINERAL EXTRACTION

tonnes	1980/81	1981/82	1982/83	1983/84	1984/85
Tin concentrates	739	955	1,038	916	1,016
Tungsten concentrates	623	473	525	472	411
Mixed tin/tungsten	2,319	2,280	2,561	3,130	3,602
Refined lead	6,488	5,665	8,001	7,505	7,469
Zinc concentrates	7,167	9,015	7,650	7,745	9,329
Refined silver	530	576	576	577	492

Source: Central Statistical Office, Government of Burma

Burma's established deposits of crude oil have been showing signs of exhaustion in recent years, and production fell by 12% between 1979/80 and 1983/84. But there are promising new onshore finds of petroleum at Kyontani, and the centre of interest in 1986 has been the huge offshore gas deposit south of Rangoon, located by a Japanese company.

It is unlikely that Burma will ever be an exporter of fuels, since all local deposits (including the rather poor-quality coal) are urgently needed by the domestic industries. The country is well endowed with hydro-electric generating potential, and is investing in this sector as far as its limited means allow.

Kampuchea

Like most other countries in Indochina, Kampuchea derives virtually all of its national income from the agricultural sector. The lack of industrial development is partly due to the severe lack of even basic transport or other infrastructural amenities, but more specifically to the chaos wreaked by the unending wars and changes of direction since the late 1960s.

Agriculture centres heavily on the cultivation of rice, particularly wetland rice in the lowlands of the Mekong and Tonle Sap (the two

TABLE 5.18 KAMPUCHEA: AGRICULTURAL PRODUCTION

'000 tonnes	1979	1980	1981	1982	1983
Rice	850	1,470	1,160	1,400	1,700
Maize	70	100	98	46	60
Sweet potatoes	14	15	14	17	25
Cassava	143	150	145	61	75
Dry beans	12	14	23	26	29
Soya beans	2	3	1	1	1
Groundnuts	10	13	4	5	6
Sesame seed	3	4	3	3	5
Coconuts	26	30	28	30	33
Sugar cane	115	130	143	170	181
Bananas	55	65	70	75	82
Oranges	20	22	23	25	30
Mangoes	7	8	10	12	14
Pineapples	5	6	5	6	7
Natural rubber	10	10	5	8	8
Tobacco	4	5	5	5	7
Jute	3	4	4	4	5
Grapefruit	1	1	1	1	2

Source: FAO

major watercourses of the country); there is, however, a wide range of fruit and vegetable products, without which the country would have been in even deeper trouble by the mid-1980s. As it was, the country was forced by crop failures in the early 1980s to appeal for assistance from multilateral aid organisations. It has been estimated that fertiliser output is insufficient to cover more than a quarter of all requirements, and in 1986 it still seems improbable that adequate provisions can be imported—certainly not from the occupying Vietnamese, who have supply problems of their own.

There have been signs of a stabilisation in Kampuchean agriculture since 1980, however, and improvements have been reported particularly in the cultivation of sugar cane and in the meat and livestock sector.

The country's heavy dependence on agriculture is no accident; the

TABLE 5.19   KAMPUCHEA: CATTLE AND LIVESTOCK

'000 head	1980	1981	1982	1983	1984
Cattle	798	956	1,040	1,148	1,357
of which: dairy	85	90	92	92	n.a.
Buffaloes	404	404	406	468	554
Pigs	222	260	487	717	974
Horses	8	8	8	9	10
Sheep	1	1	1	1	n.a.
Goats	0	0	1	1	1
Chickens (mn)	4	4	4	4	n.a.
Ducks (mn)	1	2	2	2	n.a.

Source: FAO

TABLE 5.20   KAMPUCHEA: ANIMAL PRODUCTS

'000 tonnes	1979	1980	1981	1982	1983
Beef and veal	10	11	12	13	14
Buffalo meat	6	6	6	6	7
Pigmeat	5	9	11	15	18
Poultry	12	12	12	14	15
Cows' milk	12	14	15	16	16
Hens' eggs	2	2	3	3	4
Hide leather	3	4	4	4	5

Source: FAO

TABLE 5.21   KAMPUCHEA: FORESTRY PRODUCTS

'000 cubic metres	1980	1981	1982	1983
Total production	4,955	5,007	5,107	5,239
of which: conifers	5	5	5	n.a.
deciduous	4,950	5,002	5,102	n.a.
Sawlogs	110	110	110	110
Other industrial wood	457	457	457	457
Fuel wood	4,388	4,440	4,540	4,672

Source: FAO

TABLE 5.22 KAMPUCHEA: FISHERY PRODUCTION

tonnes

	1979	1980	1981	1982	1983
Inland	21,900	44,500	62,600	53,050	58,550
Sea	7,550	6,610	5,670	5,200	4,820
Crustaceans	550	490	430	400	380
TOTAL CATCH	30,000	51,600	68,700	58,650	63,750

Source: FAO

brutal resettlements of the mid-1970s formed part of the Khmer Rouge's ideological commitment to the abolition of supposedly degenerate urban activities. The Pol Pot regime did, at least, accomplish the forced construction of thousands of miles of irrigation channels, and most of these are still in use by farmers.

What little manufacturing industry remains in Kampuchea is centred on the agro-industrial sector. The continuing war has made it impossible since the mid-1970s to collect or issue reliable information on any aspect of the economy, and as a result all recent figures are based on foreign

TABLE 5.23 KAMPUCHEA: MANUFACTURING INDUSTRY

		1971	1972	1973
Motor spirit	'000 tonnes	2	—	—
Heavy fuel oil	'000 tonnes	11	—	—
Light fuel oil	'000 tonnes	14	—	—
Cement	'000 tonnes	44	53	78
Rubber tyres	'000	208	200	200
Shoes	'000 pairs	1,292	1,000	1,000
Soap	tonnes	469	400	400
Cotton yarn	tonnes	1,068	1,094	415
Beer	'000 hectolitres	26	23	18
Spirits	'000 hectolitres	45	55	36
Non-alcoholic beverages	'000 hectolitres	25	25	25
Cigarettes	mn	3,413	2,510	2,622

Source: Government of Kampuchea (latest available statistics).

estimates. As Table 5.23 shows, however, the level of industrial production was in decline even before the present troubles began.

Kampuchea has only very limited mineral resources, of which phosphates represent the only viable option in the mid-1980s. Exploitation of other deposits is hampered by the inadequate road and rail structure, and no long-term improvement is in sight despite the restoration of rail services in some parts of the country.

TABLE 5.24   KAMPUCHEA: ELECTRICITY GENERATION

mn kilowatt hours					
	1970	**1975**	**1980**	**1981**	**1982**
Thermal	107	150	50	75	80
Hydro-electric	26	0	50	54	56
TOTAL	133	150	100	129	136

Source: West German Government

Laos

Agriculture represents by far the largest single element of the Laos economy and provides employment for about 85% of the workforce, although much of this is thought to be on a subsistence basis. Laos has a

TABLE 5.25   LAOS: COMPOSITION OF NATIONAL INCOME

mn kip, at 1982 prices					
	1980	**1981**	**1982**	**1983**	**1984**
Total National Income	8,974	9,564	9,746	9,422	10,189
Agriculture, forestry and fisheries	7,428	8,085	7,933	7,616	8,372
Manufacturing industry	679	660	682	675	686
Construction	255	203	331	331	331
Trade and commerce	334	368	517	517	517
Transport and communications	191	156	166	166	166
Other merchandise	87	92	117	117	117

Source: West German Government

fairly good land structure for farming, particularly in the south, but the country's potential has been severely limited by the impact of years of fighting; since 1980, moreover, successive problems have arisen with flooding, drought and insect infestations, so that production is barely up to the levels of the late 1960s.

Although the national economy is centralised, collective farming is still the exception rather than the rule, and land is owned and worked mainly on a family basis. Because of this factor, together with the vagaries of the climate, it has been virtually impossible to control or co-ordinate agricultural development with any success. Even large cities like Vientiane, the national capital, are periodically left without supplies and have to undertake local imports of foodstuffs.

It follows, therefore, that the mechanisation of agriculture will

TABLE 5.26   LAOS: AGRICULTURAL PRODUCTION

'000 tonnes	1980	1981	1982	1983
Rice	1,053.1	1,154.7	1,092.4	1,001.4
of which: Season	705.0	782.2	730.5	700.0
Irrigated	11.1	12.3	12.4	12.5
Others	377.0	360.2	349.5	31.9
Maize	18.3	32.8	34.7	31.9
Sweet potatoes and cassava	80.3	97.1	95.8	100.0
Vegetables and beans	42.6	43.6	44.9	44.3
French beans	1.6	1.7	1.8	1.8
Soya beans	3.3	3.9	4.2	5.5
Groundnuts	7.9	8.7	9.2	8.7
Tobacco	16.6	19.1	19.7	15.5
Cotton	4.9	5.0	5.7	5.0
Coffee	4.4	5.0	5.2	5.5
Tea	0.3	0.5	0.5	0.6
Fruit	15.2	15.6	16.0	16.0
TOTAL PRODUCTION	1,224.4	1,950.2	1,307.8	1,211.0

Source: Laotian State Planning Committee
Note: Figures vary slightly from those offered by the FAO.

remain at a low level for the foreseeable future. The government is, however, trying to promote its 'mutual aid teams' in the villages, and has instituted, with varying degrees of success, a system of minimum farm-gate prices in an attempt to bring agriculture within the official cash economy.

Rice is grown particularly in the Mekong areas to the south, and it remains the staple diet of most Laotians, supplemented by fish and vegetables when available. Measures to encourage diversification of crops are bearing promising results, but in the mid-1980s the country was still a net importer of food and was heavily dependent on foreign food aid, particularly from the Soviet Union.

TABLE 5.27   LAOS: LIVESTOCK

'000 head				
	1980	**1981**	**1982**	**1983**
Buffaloes	853.3	879.6	897.2	916.0
Cows	446.9	455.0	472.7	486.0
Pigs	1,111.1	1,176.0	1,223.0	1,300.0
Goats and sheep	48.6	54.0	56.2	60.0
Poultry	4,601.4	5,568.0	5,863.0	6,654.0

Source: Laotian State Planning Committee

The government has paid particular attention to improving the quality of livestock in recent years, and has promoted small-scale irrigation schemes as well as new strains of double-cropping rice. Export crops are very limited but include tea and coffee, soya beans and cotton. Finally, opium cultivation is still an important source of income for farmers in the north, adjoining Thailand, and makes an unseen but doubtless substantial contribution to the country's international trade. The government's efforts to curb this perfectly legal crop have been merely nominal to date.

Forestry has been a traditional source of foreign currency for Laos, but the industry has suffered appalling problems from the years of war, as whole stands have been destroyed by defoliation. Elsewhere, traditional methods of dry rice cropping, involving huge and wasteful amounts of land clearance, have contributed to the pressure on the forests. But government measures to promote logging, combined with a recovery of market prices, have helped to revive interest in the business since 1980.

TABLE 5.28 LAOS: FORESTRY

'000 cubic metres	1981	1982	1983
Sawlogs, for sleepers etc	130	130	130
Other industrial wood	95	97	100
Fuel wood	3,516	3,609	3,690
TOTAL SAWNWOOD	46	56	41

Source: FAO

Despite its landlocked position, Laos is fortunate in possessing extensive fishery potential in the Mekong districts of the south, and efforts are under way to promote artificial fish-farming techniques elsewhere. For many Laotians fish is virtually the only animal protein in their diet.

Industry remains very limited in scale, mainly because of the shortage of investment but also because of the legacies of war and the limited number of suitable quality roads; at present the whole sector is thought to account for under 6% of GDP. By far the most important manufacturing activity is the processing of timber; but almost as significant in the 1980s has been the generation of hydro-electric electricity—one of the few real exports which Laos has to offer its neighbour Thailand. The government has been planning a major expansion of capacity with the aim of fostering industrial growth while maintaining its external trade volume.

TABLE 5.29 LAOS: MANUFACTURING INDUSTRY

		1980	1981	1982	1983
Electricity	mn kWh	895.7	844.5	921.9	850.9
Tin	tonnes	417.4	254.0	305.0	352.0
Timber	'000 cu m	168.7	128.7	140.8	181.3
Sawnwood	'000 cu m	31.2	20.8	30.2	57.1
Plastic products	tonnes	44.5	69.0	207.0	185.1

TABLE 5.29   LAOS: MANUFACTURING INDUSTRY *(continued)*

		1980	1981	1982	1983
Detergent	tonnes	602.0	444.0	987.0	970.0
Oxygen	'000 tubes	3.0	1.7	3.0	4.5
Bricks	mn	2.3	4.1	5.6	10.9
Salt	tonnes	4,600.0	3,213.0	8,949.0	6,860.0
Cigarettes	mn pkts	14.6	15.1	13.0	12.0
Beer	hectolitres	6,598.0	12,019.0	13,103.0	13,000.0
Non-alcoholic drinks	hectolitres	12,482.0	15,365.0	12,643.0	12,370.0
Textiles	'000 metres	635.0	954.7	1,214.0	1,451.4
Clothing	'000 pieces	230.0	376.7	384.0	474.9
Fermented fish	tonnes	n.a.	336.0	101.0	233.0
Perfumed soap	'000 pieces	1,621.0	1,779.0	6,329.0	3,928.0
Wood products	'000 kips	10,168.0	16,918.0	13,133.0	28,040.0
Handicrafts	'000 kips	1,686.0	529.0	1,737.0	n.a.
Tinplate	'000 sheets	865.0	1,253.0	650.0	1,000.0
Motor tyres	'000 pieces	422.0	728.0	638.0	1,000.0
Animal feed	tonnes	1,800.0	3,500.0	6,006.0	3,000.0
Medicines	'000 kips	5,307.0	2,694.0	10,070.0	20,000.0
Vaccines	'000 pieces	n.a.	3,619.0	7,587.0	1,000.0
Ice	tonnes	7,912.0	9,427.0	10,515.0	12,700.0
Bread	tonnes	288.0	110.0	270.0	141.6

Source: Laotian State Planning Committee

Laos is fairly well endowed with mineral resources, but because of transport problems only tin is mined in commercial quantities. Deposits of coal and even petroleum are known to exist, as well as substantial

TABLE 5.30   LAOS: MINERAL PRODUCTION

tonnes	Tin (ore)	Salt (unrefined)	Gypsum
1980	417	20,000	30,000
1981	254	20,000	40,000
1982	305	9,000	40,000
1983	352	10,000	70,000
1984	486	n.a.	80,000

Source: West German Government

amounts of iron ore near Vientiane, and small deposits of gold, silver and certain gemstones are periodically located throughout the mountainous part of the country.

Vietnam

Detailed official figures on economic performance are not usually released in Vietnam, and the statistics given in this section are entirely collated from outside sources. It is pertinent to remember that a large proportion of the rural population lives entirely outside the cash economy; that smuggling and undeclared sales are widespread; and that the entire black economy may equal the official economy in size.

Agriculture accounts for around three-quarters of GDP, and employs two-thirds of the workforce. Vietnam has a chronic shortage of suitable land for cultivation, and successive government plans have centred on the expansion of the available acreage, particularly for export crops such as rubber, tea and coffee.

This shortage is largely due to the after-effects of aerial bombardment during the civil war, which both defoliated part of the southern half of the country and destroyed irrigation systems and other elements of the rural infrastructure; as many as 2,000,000 hectares are still thought to be too poisonous for cultivation in the mid-1980s. More than a decade after the ending of hostilities, agriculture in the north of the country is still ahead of the south—although this also reflects the fact that the north has had longer to develop within the dominant socialist framework of the economy.

Lack of land has also resulted historically from a lack of incentives for farmers to expand. Farm-gate prices were until recently kept to an unacceptably low level, with the result that new acreage was slow in appearing—although it should be added that the same factor served to drive part of the harvest out of the official and recorded economy and into the cashless private market, depressing official results.

As Table 5.31 indicates, rice is the most plentiful of Vietnam's food crops, with as many as three harvests a year in the most fertile central and southern districts. In a normal year Vietnam's rainfall is amply sufficient for wetland growing in most of the lowland areas, and the government is promoting the spread of the improved strains which have already been used for some time in the north.

TABLE 5.31   VIETNAM: AGRICULTURAL PRODUCTION

'000 tonnes	1980	1981	1982	1983	1984
Rice	11,679	12,570	14,169	14,732	15,416
Maize	418	460	437	420	n.a.
Sorghum	37	35	40	42	44
Potatoes	862	700	418	500	n.a.
Sweet potatoes	2,358	2,100	1,665	1,700	n.a.
Cassava	3,290	3,165	2,665	2,700	n.a.
Dry beans	56	57	60	62	66
Onions	130	134	138	145	149
Soya beans	32	56	100	107	110
Groundnuts	98	80	85	87	87
Cottonseed	3	3	3	3	3
Cotton (lint)	2	2	2	2	n.a.
Coconuts	311	350	355	360	n.a.
Melons	95	97	100	110	n.a.
Oranges	87	90	92	95	n.a.
Pineapples	320	350	360	380	n.a.
Bananas	895	900	1,100	1,100	n.a.
Sugar cane	4,388	3,900	4,400	4,600	n.a.
Coffee	6	7	8	9	n.a.
Tea	22	23	25	28	n.a.
Tobacco	25	28	30	32	n.a.
Jute and substitutes	31	35	36	38	39
Natural rubber	45	40	40	45	50

Source: FAO, West German Government

Rice cultivation was severely hit by the disastrous weather conditions of 1978–80, when drought and typhoons combined to wreck the country's hopes of self-sufficiency in food crops. Dry-land crops such as sweet potatoes, cassava, sorghum and potatoes should in theory provide some protection from the destructive effects of climatic change upon the vulnerable rice crop; in practice, however, it would appear that the output of most non-rice food crops has actually been falling since 1980 while that of rice has resumed levels comparable with the 15 mn tonne targets of the 1970s. In other words, the country appears in the mid-1980s to be growing more rather than less vulnerable to climatic factors.

Production of fertiliser, which was cut following attacks by the Chinese in 1979, has shrunk by around 15% since 1980.

Vietnam has, however, been successful in developing such export crops as bananas, coffee, tea, jute and rubber, and several such crops have provided the basis for industrial expansion (in fact, virtually the whole of Vietnam's industry depends on the processing of agricultural raw materials).

TABLE 5.32   VIETNAM: LIVESTOCK

'000 head

	1980	1981	1982	1983	1984
Cattle	1,661	1,765	1,970	2,000	n.a.
of which: dairy	33	35	38	37	n.a.
Buffaloes	2,316	2,478	2,500	2,390	n.a.
Horses	127	130	140	140	n.a.
Pigs	10,000	10,000	10,494	10,785	n.a.
Sheep	14	15	16	18	18
Goats	200	170	196	219	256
Chickens	51,000	49,000	54,000	57,000	62,000
Ducks	29,000	25,000	24,000	27,000	n.a.

Source: FAO

The country has some 13,400,000 hectares of forested land, but the forestry and wood-processing industries have made only rather disap-

TABLE 5.33   VIETNAM: FORESTRY

'000 cubic metres

	1980	1981	1982	1983
Total production	22,200	22,676	23,191	23,676
of which: conifers	112	112	112	112
deciduous	22,088	22,564	23,079	23,564
Sawlogs	1,312	1,312	1,312	1,312
Other industrial wood	1,427	1,459	1,526	1,562
Fuel wood	19,461	19,905	20,353	20,802
Total sawn wood	520	520	520	520

Source: FAO

pointing progress since 1980, in the light of the government's conservation and reafforestation programmes. The effects of defoliation have
been exacerbated, as in Laos, by the strip-and-burn cultivation
techniques used by traditional hill farmers, and there has been pressure
on the government to discourage these activities. Under normal
circumstances the Vietnamese reckon to process about 10% of all
timber for industrial purposes, and they also extract resins and certain
ingredients for use in medicines.

Fisheries provide a most important source of protein, being consumed
not only fresh but also in dried form, or as fish sauce, and the
government has been working to expand both inland and offshore
fisheries. In 1984 the national fishing fleet comprised 26 ships of over
100 tonnes each, with a total deadweight of 6,530 tonnes.

TABLE 5.34   VIETNAM: FISHERY PRODUCTION

'000 tonnes	1979	1980	1981	1982	1983
Inland catches	185	190	195	200	205
Sea catches	341	348	351	362	415
Crustaceans	51	52	53	54	62
Others	23	23	24	24	28
TOTAL	600	613	622	640	710

Source: FAO

Manufacturing industry has made fairly good progress since 1980,
despite serious shortages of energy and disruptions to the supply of raw
materials. This growth is due partly to the assistance provided by the
Soviet Union and by East European countries, but it also reflects the
recent impact of productivity bonuses, the decentralisation of decision-
making and the promotion of locally-oriented structures which are more
readily adjusted to meet local conditions.

Although most of the larger industrial concerns are owned by the
state, manufacturing is by no means limited to the public sector. There
is a very large number of small private companies and craft workshops,
as well as co-operatives and other ventures in which both private and
state holdings are represented.

TABLE 5.35   VIETNAM: MANUFACTURING INDUSTRY

		1980	1981	1982	1983
Cement	'000 tonnes	641	538	710	907
Steel	'000 tonnes	62	34	47	48
Fertilisers	'000 tonnes	313	273	224	265
Paper and card	'000 tonnes	48	53	53	49
Refined sugar	'000 tonnes	114	246	222	306
Cotton fibres	'000 tonnes	29	31	44	45
Copra	'000 tonnes	39	58	58	64
Dried fish	'000 tonnes	385	404	445	513
Processed timber	'000 cu. m.	520	520	520	520
Beer	'000 hl.	606	561	561	527
Cigarettes	'000,000	7,900	11,300	12,800	18,200
Bicycle tyres	'000 pieces	4,917	5,667	11,045	10,460
Ploughing equpt.	'000 pieces	311	327	351	448

Source: West German Statistical Office

TABLE 5.36   VIETNAM: MINERAL PRODUCTION

'000 tonnes	1977	1978	1979	1980	1981	1982
Hard coal	6,200	6,000	5,500	6,300	6,500	6,100
Phosphates	1,500	1,800	400	500	550	500
Salt (unrefined)	580	530	525	520	500	599

Sources: United Nations, West German Government

V   Foreign trade and investment

Burma

Burma has a long tradition of international trade, and maintains adequate port facilities at Rangoon with easy access to the Indian Sub-Continent and the Middle East. The overland transport of export goods is barely practicable for geographic and political reasons; the long border with Thailand, for example, is permanently closed.

Nevertheless, south-east Asian and Pacific countries such as Singapore, Japan and Malaysia are among Burma's principal export markets. Virtually all official trade is conducted through state trading agencies such as the Myanma Export-Import Corporation—although, as already mentioned, extensive smuggling complicates the picture. Rice, followed by teak and rubber, are the main export commodities, while machinery and transport equipment tops the list of import requirements.

TABLE 5.37   BURMA: BALANCE OF PAYMENTS

'000 kyat	1979/80	1980/81	1981/82	1982/83	1983/84*	1984/85*
Merchandise exports	26,340	31,800	34,621	28,914	32,917	36,000
Merchandise imports	42,701	46,027	59,514	68,699	48,953	56,500
Merchandise balance	−16,361	−14,227	−24,893	−39,785	−16,036	−20,500
Main balance†	−17,533	−15,353	−27,129	−42,471	−18,660	−22,345
Net grants	−4,304	−6,394	−4,285	−6,018	−5,281	−6,352
Net loans	19,454	11,081	18,428	23,991	14,612	17,830
Current account	6,203	1,301	−4,418	−12,470	632	1,196
Overall balance	6,024	2,182	−3,082	−9,639	2,515	−474

Source: Euromonitor calculations, based on government statistics
Notes: *Estimates
        †Including transport, insurance, private and government services, diplomatic
        costs and miscellaneous expenses.

TABLE 5.38   BURMA: FOREIGN TRADE

kyat mn	1979/80	1980/81	1981/82	1982/83	1983/84
Domestic exports	2,679.0	3,176.4	3,432.3	3,003.4	3,386.4
All exports*	2,696.0	3,225.1	3,552.8	3,036.3	3,419.5
All imports	4,309.5	4,635.0	5,611.3	6,313.6	5,197.3
Trade balance	−1,613.5	−1,409.9	−2,058.5	−3,277.3	−1,777.8

Source: Central Statistical Office, Government of Burma
Note: *i.e. including re-exports

In accordance with its socialist traditions, the government has hitherto discouraged foreign investment in all its forms, but there have been

TABLE 5.39   BURMA: PRINCIPAL IMPORTS

kyat mn

	1979/80	1980/81	1981/82	1982/83	1983/84
Capital goods	2,765.7	2,496.3	2,930.8	3,742.8	3,172.8
Intermediate goods	1,333.8	1,863.1	2,209.1	2,044.5	1,648.2
Consumer goods	210.0	275.6	471.1	526.3	376.3
of which: wheat flour	26.1	29.0	10.1	0.1	60.2
TOTAL	4,309.5	4,635.0	5,611.3	6,313.6	5,197.3

Source: Central Statistical Office, Government of Burma

TABLE 5.40   BURMA: PRINCIPAL TRADING PARTNERS

US$ mn

	1980	1981	1982
Exports			
Singapore	63.26	59.43	55.04
Japan	69.58	57.49	44.32
Hong Kong	26.46	35.44	27.78
Malaysia	29.51	24.80	22.94
USA	29.51	24.80	22.94
Sri Lanka	8.27	14.54	16.27
China	—	—	13.63
South Korea	3.10	34.57	13.14
United Kingdom	11.36	9.41	8.40
Imports			
Japan	236.52	274.03	253.68
Singapore	73.76	75.93	95.15
United Kingdom	52.39	40.46	85.46
West Germany	70.36	53.59	76.71
USA	31.68	37.40	37.29
France	6.33	24.37	35.40
China	—	—	34.01
South Korea	6.58	14.75	32.02
Netherlands	14.85	33.50	25.32

Sources: IMF, BOTB (British Overseas Trade Board)

signs in the mid-1980s of a change of policy, of which financial liberalisation has been the most obvious sign so far. Foreign involvement will
be essential if it is to exploit the offshore deposits of natural gas which
have recently been located in the Gulf of Martaban. But by the start of
1986 only one joint-venture scheme, involving a West German machine
manufacturer, had been allowed to go ahead.

Burma does, however, accept assistance from multilateral agencies
such as the IMF, the World Bank and the Asian Development Bank; it
is also aided by Japan, the United States and West Germany.

Despite its years of concentrating on self-sufficiency, Burma is
nowadays increasingly feeling the weight of its foreign debt, which
exceeded US$ 1.8 bn in 1985—or about four times its annual export
earnings. The resolution of this problem appeared in 1986 to be a pre-
requisite of any further progress in the country's economic development,
and seemed likely to define Burma's options for some time to come.

TABLE 5.41   BURMA: FOREIGN EXCHANGE RESERVES

'000 kyat, at end of March			
	Gold	Foreign exchange	Total
1974	405	5,612	6,017
1975	541	10,241	10,782
1976	541	8,392	8,933
1977	576	7,014	7,590
1978	672	8,024	8,696
1979	710	10,031	10,741
1980	748	16,017	16,765
1981	748	18,199	18,947
1982	748	15,117	15,865
1983	748	5,478	6,226
1984	748	7,993	8,741
1984*	748	7,412	8,160

Source: Government of Burma
Note: *End of September

Kampuchea

Because of the continuing absence of official trade statistics, practically all information has to be painstakingly collated from Kampuchea's trade partners—not all of whom are themselves able or indeed willing to present accurate accounts. It is certainly true, however, that the country is still almost totally dependent on foreign aid for manufactured goods, and that the limited assistance provided by the Vietnamese can largely be traced back to the Soviet Union. All external transactions, including multilateral aid, are channelled through the state organisation Kampexim, which is based in Phnom Penh. There is also, however, a National Trade Commission whose responsibilities extend to external as well as internal economic co-ordination.

TABLE 5.42   KAMPUCHEA: FOREIGN TRADE BALANCE

US$ '000, USSR and OECD members only						
	1978	1979	1980	1981	1982	1983
Imports	2,561	7,046	72,442	110,529	86,023	102,388
Exports	1,111	851	3,843	4,132	5,449	6,420
Trade balance	−1,450	−6,195	−68,599	−106,397	−80,574	−95,968

Source: West German Government, based on information from trade partners

TABLE 5.43   KAMPUCHEA: PRINCIPAL IMPORTS

US$ '000, OECD countries only					
	1979	1980	1981	1982	1983
Foodstuffs and live animals	1,244	48,263	19,231	7,436	4,204
of which:					
Meat and meat products	280	175	—	147	87
Dairy produce and eggs	198	830	10	306	99
Grain and grain products	383	46,800	19,198	6,597	3,946
Tobacco and beverages	88	409	15	288	64
Raw materials (excl. food and minerals)	26	28	55	175	61
of which: Cork and wood	25	11	—	66	39
Mineral fuels and lubricants	—	1,324	35	3	1
Animal and vegetable oils, etc.	13	5,624	—	16	2,209
Chemical products	748	5,530	4,030	1,699	659
of which:					
Medical and pharmaceutical products	—	—	420	—	462

TABLE 5.43   KAMPUCHEA: PRINCIPAL IMPORTS *(continued)*

US$ '000, OECD countries only

	1979	1980	1981	1982	1983
Manufactured goods	647	1,102	978	849	973
of which:					
Paper and card	31	161	331	223	75
Mineral-based products	179	90	55	168	169
Iron and steel	154	62	—	112	107
Machines, electrical goods and					
transport equipment	3,822	6,588	2,903	1,254	1,803
of which: Vehicles	3,236	4,668	1,530	554	334
Other manufactures	428	1,106	353	524	692

Source: West German Government, based on information from trading partners

TABLE 5.44   KAMPUCHEA: PRINCIPAL TRADE PARTNERS

US$ '000

	1979	1980	1981	1982	1983
Imports					
Soviet Union	n.a.	2,464	82,589	73,476	91,219
Japan	744	25,459	10,419	5,137	3,475
United States	148	25,916	11,473	1,613	2,485
European Community	4,639	8,776	3,627	3,358	3,526
of which:					
France	573	1,939	569	1,587	1,585
United Kingdom	854	1,919	1,261	834	1,251
West Germany	682	3,976	851	355	234
Australia	1,055	8,198	364	1,468	967
New Zealand	216	10	—	294	331
Sweden	44	23	144	126	148
Exports					
Soviet Union	n.a.	2,466	2,634	3,170	5,398
Japan	315	568	670	573	423
European Community	204	400	221	1,568	401
of which:					
United Kingdom	178	170	184	160	278

Source: West German Government, based on information from trading partners

Aid from the United States, the former mainstay of the economy, was refuted by the then Cambodian government as long ago as 1963. All vestiges of industrial investment from abroad (notably from the People's Republic of China) had ceased by the time of nationalisation, and non-communist involvement has of course been barred for many years. As a result, industrial development has been slow to say the least, and such is the strength of international feeling about the Vietnamese invasion of 1979 that it is doubtful whether foreign industrial investment would be forthcoming even if it were permitted.

TABLE 5.45   KAMPUCHEA: TRADE WITH THE SOVIET UNION

US$ '000			
	1981	**1982**	**1983**
Imports			
Petroleum and petroleum products	19,921	19,538	28,792
Cotton yarns	2,905	2,889	2,960
Cotton textiles	1,937	2,614	2,691
Textiles from artificial fibres	1,383	3,027	3,094
Machinery, electrical and transport equipment	27,253	26,418	36,595
of which: trucks	1,522	1,651	9,956
Exports			
Natural rubber	2,634	3,179	5,398

Source: West German Government, based on Soviet information

Laos

Although not a formal member of the Soviet-based Council for Mutual Economic Assistance (CMEA, or Comecon), Laos shares close affiliations with Vietnam and the Soviet Union and may join in the foreseeable future. Certainly, it already obtains most of its foreign aid through these channels. Assistance from the People's Republic of China and North Korea has completely ceased since the installation of the pro-Vietnamese administration in Vientiane.

Laos also receives aid from multilateral agencies such as the International Development Association and the Asian Development Bank, which have both offered concessionary project finance.

All foreign trade figures emanating from Vientiane are subject to considerable qualification because of the high volume of smuggling across the borders with Burma and Thailand. Perhaps surprisingly for such a staunchly communist state, Laos does most of its officially-acknowledged foreign trade with Japan and with Thailand. Theoretically, the country is open to foreign investment, but in practice the political and strategic issues have deterred virtually all involvement from non-communist countries.

TABLE 5.46 LAOS: FOREIGN TRADE

Foreign trade index: 1980=100				
	1980	1981	1982	1983
Total exports	100.0	110.2	171.2	285.2
Total imports	100.0	82.2	84.3	113.6
Exports to socialist countries	100.0	225.0	417.9	518.1
Imports from socialist countries	100.0	50.8	76.4	432.2

Source: Government of Laos

TABLE 5.47 LAOS: BALANCE OF PAYMENTS

	1981	1982	1983	1984
Exports (fob)	19.4	39.8	42.8	36.2
Imports (cif)	109.5	132.2	135.1	98.4
Trade balance	−90.1	−92.4	−92.3	−62.2
Current account balance	−57.7	−65.3	−76.0	−51.6
Capital balance	−61.7	−60.3	−72.1	−52.3
Change in currency reserves	−4.6	−5.0	10.3	1.0

Source: West German Government

Vietnam

As already noted, Vietnam depends on aid from within the CMEA area for much of its industrial expansion. Weakened by its costly armed occupation of neighbouring Laos and Kampuchea, it has little foreign currency to spare and would sometimes fail to meet all of its food requirements without the aid of the IMF and World Bank.

As Table 5.48 shows, the vast majority of Vietnam's foreign trade takes place with its CMEA partners, which also provide most of what little foreign investment there is. The country has so far permitted a small amount of investment from non-communist countries (a new paper mill, for example, is being run by a Swedish company); however, it is not expected to seek a substantal increase in foreign involvement during the mid-1980s.

TABLE 5.48   VIETNAM: FOREIGN TRADE

US$ mn	1979	1980	1981	1982	1983
Imports					
Soviet Union	681.1	700.7	1,002.4	1,017.0	1,216.4
Japan	117.7	113.1	109.4	92.3	119.1
Hong Kong	18.0	30.0	27.0	60.0	55.0
Singapore	48.0	49.0	72.0	35.0	45.0
Czechoslovakia	45.3	47.8	58.0	41.7	39.5
USA	0.5	1.1	10.1	32.0	20.7
France	99.9	59.6	76.0	22.5	31.5
Italy	52.8	42.3	18.5	15.0	12.5
West Germany	54.1	18.8	18.4	7.4	2.7
Poland	39.6	51.6	21.4	13.7	15.7
Sweden	56.0	51.0	22.2	21.8	11.5
Hungary	28.4	39.8	32.8	18.8	11.4
Exports					
Soviet Union	225.1	242.7	231.8	284.8	317.0
Hong Kong	17.0	22.0	33.0	81.0	70.0
Japan	48.2	48.6	37.3	36.0	37.7
Czechoslovakia	12.6	19.4	19.7	26.0	34.4
Singapore	16.0	18.0	13.0	21.0	33.0
Poland	15.4	14.3	17.8	14.8	18.3
Bulgaria	7.1	9.9	13.1	11.5	12.7
Hungary	8.0	6.7	5.3	8.3	9.6
France	5.7	4.9	7.3	5.8	7.7
Belgium/Luxembourg	1.3	0.0	0.0	0.1	5.3
West Germany	4.8	6.5	5.5	3.9	2.8

Source: West German Statistical Office, based on information from trading partners

Chapter Six

INDIAN SUB-CONTINENT

I Population

India

The last census, conducted in March 1981, put India's total population at 685.2 mn, having grown at an average annual rate of 2.25% during the preceding decade. The UN estimates that by 1984 the population had expanded by another 9% to 746.7 mn.

Bombay is India's largest city, home to 8.2 mn people or 1.2% of the 1981 population. Delhi, the second largest, stood at 4.9 mn, barely half Bombay's size, whilst New Delhi, the national capital, had just 273,036 inhabitants.

Ten Indian cities have populations greater than 1 mn, but together they contain just 4.4% (30.3 mn) of the total. Another six cities have populations greater than 750,000, with a further fifteen exceeding 500,000 inhabitants.

TABLE 6.1 INDIA: POPULATION

	1981	1982	1983	1984
Population (mn)	703.3	77.8	732.3	746.7
of which: males (%)	51.7	—	—	—
females (%)	48.3	—	—	—
Birth rate ('000)	33.9	33.8	33.6	—
Death rate ('000)	12.5	11.9	11.9	—
Registered unemployed ('000s)	17,930	19,753	21,290	23,500
% of labour force	6.7	7.3	7.7	8.3

Source: National Statistics

Population densities vary widely within and between rural and urban areas. In agricultural areas there are high densities in rice growing areas, for example, whilst at the other extreme the Himalayas and

INDIAN SUB-CONTINENT

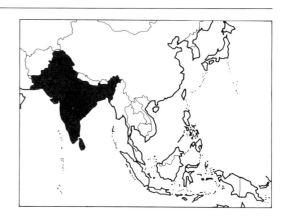

India
Pakistan
Bangladesh
Sri Lanka

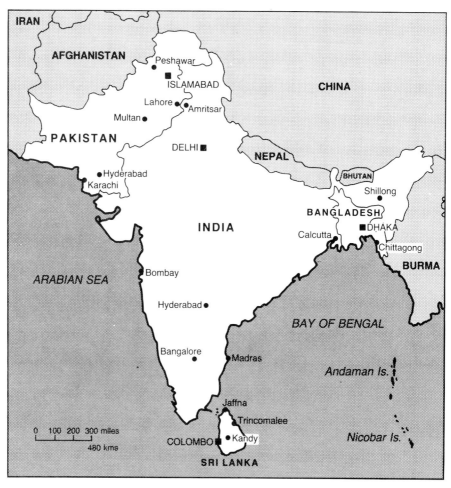

Rajasthan are very thinly populated. The southern state of Tamil Nadu, with its capital, Madras, had a 1983 population of 48.3 mn, giving a density of 372/sq km, whilst Rajasthan's 34.3 mn inhabitants are spread much more thinly at 100/sq km.

High levels of average population growth have become of considerable political (as well as economic) significance, with much of the impact of India's past economic improvement dissipated by population expansion. Already large expanses of India are overpopulated. Sharp reductions in the birth rate and increases in the penetration of modern family planning techniques are officially expected to keep the population down to 950 mn by the end of this century—but recent failures in family planning policy make 1 bn more likely.

In inter-communal terms two socio-political institutions dominate the average Indian's life: caste and religion. Every Indian enters a caste (class) irretrievably at birth, and it still largely determines day-to-day status and often career potential. Religious differences, especially the competition between Hindus and Muslims in northern India that all too often erupts into bloody violence, are frequently the root cause of much of India's communal strife. Nonetheless most of the population is strongly aware of the unity of Indian cultural heritage, and this acts as a strongly cohesive force in the face of so much diversity otherwise.

TABLE 6.2   INDIA: DISTRIBUTION OF EMPLOYMENT

	1971 census	
	'000s	%
Agriculture, fisheries etc.	130,058	72.1
Mining	923	0.5
Manufacturing	17,069	9.5
Utilities	535	0.3
Construction	2,219	1.2
Commerce	8,831	4.9
Transport and communications	4,403	2.4
Financial and business services	1,209	0.7
Community, social and personal services	15,238	8.4
TOTAL	180,485	100.0

Source: National Statistics

Despite India's remarkable technical expertise, agriculture, much of it subsistence, continues to provide a living for the vast majority of the population. In 1982, 82.2% of a labour force of 276 mn were employed in rural areas. By 1988 the workforce may have grown to 325 mn, and this very rapid rate of expansion, in conjunction with an inadequate rate of expansion in formal employment opportunities, will add greatly to the labour surplus burden that must then be absorbed by new, informal opportunities in the agricultural sector.

There are no truly reliable estimates of unemployment (under-employment would, in any case, seriously hamper any meaningful attempt), but official figures put the registered jobless at 23.5 mn in late 1984; however a figure three times higher is likely to be more realistic.

Pakistan

As elsewhere in the Indian Sub-Continent, lengthening life expectancies have dramatically raised Pakistan's population growth, from the pedestrian 1.7% or so of the 1950s to more than 3% today. As a consequence a census-verified March 1981 population of 83.8 mn was thought to have risen by 11% to 93.3 mn by mid-1984.

TABLE 6.3   PAKISTAN: DEMOGRAPHIC CHARACTERISTICS (1981)

| | Population | |
	mn	%
TOTAL	82.06	100.0
Male	43.09	52.5
Female	38.97	47.5
Rural	58.21	70.9
Urban	23.84	29.1
0–14 years	36.52	44.5
15–54 years	38.19	46.5
55 and above	7.34	9.0

Source: Census Organisation
Note: Excludes population of Federal Administered Tribal Areas

There is a very high degree of religious homogeneity, and 98% of all Pakistanis are Muslims—70% of those being Sunnis, 20%–25% Shia, with the remainder adhering to the Ahmadiya sect.

In 1981 almost 30% of the population lived in urban areas, the largest of which was (and still is) Karachi, home to approximately 5.1 mn people (6% of the total population). Pakistan's second largest city is Lahore with 2.9 mn people, and the top ten cities together 'house' an estimated 13.3 mn, or 56% of the urban total. The capital, Islamabad, had a 1981 population of just 201,000 despite having trebled in size during the preceding decade.

According to administrative divisions (four 'provinces', a 'Federal Administration Tribal Area' on the border with Afghanistan, and the Capital Territory around and including Islamabad), the Punjab was, in 1981, by far the most populous with 47.3 mn inhabitants. Sind, in the south-east, had 19.0 mn and the North-West Frontier Province (NWFP) had 11.1 mn.

TABLE 6.4   PAKISTAN: DISTRIBUTION OF CIVILIAN EMPLOYMENT (1982/83)

	%
Agriculture, forestry and fisheries	52.7
Mining	0.1
Manufacturing	13.4
Construction	4.8
Electricity, gas and water	1.1
Commerce	12.0
Transport and communications	4.6
Financial and business services and real estate	0.8
Other services	10.2
Other activities	0.3
TOTAL	100.0

Source: Federal Bureau of Statistics

According to the International Labour Office (ILO) the Pakistani workforce reached some 27.7 mn people in 1984, having grown by 1.2% in the previous year. It is predominantly male with only about 12% of the total accounted for by women. Slightly more than half the workforce find employment in the agricultural sector, whilst the manufacturing, commerce, and social/personal services sectors absorb between 10% and 13% each.

TABLE 6.5 PAKISTAN: UNEMPLOYMENT RATES ACCORDING TO SEX, RURAL/URBAN SPLIT (1981 CENSUS)

	'000s	% of labour force
Labour force	22,623	100.0
of which: Male	21,782	96.4
Female	824	3.6
Rural	16,591	73.3
Urban	6,032	26.7

	'000s	Jobless category rate
Total unemployed	2,579	11.4
of which: Rural	1,339	8.1
Urban	1,240	20.6

Source: Pakistan Economic Survey
Note: Figures do not include FATA

The ILO put 1984 unemployment at an optimistic 3.9%, an 11.8% rise in absolute terms (to 1.1 mn) but only a small increase in proportional terms from 1983's 3.5%.

Bangladesh

Bangladesh has only one truly large and expanding conurbation: Dhaka, the capital. According to the census of March 1981 the capital was home to 3.4 mn Bangladeshis, 3.9% of that year's official population of 87.1 mn. However this census figure is widely held to be grossly underestimated. The government itself estimated a 1981 population of almost 90 mn on the basis of that year's census, but even that 3% upward revision was probably inadequate accommodation. By 1984 the IMF was purporting a mid-year estimate of 96.73 mn.

The second largest city, and the only other to exceed 1 mn inhabitants, is Chittagong with 1.4 mn in 1981. And, taken together, the ten largest urban areas had, in 1981, a total population of 6.7 mn or 7.4% of the total.

Not surprisingly in a country so poor, 77% of a labour force of 30.9

mn is employed in the agricultural sector, whilst manufacturing, the principal activities of which are, in any event, powered by agricultural inputs, accounts for just 4.6%.

Unemployment and underemployment are both thought to be high indeed. The latter not least of all because of the large proportion of the population dependent on subsistence agriculture for a livelihood. Official figures, which despite the bleak scenario manifested could well understate the problem, put the 1982/83 jobless total at 12.3 mn or 37%.

Sri Lanka

Sri Lanka's population (estimated at 15.6 mn in mid-1984) is very unevenly distributed, with all the densest rural populations and the largest cities in the wet zone, the south-western corner of the island.

The largest urban concentration is the capital, Colombo, which, with an estimated 623,000 inhabitants in 1983, contained 4% of the population. In addition Dehiwala-Mount Lavinia had 181,000, Jaffna (capital of the predominantly Tamil north) 128,000, Kandy 114,000, and Galle 88,000.

TABLE 6.6   SRI LANKA: POPULATION, BIRTH AND DEATH RATES

	1971	1981*	1982*	1983*	1984*
TOTAL POPULATION (mn)	12.6	15.0	15.2	15.4	15.6
of which: Males	6.5	7.7	7.7	7.9	8.0
Females	6.1	7.3	7.5	7.5	7.6
Birth rate (per '000)	32.7	28.0	26.8	26.2	24.8
Death rate (per '000)	8.2	6.0	6.1	6.1	6.5
Population growth rate (%)	2.2	1.9	1.5	1.3	1.3

Source: CBC
Note: *provisional

There are 24 administrative districts, four of which have more than 1 mn inhabitants: Colombo 1.8 mn, Gampaha 1.4 mn, Kurungela 1.3 mn and Kandy 1.2 mn. As well as being the most populous, Colombo is also the most densely populated, with 2,699 people to each of its 652.4 sq km; more than ten times the national average (238/sq km).

In ethnic terms Sri Lanka is essentially dualistic. There are groups of Muslims (Moors) and Christians, but the most notable division is between the Buddhist Sinhalese (74% of the total in 1981) and the Hindu Tamils (18%—almost three-quarters of which are of distant Sri Lankan origin with the remainder being more recent arrivals from the Indian mainland).

The two communities are divided on linguistic as well as religious grounds and the rise of Sinhalese nationalism in the second half of the 1950s gave rise to occasional inter-communal violence that most recently erupted in 1983 after Tamil terrorists disrupted local government elections in Jaffna.

Reliable employment data are not available, and the figures included in the 1981 census are estimates based on a sample of just 10% of the population. The labour force at present numbers some 5.4 mn, 7.7% more than in 1981 when 87% worked in agriculture, 8.3% in manufacturing, and the unemployment rate was 17.8%. By 1982 the jobless total had fallen to 11.7% helped by the government's development programme and labour migration to the Middle East. In 1981, 25% of the labour force and 44% of the unemployed were women.

II Government policy

The democracies of India and Sri Lanka are flanked by military dictatorships in Pakistan and Bangladesh. All four countries gained initial independence (from the British empire) during 1947–48. Sri Lanka subsequently declared itself a republic in 1972, thus severing its last constitutional link with the British monarchy, whilst Bangladesh recorded a second independence day when Indian armed forces helped it (then known as East Pakistan) to escape the grasp of a geographically separate West Pakistan.

The two democracies differ markedly in that India retains a bicameral parliamentary system with the prime ministerial office supported by a cabinet, whilst Sri Lanka adopted a presidential system in 1978 after almost 50 years of parliamentary government along the lines practised in Westminster.

178

Sadly, a domestic political characteristic that the two democracies do share is an often dangerous measure of intercommunal strife. And for both countries such tensions have reached new peaks of destruction in very recent years.

All four countries are developing their economies via some form of medium-term economic planning, with traditional five-year-planners Pakistan and Bangladesh on their sixth and third respectively, whilst India and Sri Lanka now operate systems of rolling five year plans.

India

TABLE 6.7   INDIA: GOVERNMENT FINANCE*

Rs bn

	1980/81	1981/82	1982/83	1983/84	Estimate 1984/85
Total expenditure	368.5	437.4	527.5	617.1	689.2
Developmental	244.3	286.5	335.9	395.4	451.0
Non-developmental	124.2	150.9	191.6	221.6	238.1
of which: Defence	38.7	46.5	54.1	63.5	68.0
Interest payments	29.6	37.5	46.4	57.1	65.4
Costs of tax collection	5.0	5.6	6.6	8.2	8.4
Police	11.6	13.8	16.3	18.7	19.7
Others	39.3	47.5	68.1	74.2	76.6
Current revenue	245.6	304.3	358.0	416.4	475.9
Non-tax	47.2	62.8	85.5	98.2	121.6
Tax	198.4	241.4	272.4	318.2	354.3
of which: Income and corporation	28.2	34.5	37.5	42.4	43.1
Customs	34.1	43.0	51.2	58.8	71.0
Union excise duties	65.0	74.2	80.6	101.3	109.7
Sales tax	40.2	50.6	56.7	64.4	73.4
Others	31.0	39.1	46.4	51.4	57.1

Source: Economic Survey
Note: *Includes Central and State governments and union territories.

Traditional antagonisms between Hindus and the Sikh minority (the most extreme members of the latter clinging fanatically to the principle of comprehensive self-determination) cost the country its charismatic though rather autocratic prime minister, Mrs Indira Ghandi. Sikh members of her personal bodyguard assassinated her in revenge for the Indian army's storming of the holiest of Sikh shrines, the Golden Temple of Amritsar, in pursuit of armed Sikh extremists. Mrs Ghandi had dominated Indian politics since shortly after the death of her father, India's first premier, Jawaharlal Nehru, in May 1964.

The first year or so of administration by Mrs Ghandi's successor, her son Rajiv, has been a quite remarkable political success. In the 1985 general election, called very soon after his mother's death, Mr Ghandi increased his party's holding in the Lok Sabah by 14% to 400 seats, almost 80% of the 508 contested. Elections in some constituencies were postponed because of violent unrest, but Rajiv Ghandi's self-evident popular appeal helped Congress to the largest parliamentary majority since independence. His power has been further consolidated by local election victories, and Mr Ghandi's political strength (popularity) has allowed a fair measure of economic reform to be initiated, including increased competition, management shake-ups in the public sector, and a general deregulation of the economic environment.

For a long time after independence Indian economic development was deeply rooted in very strong centralised planning, with regulation of the private sector, widespread public ownership and tight control of trade and capital flows simplifying the planning process. Only recently, gently under Mrs Ghandi and now more vigorously under her son, has the Indian economy's regulatory framework begun to loosen up.

The country began the planning process in 1951 with an intention to concentrate principally on development of agriculture in general and irrigation systems in particular; national income grew by 3.6% per annum (1.9% in per caput terms) with agricultural output 4.1% higher and industrial output up 7.3%. Successive plans running through 1956/57–1960/61 and 1961/62–1965/66 shifted the focus to heavy industry and the transportation sector. And whilst the shift of emphasis is clear in falling agricultural output growth figures (annual averages of 4.0% and 1.4% respectively), no counterbalancing industrial improvement was evident, and average annual growth for this sector fell to 5.6% and 2.0% respectively.

Real national income growth improved slightly to 4% per annum during 1956/57–1960/61, but fell sharply under the following plan to just 2.2% (zero in per caput terms). The next plan (1966/67–1970/71) was abandoned in 1968 as slower aid flows began to make many of its targets unattainable. Its successor (the fourth, 1969/70–1973/74) recognised difficulties in the distribution of the developmental progress already made by India, and thus gave equal weight to growth and distribution. But the farm sector again put in weak performances (average annual growth of 2.9%) after crop failures in 1971/72 and 1972/73, though industry did strengthen its expansion to 4.7% from 2.0% during the 1966/67–1968/69 period.

The fifth plan promised all-round improvements in performance despite getting off to a bad start with a severe inflationary push given by the aforementioned crop failures. Between 1974/75 and 1978/79 the average annual growth of real national income improved to 5.3% (from 3.4% under the previous plan), taking per caput income growth to a high of 2.9%, whilst agricultural growth rose by 1.3 points to 4.2% and industrial output registered average annual increases 1.1 points higher at 5.8%.

In 1979/80 a system of more flexible, 'rolling', five-year plans was introduced. The recent emphasis (including the seventh plan approved by cabinet in November 1985) has been on energy supplies, and, whilst the inaugural year of the sixth plan saw nothing short of dismal performances all round, by 1984/85 provisional figures suggested that the 5.2% annual growth target had been all but met (5.1%), with annual growth in per caput income up to 2.8%, farm output 6.8% and industry 5.5%.

The seventh plan has been the subject of much controversy. It is aiming for 4% per annum overall growth, made up of 4% on farm output and 8% on industry. But in addition to a rather optimistic industrial output growth figure the plan has also attracted criticism for the size of the spending to be financed; total investment of Rs 3,224 bn.

Pakistan

In Pakistan General Mohammed Zia ul-Haq seized power on 5 July 1977 with the country seemingly on the verge of civil war after seven years of increasingly dictatorial civilian rule under President Zulfikar ali Bhutto. Bhutto was found guilty of instigating the murder of political opponents, and hanged. General Zia promised a swift return to constitutional government but general elections have been repeatedly

TABLE 6.8   PAKISTAN: GOVERNMENT EXPENDITURE

Rs mn

	1980/81	1981/82	1982/83	1983/84	1984/85*
Expenditure met from revenue of which:	31,861	37,886	51,357	64,348	70,736
General administration	1,802	2,062	2,444	2,982	3,738
Defence	15,300	18,631	24,566	26,751	29,191
Law and order	932	1,086	1,286	1,516	1,702
Community services	744	837	955	1,219	1,402
Social services	1,350	1,496	1,804	2,180	2,618
of which: Education	593	651	774	1,021	1,223
Health	141	210	193	266	329
Economic services	1,053	1,181	2,172	1,466	1,539
of which: Agriculture and irrigation	103	128	139	160	189
Transport	218	181	135	72	47
Subsidies	1,425	1,310	1,727	4,635	3,870
Debt servicing, investable funds and grants	9,239	11,270	16,398	23,593	25,720
Unallocable	16	13	5	6	956

Source:

Note: *estimate

delayed, and a referendum on islamicisation has been cited by the general as legitimising his rule even though no such question was ever put to the electorate.

The country is mid-way through its sixth (1983/84–1987/88) five-year plan. The first three all concentrated on the twin goals of growth and industrialisation, but, with the arrival of the Bhutto government in 1972 (elected on a socialist manifesto promising socio-economic revolution), the fourth plan emphasised social and economic justice, which, said the government, required an extensive programme of nationalisation. Infrastructure was neglected and considerable output gains during the 1960s (5.2% per annum in agriculture, and 9.1% in industry) were soon eroded (2.3% per annum in both sectors during 1970–78). The Bhutto regime, faced with considerable political and social unrest, was then forced to resort to a series of one-year plans with no medium-term perspective. However, with the forced removal of this increasingly undemocratic civilian government in July 1977, five year plans were restored.

The following (fifth) plan sought to restore swift and balanced growth, improve basic needs (i.e. health, water and education) in backward areas, and boost investment through stimuli to the private sector including some denationalisation. With real GDP growth averaging 6.2% per annum it was declared a success. More recently, the current (1983/84–1987/88) plan aims for continued strong growth (with a 6.5% per annum target), but with a more committed approach to social expenditure (especially education), infrastructure (especially electricity generation and energy exploration. Through these it is hoped Pakistan's three principal constraints to growth will be tackled: low investment and savings ratios; low agricultural productivity; and a very weighty fuel imports burden.

Bangladesh

TABLE 6.9   BANGLADESH: GOVERNMENT FINANCE

mn taka	1982/83	1983/84*	1984/85*
Revenue	28,666	30,230	34,650
of which: Income tax	4,324	3,297	3,688
Customs duty	10,386	10,000	11,600
Sales tax	2,705	3,450	3,900
Railways	1,505	1,540	1,620
Other	9,746	11,943	13,842
Expenditure	20,219	25,639	28,411
of which: General administration	3,548	4,792	5,131
Defence	2,470	3,281	3,573
Education	2,337	3,104	3,381
Manufacturing and construction	1,944	2,586	2,840
Justice and police	1,895	2,517	2,741
Railways	1,539	1,699	1,978
Health	899	1,194	1,299
Other	5,587	6,466	7,468

Source: Ministry of Finance
Note: *Expenditure figures estimated

183

On 17 December 1971 Pakistani government troops surrendered in East Pakistan, the Bangladeshi flag having been first raised nine months earlier. But Shaikh Mujib Rahman's return from detention in West Pakistan to become the first Bangladeshi prime minister also presaged a slide towards anarchy that not even his resounding victory in the March 1973 elections (winning 292 out of 300 seats contested) could halt. A state of emergency, declared in 1974, and the assumption of dictatorial powers in early 1975 (including the imposition of a one-party system), prompted a coup in late 1975. The present military incumbent of the presidential office, Lt-General Ershad, acquired the job in a bloodless March 1982 coup after Rahman was assassinated ten months earlier. At first it seemed clear that the military envisaged a return to civilian rule, but the rescheduling of the October 1984 elections to March 1985 proved to be but the first of many. However, Ershad remains committed to democracy and has a strong desire to remain in the vanguard of Bangladeshi politics.

Economic policy and planning in Bangladesh are dominated by two issues—a rapidly expanding population's demand for food grains, and a very narrow natural resource base—which together make economic diversification very difficult, and saddle the country with a structural trade deficit and heavy dependence on foreign aid. These obstacles to development are recurrent in Bangladesh's short history as an independent nation, and its first five year plan (1973/74–1977/78), with a 5.5% per annum average real GDP growth target, had to be disbanded as oil price hikes, flooding and political disorder made it totally unattainable. A two-year intermediate evaluation was then drawn up and during this period the development effort was concentrated on expanding food production, boosting rural employment opportunities and completing projects already underway.

Bangladesh's second plan finally came into being in 1980/81 with total spending set at Tk 256 bn (about US$17 bn) of which 21% would be provided by the private sector and 54% would come from foreign capital inflows. Overall GDP growth was to be 7.2% per annum, with agriculture growing by 6.3% (rice and wheat by 7.1%) and the industrial sector by 8.6%. Per caput income growth was expected also to benefit from falling population growth and thus average 4.9% annually. In the event almost every area underachieved, with real GDP coming close to the 7.1% target in only one year (1980/81, 6.7%), and per caput income managing to come close in only two of the five (1980/81, 4.5% and 1984/85, 4.0%). According to provisional figures for 1984/

85 real GDP grew by just 20% during the life of the plan against a target of almost 42%, whilst real per caput income was approximately 13% higher, 14 points less than targeted.

TABLE 6.10   BANGLADESH: GOVERNMENT DEVELOPMENT EXPENDITURE

mn taka

	1981/82	1982/83	1983/84*	% 1983/84
Power, scientific research, natural resources	5,043	5,042	8,168	26.9
Water and flood control	4,219	4,124	5,368	17.7
Agriculture	5,969	3,946	4,816	15.8
Transport	3,633	3,183	3,406	11.2
Industry	2,225	1,963	2,342	7.7
Physical planning and housing	466	1,088	1,550	5.1
Education	828	1,009	1,338	4.4
Population planning	519	788	816	2.7
Health	628	719	717	2.4
Communications	787	698	702	2.3
Rural development	913	663	505	1.7
Employment	69	233	359	1.2
Social welfare	204	145	102	0.3
Other	26	91	217	0.7
TOTAL	25,529	24,292	30,406	100.0

Source: Ministry of Finance
Note: *estimate

Sri Lanka

In Sri Lanka the ethnic divide separates the majority Sinhalese (Buddhists) from the Tamil (Hindu) communities predominantly situated in the north. It is ironic that President Jayawardene (Prime Minister Jayawardene between July 1977 and September 1978) may yet be best remembered for the unprecedented level of inter-communal violence that broke out in July 1983 despite first being responsible for a significant degree of Tamil social integration and Tamil human, political and civil rights under the constitutional amendments of 1978.

TABLE 6.11   SRI LANKA: GOVERNMENT FINANCE

Rs mn

	1981	1982	1983	1984*	Approved estimates 1985
Revenue	16,228	17,809	25,210	37,731	38,041
Expenditure	31,094	37,900	46,816	53,592	59,498
of which: Capital	13,373	18,669	21,733	21,750	29,534
Budget deficit	14,866	20,091	21,606	15,861	21,457
Deficit as % GDP	15.1	17.0	15.4	9.8	—
Financing of deficit					
Domestic non-market borrowing	400	1,713	2,385	904	—
Domestic market borrowing	6,296	9,899	8,965	3,041	9,100
Foreign finance	8,208	8,794	10,950	11,250	14,071
Use of cash balances	−38	−315	−694	666	−1,714
TOTAL FINANCING	14,866	20,091	21,606	15,862	21,457

Source: CBC
Note: *provisional

Under the stewardship of President J R Jayawardene the economy of the country is more liberal and open, where economic management aims to achieve a shift of resources away from consumption and towards investment. Import restrictions, price controls and food subsidies have all been lowered, whilst public investment plans have been expanded. The planning system now operates on 'rolling' five-year targets, and the 1985–89 expenditure total of US$10.6 bn will emphasise infrastructure and rehabilitation of the cash crop sector.

III   Economic performance and structure

India

Few economies boast a degree of developmental duality as profound as does India. On the one hand it has a lofty standard of homespun technological achievement—spanning nuclear power, satellite communications, the manufacture of silicon chips, and armaments—whilst

186

at the other extreme is the low-tech, all too often calorie-deficient India of the majority.

TABLE 6.12   INDIA: REAL GROWTH OF GDP (FACTOR COST) BY SECTOR

	1979/80†	1980/81†	1981/82†	1982/83†	1983/84*
Agriculture, fishing, mining, etc.	−12.5	12.2	3.4	−2.2	9.0
Manufacturing, construction, utilities	−2.3	2.3	3.6	2.8	4.4
Transport, communications, trade	−0.5	5.9	6.6	2.8	6.0
Financial, personal, business services and real estate	1.3	3.0	5.1	8.3	5.2
Public administration, defence, etc.	9.1	8.3	9.0	11.0	10.8
GDP at factor cost	−5.0	7.6	4.8	2.1	7.4

Source: Economic Survey
Notes: †provisional   *estimate

During the first 20 years after independence India was among the developing world's underachievers, with 3.4% average annual economic growth reduced by galloping birth rates to just 1.2% in per caput terms. Over the last five years or so more promising rates have been established and the sixth (most recent) five year plan even achieved its growth target of 5.2% per year (raising the per caput figure to a more tangible 2.8%).

TABLE 6.13   INDIA: BREAKDOWN OF GDP BY SECTOR

	1979/80 %	1980/81 %	1981/82 %	1982/83 %	1983/84 %
Agriculture, fishing, mining, etc.	39.8	41.5	40.9	39.3	39.8
Manufacturing, construction, utilities	22.9	21.8	21.6	21.7	21.2
Transport, communications, trade	19.2	18.8	19.2	19.3	19.0
Financial, personal, business services and real estate	6.9	6.6	6.6	7.0	6.9
Public administration, defence	11.2	11.3	11.7	12.7	13.1
GDP at factor cost	100.0	100.0	100.0	100.0	100.0

Source: Economic Survey

Agriculture (40% of GDP, 30%–35% of exports, and more than 70% of employment) remains the backbone of the economy. The significant improvement in overall economic performance under the sixth five year plan was due largely to agricultural growth averaging 4.2% per annum. But, despite considerable improvements in irrigation techniques, seed quality and fertiliser usage, this sector continues to be very vulnerable to the monsoons.

In the last fifteen years there has been a marked shift in economic emphasis away from the farm sector, with the contribution to output made by primary activities (agriculture and mining) falling from 51% in 1970/71 to 40% in 1983/84.

The contribution made by industry benefited little from this reduction, and in 1983/84 industrial output made up 21% of GDP, only slightly higher than the 20% of 1970/71. Meanwhile the service sector has grown from 30% to 39% (with transport and communications being among the most noteworthy growth areas) as rising incomes and falling food prices have raised disposable incomes.

Activities in Indian agriculture are dominated by the production of food, with grain crops accounting for almost three-quarters of the total

TABLE 6.14   INDIA: AGRICULTURAL PRODUCTION

mn tonnes

	1979/80	1980/81	1981/82	1982/83	1983/84
Rice	42.3	53.6	53.3	47.1	60.0
Wheat	31.8	36.0	37.5	42.8	45.2
Pulses	8.6	10.6	11.5	11.9	12.7
Kharif foodgrains	63.3	77.7	79.4	69.9	89.1
Rabi food grains	46.5	51.9	53.9	59.6	62.4
All food grains	109.7	129.6	133.3	129.5	151.5
Groundnuts	5.8	5.0	7.2	5.3	7.3
Rapeseed and mustard	1.4	2.3	2.4	2.2	2.6
Oilseeds	8.7	9.4	12.1	10.0	12.8
Sugar cane	128.8	154.3	186.4	189.5	177.0
Cotton (mn bales)	7.7	7.0	7.9	7.5	6.6
Jute and mesta (mn bales)	8.0	8.2	8.4	7.2	7.4

Source: Economic Survey 1984/85

cropped area. Principal cereal crops include milled rice, wheat, sorghum, maize and cat-tail millet.

The main Indian cash crops are cotton, jute, tea and sugar cane, and 1983/84 was a year of mixed performances in this sector. Output of cotton lint fell by 12.6% to 6.6 mn bales, and sugar cane output fell by 6.6% to 177.0 mn tonnes, but jute production was 1.9% higher at 6.1 mn bales and the tea crop was 4.8% more plentiful. India is also the world's largest producer of groundnuts (7.3 mn tonnes in 1983/84), rapeseed (2.6 mn tonnes) and sesame seed (618,000 tonnes). In 1984/85 the total oilseeds crop reached 11.3 mn tonnes, 11.7% lower than in the previous year.

With a large domestic market Indian tea producers have not suffered as much as they might have under the pressure of competition from newer arrivals in the international market place (Kenya, Indonesia and China, for example). Sharp increases in sugar production meant that, in the face of quota impositions by importers, there have been difficulties selling surplus sugar stocks, but in the mid-1980s India is again importing sugar (as well as cotton and oilseeds). Meanwhile, jute sales have been pressurised by a greater Chinese presence as well as the continued encroachment on traditional markets by synthetic substitutes manufactured in the industrial countries.

Though India has had some problems of late selling its cash crops, it is with food production that its most serious difficulties arise. The problems that face Indian food production are in spite of an almost meteoric increase in cereals harvests, thus allowing enough to be kept in reserve to cover two consecutive bad monsoons. Indeed by 1985 stocks had begun to exceed storage capacity, and the level of stocks in the face of widespread malnutrition has become a political issue of some importance. There is an urgent need to increase storage facilities, but the addition of more than 1 mn tonnes in 1985/86 would be unlikely even with a crash programme of construction. The current five year plan only envisages the creation of an extra 1.5 mn tonnes of capacity during its lifetime.

Cash crop farmers enjoy a degree of insulation from the vicissitudes of the market that foodgrain producers must envy. Through buffer stocking and comprehensive price support against the cycle of surplus and shortfall, the microeconomic burden is lifted. For both jute and cotton a period of critical scarcity is now giving way to excess supply.

Two agricultural shortcomings remain. Indian food production in general (food grains notwithstanding) continues to fall well short of the nation's considerable potential; production of the staple food of the masses, pulses, has stagnated during the last ten years. And secondly, with so many Indians living well below even the most pessimistic poverty line, few officials can be happy with the distribution of what food production gains have been made.

TABLE 6.15   INDIA: IRRIGATED AREA UNDER VARIOUS CROPS

mn hectares	1971/72	1979/80	1980/81
Rice	14.1	16.9	16.3
	(37.2)	(42.8)	(40.5)
Wheat	10.4	15.0	15.5
	(54.5)	(67.9)	(69.7)
Maize	0.8	1.4	1.2
	(14.3)	(23.5)	(19.7)
Total cereals	28.1	35.8	35.6
	(28.0)	(34.7)	(33.8)
Total pulses	2.0	2.0	2.0
	(8.8)	(8.8)	(8.9)
Total food grains	30.1	37.8	37.6
	(24.5)	(30.1)	(29.4)
Oilseeds	1.2	1.9	2.3
	(7.7)	(12.5)	(14.3)
Cotton	1.7	2.2	2.1
	(26.7)	(27.4)	(27.1)
Sugar cane	1.7	2.1	2.3
	(71.8)	(76.9)	(80.8)

Source: Directorate of Economics and Statistics
Note: Figures in brackets show irrigated area as % of total under that crop.

Improved irrigation, fertilisers, double cropping and the like could, in theory, quadruple output in important areas such as rice—as has been done in the case of wheat. Rice is of particular importance because it is India's main crop (43% of the cereals total), but it remains an underachiever because the principal rice growers are either too big and therefore too detached to be touched by the socio-economic importance of boosting production or too small to be able to afford the technology of higher output. In addition farm credit is too hard to come by.

The industrial sector, though small, has been remarkable, if not for its growth then for the technological heights it has scaled. At the granting of independence (1947) the industrial sector was made up entirely of textiles, jute processing and a steel mill dating from the turn of the century. Today India produces a wide range of sophisticated products including microchips and telecommunications equipment.

TABLE 6.16 INDIA: PRINCIPAL INDUSTRIAL PRODUCTS

'000 tonnes	1981	1982	1983
Cotton cloth (mn metres)	8,294	7,948	8,334
Refined sugar	5,148	8,436	8,238
Jute goods	1,365	1,293	1,335
Paper and board	1,235	1,236	1,198
Sulphuric acid	2,133	2,076	2,076
Soda ash	641	597	752
Fertilisers	4,092	4,378	4,338
Petroleum products	27,575	29,993	32,948
Cement	20,772	22,655	25,736
Pig iron	9,465	9,613	9,087
Finished steel	6,758	6,700	6,196
Aluminium	213	216	203

Source: Ministry of Industry and Commercial Affairs

India's infant planners saw the nation's diverse resources and potentially huge domestic market and set about development by importing a comprehensive heavy capital base, whilst keeping one eye on raising average incomes in order to expand that home market. At first the strategy worked well with real industrial output growth averaging more than 9% in the 15 years to 1965.

But in the subsequent decade industrial growth rates were reduced sharply as average growth in gross manufacturing output dropped below 3%, with the capital goods industry worst hit, growing by just 1.5% per annum. The main reasons for this slowdown were the relatively slow pace of expansion of domestic market size and the absence, because of planners' concentration on import substitution (self-sufficiency), of a thriving export sector to absorb the overflow. At the same time inefficiencies in investment allocation and slower growth in non-industrial sectors compounded the problem. This sector has picked up in recent years, with growth averaging about 7% per annum in the first half of the 1980s, but some major structural problems are yet to be solved.

There appears to be a fairly optimistic Indian attitude to industry prevalent at the moment, but this is in spite of an almost complete absence of evidence to indicate the timing of sufficient revival for the

TABLE 6.17   INDIA: MINERAL OUTPUT

'000 tonnes	1982	1983	1984
Coal	128,504	136,274	144,513
Lignite	6,673	7,310	7,681
Iron ore	42,721	38,672	41,943
Manganese ore	1,490	1,277	1,130
Bauxite	1,920	1,925	2,036
Fireclay	878	700	596
China clay	555	583	610
Dolomite	2,186	2,165	2,319
Gypsum	962	988	1,258
Limestone	34,274	38,336	45,059
Crude petroleum	19,734	25,148	28,046
Sea salt	7,308	7,005	7,725
Chromium ore	364	365	442
Phosphorite	613	776	868
Kyanite	38	42	38
Magnesite	419	436	418
Copper ore	3	3	4
Lead conc.	22	36	35
Zinc conc.	53	76	85
Gold (kg)	2,244	2,156	1,988
Diamonds (carats)	13,022	14,286	15,887
Natural gas (mn cu. m.)	2,599	3,432	3,236

Source: Indian Bureau of Mines

seventh five year plan's 8% per annum target to be met. A recent survey reported that 40% or so of the manufacturing companies interviewed had capacity utilisation rates between 35% and 65%, with low demand or poor infrastructure most commonly blamed. The prevalence of geriatric technology was also clear in the survey, with the average age of individual fixed capital bases put at 23 years.

With a per caput energy consumption level of 231kg of coal equivalent (among the lowest in the world) it is not surprising that India produces about 85% of its domestic energy requirements, with half of that coming from solid fuels. Coal reserves are estimated at approximately 114 bn tonnes, of which 23% (26 bn tonnes) are proven.

Oil imports fill the energy gap and despite indigenous oil reserves, there is little chance of domestic production ever satisfying demand. The seventh five year plan sees production rising to 42 mn tonnes in 1989/90 from 1984/85's 29 mn, but even that would leave a 12–14 mn tonnes supply shortfall. Looking further into the future, an output

TABLE 6.18   INDIA: ENERGY PRODUCTION

	1980/81	1981/82	1982/83	1983/84	1984/85*
Coal					
Production (mn tonnes)	114.0	124.2	130.5	138.2	101.6
Output growth (%)	9.6	8.9	5.1	5.9	6.9
Pit head stocks (mn tonnes)	18.3	21.1	23.3	23.0	22.0
Stock growth (%)	30.7	15.3	10.4	−1.3	31.0
Electricity (utilities only)					
Installed capacity ('000 mW)	30.2	32.3	35.4	39.4	41.3
% change	6.3	7.0	9.6	11.3	10.4
Generation (bn kWh)	110.8	122.1	130.2	139.9	116.1
% change	5.9	10.2	6.6	7.5	13.5
Petroleum					
Crude oil output (mn tonnes)	10.5	16.2	21.1	26.0	21.1
% change	−11.0	54.3	30.2	23.2	10.2
Refinery throughput (mn tonnes)	25.8	30.1	33.2	35.3	25.9
% change	6.2	16.7	10.3	6.3	−0.5

Source: Economic Survey 1984/85

Note: *1984/85 data refer to April-December, growth rate calculated on basis of same period of previous year.

ceiling of 50 mn tonnes per year, expected to be reached in 2004, will by that time be dwarfed by annual demand for more than 100 mn tonnes. Gas reserves have been variously estimated at between 1.5–4.5 bn tonnes of oil equivalent. Proven reserves are thought to contain 885 bn cubic metres (38% associated gas), thanks to several large finds that have increased the total fourfold in recent years.

Total installed electricity generating capacity was 41,300 mW in 1984/85: 33.6% hydro, 2.6% nuclear, 63.8% thermal. The government plans to add another 22,000 mW under the seventh five year plan. But annual additions to capacity are already falling short of target, and it is widely believed that if anything power shortages (11% in 1984/85) will worsen.

Pakistan

Real economic growth during the post-independence period (i.e. since 1947) has averaged slightly more than 5% per annum. This average was dragged down principally by the stagnation of agricultural output during the 1950s, when average real GDP growth fell to little more than 3%. In

TABLE 6.19   PAKISTAN: GDP AT CURRENT FACTOR COST

mn rupees

Sector	1979/80	1980/81	1981/82	1982/83 (revised)	1983/84 (provisional)
Agriculture	62,504	70,346	81,393	89,815	91,837
Mining and quarrying	2,239	3,149	3,553	4,164	5,458
Manufacturing	37,192	45,167	52,799	61,083	75,061
Construction	11,906	13,659	14,554	15,581	19,120
Electricity and gas distribution	4,789	5,684	6,288	7,051	8,053
Transport, storage and communications	15,464	19,004	22,789	25,347	29,108
Wholesale and retail trade	32,571	39,038	47,843	53,310	61,036
Banking and insurance	5,356	6,035	7,233	9,174	10,651
Ownership of dwellings	7,137	8,309	9,470	10,251	11,447
Public administration and defence	16,263	19,257	21,466	25,553	32,750
Services	17,950	21,325	24,734	27,398	31,172
TOTAL GDP	213,371	250,973	292,122	328,727	375,693

Source: National Statistics Yearbook

addition, the years of the Bhutto administration (which came to power on a socialist manifesto but subsequently neglected both the nationalised sector that it expanded and the nation's infrastructure), saw the average fall again, this time to slightly less than 4%. During the 1960s (6.8%) and since the military intervention in 1977 (6.5%) economic expansion has been significantly higher.

The military intervention under General Zia led to the reversal of many of Bhutto's economic policies, with some degree of denational-isation and the abandonment of nationalisation as a serious policy option. The 6.5% average of the last pair of five year plans conceals a sharp slowdown in 1983/84 (with real GDP growth down to just 4.4%), but there was a notable 8.4% growth in 1984/85.

Agriculture still dominates the Pakistani economy even though its share in GDP has fallen from more than one half at independence, through slightly more than one-third in the early 1970s, to less than one-quarter in 1984/85. The farm sector is now possessed of a more modern institutional, infrastructural and technological identity, and, as well as being the principal employer, it is also of critical importance as a source of industrial inputs and exportable outputs.

Under the Zia regime among the fastest growing sectors has been manufacturing (10% per annum), and as a consequence the proportional significance of this sector has grown from barely more than 15% of GDP to 20.0% in 1984/85.

The service sector's share in output has also grown in recent years, so that by 1984/85 it had reached 47.5% of GDP, up from 41.8% at the beginning of the 1970s. Regional tensions heightened by the Soviet invasion of neighbouring Afghanistan are probably visible in an increase in the relative burden of public administration and defence, from 6.9% of GDP in 1971/72 to 8.7% in 1984/85.

1984/85 was a far from typical year in terms of individual sectors' performances, and the most notable was the small mining industry (1.4% of GDP). This sector's real output growth of 14.7% was more than double the 6.8% annual average registered over the 1976/77–1983/84 period. This unprecedented expansion was principally the result of swifter development of oil and gas reserves, but Pakistan also mines chromite (4,850 tonnes in 1983/84), limestone (4 mn tonnes), gypsum (313,000 tonnes), fireclay (94,929 tonnes), silica sand (124,000 tonnes),

TABLE 6.20   PAKISTAN: REAL SECTORAL GROWTH RATES

	1979/80	1980/81	1981/82	1982/83	1983/84*
	%	%	%	%	%
Agriculture	6.7	3.8	3.9	3.7	−4.6
Mining	13.1	13.2	8.1	6.9	8.0
Manufacturing	9.9	10.3	11.2	8.9	7.7
Construction	11.5	4.2	3.2	0.7	10.2
Electricity and gas distribution	12.1	10.9	4.7	7.8	9.2
Transport and communications	6.7	8.0	7.1	6.7	6.5
Commerce	7.3	6.6	10.9	6.9	5.8
Financial services	−1.9	−0.8	7.5	21.0	6.8
House ownership	3.6	3.6	3.6	3.6	3.6
Public admin. and defence	6.2	10.6	1.4	5.6	15.5
Services (n.e.s.)	5.7	5.7	5.7	5.7	5.7
Gross domestic product	7.3	6.5	6.6	6.1	4.4
Net factor income from abroad	2.8	−10.7	1.0	43.6	7.6
GNP	7.0	5.5	6.3	7.8	4.6

Source: Pakistan Statistical Yearbook
Note: *provisional

rock salt (554,000 tonnes) and coal and lignite (1.6 mn tonnes). In 1983/84 Pakistan produced almost 5 mn barrels of crude petroleum (an average of 13,700 bpd) and 9.9 bn cubic metres of natural gas.

Despite the optimistic picture portrayed by a superficial macro view of economic growth rates, the Pakistani economy still endures some quite serious structural shortcomings. Among them is the dependence of agriculture on the weather.

It has not merely been dependence on favourable weather conditions that has hampered this sector. During the 1950s, industry grew by 8.1% as the new leadership strove to lay down a strong industrial base. But as a consequence agriculture was at best neglected and in some cases positively deterred; farm output growth averaged just 2.3%, a pitiful performance that left per capita growth negative. Food grains output fell by 1 mn tonnes to 5 mn tonnes during the first four years of the decade, and when 'compulsory procurement' of farm produce was introduced to manage the food shortages it was done at prices so low that they acted as a strong disincentive to production.

TABLE 6.21   PAKISTAN: LAND UTILISATION

mn hectares

	1971/72	1981/82	1982/83†
Cultivated area	19.1	20.3	20.4
Fallow	4.8	4.9	4.7
Net area sown	14.3	15.5	15.7
Area sown more than once	2.3	4.3	4.4
Total cropped area	16.6	19.8	20.1
Cropping intensity*	86.9	97.5	98.5

Source:

Notes: *total cropped area
       cultivated area
    †provisional

TABLE 6.22   PAKISTAN: PRODUCTION OF MAJOR CROPS

'000 tonnes

	1970/71	1981/82	1982/83	1983/84	1984/85†
Food crops					
Wheat	6,476	11,304	12,414	10,882	11,000
Rice	2,200	3,430	3,445	3,340	3,457
Maize	718	930	1,005	1,014	1,027
Bajra	355	272	220	256	276
Jowar	329	225	222	222	234
Barley	91	158	185	140	161
Total food grains	10,169	16,319	17,491	15,854	16,155
Gram	494	294	492	522	519
Total food crops	10,663	16,613	17,983	16,376	16,674
Cash crops					
Sugar cane	23,167	36,580	32,534	34,287	32,422
Rapeseed and mustard	269	239	246	217	277
Sesamum	10	17	11	9	12
Cotton	542	748	824	495	1,017
Tobacco	113	69	65	80	80
Total cash crops	24,101	37,653	33,680	35,088	39,784

Source: Pakistan Economic Survey

Note: †estimate

In the 1960s things changed much for the better in this sector, with the end of compulsory procurement, better fertilisers and irrigation systems and easier farm credit helping the sector to more than double its average annual growth rate to 5.2%. But, as ever, more favourable weather also played an important part in the turnaround. By the end of the third five year plan (1966–70) food grains output reached 11 mn tonnes—more than double the 1954/55 level—making Pakistan almost self-sufficient. By 1982/83 only edible oils remained as a significant food import.

Pakistan came into being as a result of the partition of British India, and whilst part of the empire industry had been concentrated in the Hindu areas, Pakistan had little or no manufacturing base at the declaration of independence.

Despite humble beginnings, industrialisation proceeded at a fast pace with average industrial growth of 8.1% during the 1950s and 9.1% during the heady days of the 1960s when a much more robust agricultural growth rate (5.2%—twice the level of the 1950s) combined greatly to accelerate the expansion of overall GDP. Today manufacturing accounts for about one-fifth of total GDP and this proportion has been, and still is, rising steadily.

The sector is dominated by farm-fed operations such as textiles and

TABLE 6.23 PAKISTAN: INDUSTRIAL OUTPUT

'000 tonnes	1981/82	1982/83	1983/84
Cotton cloth (mn sq. m.)	325	336	309
Cotton yarn	430	448	440
Cement	3,657	3,938	4,502
Urea	1,224	1,832	1,798
Sugar	1,301	1,129	1,296
Vegetable ghee	531	525	595
Sea salt	224	163	205
Soda ash	107	99	107
Superphosphate	103	104	106
Sulphuric acid	59	72	81

Source: Pakistan Economic Survey

food processing, which, in 1980/81 accounted for 38.7% of total manufacturing value added. Tobacco and beverages, the other principal food product industries, added another 13.3%. In 1984/85 the cotton textiles industry alone provided 25% of total exports (40% of manufactured exports).

As already mentioned, the Bhutto years saw a sharp decline in private manufacturing activity as sectors were nationalised and strict controls were placed on investment; private sector manufacturing investment fell from 90% of total gross fixed capital formation in 1972/73 to just 26% in 1977/78 (the year Bhutto was removed from office by the military).

The present regime, for all its faults, has done much to reverse the industrial erosion endured during the first three-quarters of the 1970s. In mid-1984 the government made it quite clear that the private sector was expected to shoulder the full burden of investment, with the government acting as investor of last resort.

After manufacturing growth of just 2.9% per annum during 1970/71–1976/77, the sector has expanded on average by 9.6% per annum, and this has facilitated a welcome degree of import substitution, especially in consumer goods. In 1983/84 manufactures made up almost 60% of the rupee export total.

Pakistan does not want to remain dependent on 'traditional', consumer-oriented manufacturing activities, though the capital and intermediate goods industries remain relatively underdeveloped. However, in late 1984 the country's first steel mill (at Bin Qasr, near Karachi) was opened, which should help to lay the foundations for a more diversified industrial structure.

In 1984/85 total primary energy consumption was some 23 mn metric tonnes of oil equivalent, with two-thirds of it supplied from commercial sources and the other third accounted for by traditional fuels such as wood and cattle dung. The country is about 65% self-sufficient in commercial energy, with most (95%) of the imported balance accounted for by crude petroleum and its products.

Oil imports have thus been a substantial burden on the external account, but whilst total oil consumption has been increasing, the successful development of domestic reserves has nonetheless lowered

TABLE 6.24   PAKISTAN: OUTPUT OF PRINCIPAL MINERALS

'000 tonnes

	1982/83	1983/84
Aragonite/marble	120.6	101.0
Barytes	20.1	36.0
Bauxite	2.8	4.2
China clay	23.6	21.2
Coal	1,854.5	1,926.4
Fire clay	69.4	83.7
Fuller's earth	20.8	19.0
Gravel	418.5	84.5
Gypsum	340.7	339.0
Lime stone	4,231.6	4,696.0
Rock salt	547.5	581.0
Silica sand	140.7	99.4
Soap stone	19.1	15.6
Crude petroleum ('000 barrels)	4.7	4.9
Natural gas ('000 cubic m.)	9,826.0	9,811.0

Source: Pakistan Economic Survey

the costs of those imports. During the second half of 1985 Pakistan's oil output rose to 19,500 bpd (about a quarter of total consumption), and it is planned this will rise to 20,800 bpd in 1987/88. A total of 90 exploration wells are to be drilled in 1985/86, almost twice the 51 drilled in the previous year. Natural gas reserves are put at 449 bn cubic metres, and would last for more than 40 years at current rates of extraction.

Coal reserves are estimated to exceed 1 bn tonnes, but only one-tenth of that is proven. Most of the coal mined is low grade and used for brickmaking or domestic purposes. In 1983/84 coal output reached 1.92 mn tonnes, and it is expected that this will be raised to 2.6 mn tonnes by 1987/88.

Despite the rapid expansion of generating capacity it still lags well behind demand, and power shortages are a severe constraint on industry. This has not gone unnoticed by the government which, under the sixth five year plan, intends to raise capacity from the 4,809 mW available in 1982/83 to 8,604 mW in 1987/88.

TABLE 6.25   PAKISTAN: ENERGY SUPPLY

'000 tonnes oil equivalent	1980/81	1981/82	1982/83	1983/84	1984/85†
Oil (excluding exports)	4,868	5,175	5,855	6,436	6,512
Gas (excluding feed stock)	5,546	5,731	6,005	5,630	5,843
Coal	910	1,138	1,035	1,217	1,268
Hydro	2,109	2,261	2,701	3,046	3,322
Nuclear	33	34	43	65	72
LPG	42	50	50	72	79
TOTAL*	13,509	14,388	15,689	16,467	17,095
PER CAPITA SUPPLY	0.161	0.166	0.176	0.179	0.180

Source: Directorate General of Energy Resources [in the Pakistan Economic Survey]
Notes: *figures rounded   †estimate

Bangladesh

Bangladesh won its independence from the rest (west) of Pakistan only 15 years ago after a prolonged period during which East Pakistan was systematically exploited and, in developmental terms, neglected. By 1970 it was estimated that West Pakistanis' standard of living was as much as 50% higher than that which prevailed in East Pakistan (now Bangladesh). But independence has been expensive for the Bangladeshis, and they have only recently achieved a standard of living comparable to that prevailing in 1971. The ravages of conflict, causing considerable harm to what little infrastructure existed, were compounded first by drought and then flooding.

The first five year plan was to run from 1973/74 to 1977/78, and stated a growth target of 5.5% per annum. But again natural disasters, this time aided by the first oil price hike, put paid to such optimism at an early juncture, and the plan was virtually abandoned. Average annual growth for the period was approximately 4%, which was slow when one considers the low base from which the economy was growing. The second five year plan growth rates did not highlight any significant improvement. In 1978/79 a small acceleration over the previous five-year average was achieved (4.4%), however the average fell back to 3.6% in the following year. In 1980/81, the last year of Ziaur Rahman's administration, more favourable weather and better irrigation took overall growth to 6%; in the following year bad weather restricted growth to less than 1%. In 1982/83 the first two crops were again hit by unfavourable rains, and growth was restricted to 3.6%, well behind target.

TABLE 6.26   BANGLADESH: REAL OUTPUT GROWTH BY SECTOR

	1980/81 %	1981/82 %	1982/83 %	1983/84 %	1984/85† %
Agriculture	5.3	9.1	4.6	1.6	8.5
Industry*	5.4	1.6	−1.6	3.6	3.7
Construction	13.4	5.6	1.1	20.1	5.5
Power, gas, water etc.	11.1	18.4	53.0	7.1	14.2
Transport and communications	2.8	0.1	7.7	2.2	2.2
Trade services	1.3	−8.7	2.6	5.7	4.2
Housing services	2.2	2.4	2.3	2.3	2.4
Public administration and defence	75.8	6.6	0.4	20.7	15.4
Banking and insurance	21.8	−6.8	−5.6	5.8	5.0
Professional and miscellaneous services	5.9	6.4	6.5	6.8	6.7
GDP at market prices	6.8	0.8	3.6	4.2	3.1

Source: Bureau of Statistics

Notes: *excluding mining (sector very small indeed)   †provisional

The current (military) government, headed by Lt-General Ershad, has achieved much (not least of all considerable progress towards self-sufficiency in food grains), but the growth average over the last four years (1981/82–1984/85) has remained pitifully low at barely more than 3%. And in mid-1985 the elements again conspired to underline the fragility of the economy and its dependence on kindly weather, when cyclones and floods took thousands of lives, hundreds of thousands of homes, and affected the livelihood (i.e., crops) of some 5 mn people.

Agriculture is the most important sector of the economy, providing almost two-thirds of GDP, more than three-quarters of employment and virtually all export products (jute, tea, hides and leather goods). Industry contributes less than 10% to total GDP and is dominated by textiles processing. Other manufacturing activities almost all concentrate on the processing of agricultural goods, and, with the exception of several thousand billion cubic feet of gas and 700 mn tonnes of low grade coal, Bangladesh is conspicuously bereft of mineral reserves.

TABLE 6.27   BANGLADESH: GDP BY SECTOR

taka bn

	1981/82	1982/83	1983/84	1984/85†	1984/85 % share*
Agriculture	109.0	121.8	135.9	169.3	48.4
Mining (taka mn)	6.0	3.0	4.0	4.0	—
Industry	25.7	28.1	30.9	34.4	8.6
Construction	15.8	15.0	18.1	20.9	5.3
Power, gas, water etc.	1.0	1.6	1.9	2.4	0.6
Transport and communications	22.9	25.0	26.0	27.2	6.8
Trade services	22.1	23.2	28.5	35.0	8.8
Housing services	19.6	19.5	24.9	27.3	6.9
Public administration and defence	9.4	10.3	14.0	17.7	4.4
Banking and insurance	4.2	4.3	5.2	5.9	1.5
Professional and miscellaneous services	22.6	25.5	31.1	34.4	8.6
GDP at market prices	265.1	288.4	349.9	397.7	100.0

Source: Bureau of Statistics

Notes: †provisional   *rounded

Agriculture is dominated by the production of a single crop, jute—providing almost 60% of total exports. About half the jute crop is exported in its raw form, whilst the other half is processed in Bangladesh and exported as products (sacking and carpet backing, for example). Rice is the most important food crop.

Jute's history is a crisis-ridden one. For years after independence output volumes fluctuated violently as the government tried to resolve problems with rice output and yields; the jute crop competes with one of three rice crops for land. By the late 1970s volumes began to revive, at one point climbing to 6.5 mn bales/year. But producers found quality lacking and faced much weaker world demand. In recent years (1983–85) the jute crop has been hit hard by bad weather, and in 1984 in particular almost 1 mn bales were lost to flooding after drought had already reduced the early crop.

Jute growers face stiff competition from synthetic alternatives, and high oil prices could have meant some windfall gains. But the extreme unpredictability of jute supplies seriously undermines its case, and now with oil prices falling the outlook is far from encouraging.

In 1983/84 the rice crop was an unprecedentedly large 14.3 mn tonnes, 2.1% higher than the previous crop and 6.4% up on 1981/82. There are three rice crops: the main one in October that normally yields about 7 mn tonnes, and two smaller, 3 mn tonne crops in spring and summer.

TABLE 6.28 BANGLADESH: PRODUCTION (AND YIELD) OF PRINCIPAL AGRICULTURAL CROPS

	1982/83	1983/84	1984/85
Rice ('000 tonnes)	13,991	14,279	14,392
(tonnes/acre)	(0.63)	(0.63)	(0.64)
Wheat	1,078	1,192	1,441
	(0.84)	(0.92)	(0.86)
Pulses	216	176	201
	(0.35)	(0.35)	(0.35)
Rape and mustard	120	129	140
	(0.28)	(0.28)	(0.29)
Coconut	78	82	82
	(1.05)	(1.07)	(1.08)
Sugar cane	7,242	7,056	6,769
	(17.66)	(17.14)	(16.74)
Jute	872	931	817
	(0.62)	(0.65)	(0.55)
Cotton	10	8	5
	(0.20)	(0.19)	(0.16)

Source: Bureau of Statistics

TABLE 6.29 BANGLADESH: AGRICULTURAL PRODUCTION

1972/73 = 100

	1979/80	1980/81	1981/82	1982/83	1983/84†
Total agricultural crop	124	131	129	136	141
of which: Paddy	128	138	135	143	146
Minor cereals*	893	1,158	1,056	1,193	1,321
Jute and mesta	91	76	71	74	80
Beverages	115	122	127	127	123
Pulses	105	97	97	96	92
Spices	97	78	104	108	97
Oil seeds	103	101	106	103	110

TABLE 6.29   BANGLADESH: AGRICULTURAL PRODUCTION *(continued)*

1972/73=100	1979/80	1980/81	1981/82	1982/83	1983/84†
Fruits	91	90	99	103	90
Sugar cane	119	120	124	136	132
Vegetables	111	115	136	141	142
Livestock and poultry	154	158	160	174	172
Forestry	127	133	147	147	165
Fishery	74	74	79	83	83
All groups	126	132	132	139	144

Source: Bureau of Statistics
Notes: *e.g. wheat   †provisional

Grain imports have been a heavy burden on the balance of payments and with wheat's superior nutritional qualities there has been a drive to boost wheat production from traditionally low levels. In 1979/80 there was a sharp increase in the size of the wheat crop to 1 mn tonnes, and, despite a set-back in 1981/82 (950,000 tonnes), it has grown steadily to 1.19 mn tons in 1983/84. But in 1984/85 bad weather again raised Bangladesh's food import needs, from 1.75 mn tonnes to 2.65 mn tonnes.

Industrial performance has been very disappointing, with the effects of inefficiency compounded by poor management and market-distorting prices. Manufacturing output grew by 14.4% between 1977/78 and 1980/81, but then its performance deteriorated to stagnation in 1981/82 and a 4.9% contraction during 1982/83. More recently there has been a small revival in manufacturing fortunes, with a late rally in 1983/84 taking that year's growth to 4.4%, and a 2.1% real expansion in the following year, thanks to a dramatic 'non-foods' revival that countered a 44.6% reduction in the food industry's output.

There has been only slow movement in the broadening of Bangladesh's industrial base, and as a consequence this sector is still dominated by agricultural-product processing in general and jute processing in particular, the latter contributing one-third of total value added in manufacturing.

After the March 1982 coup Lt-General Ershad commenced a

privatisation programme and returned some 55 jute and textile mills to the private sector—under the previous regime they had been nationalised under the Bangladesh Jute Mills Corporation. However, whilst this would seem to have acted as a spur to overall textiles output, it did little for the two principal activities, jute and cotton. Cotton goods output has stagnated throughout the early 1980s, whilst jute goods output remained unmoved by the change in ownership until 1983/84 when production in fact fell by 4.4% before contracting by another 6.4% in 1984/85. Nonetheless by 1983/84 garment making had emerged as an important new recruit to the ranks of the export revenue earners, and accounted for about 5% of total exports.

Food processing (15% of total industrial output) is done largely for the domestic market, and has recently suffered severe setbacks with annual output falls during 1982/83–1984/85 of 3.4%, 15.5%, and 34.5% respectively. Ironically it is fisheries production, perhaps the most promising of these areas, that has suffered most seriously in output terms; down by more than 70% between 1981/82 and 1984/85. Fortunately exports in this area have not suffered so badly, and in 1983/84 they accounted for Tk 2,030 mn (US$81 mn) or 10.1% of the total.

Natural gas production has risen steadily throughout the 1980s, reaching 94,850 mn cubic feet in 1984/85—14.2% higher than the previous year, and more than double the 1979/80 level of 45,364 mn cubic feet. Offshore oil exploration continues in the Bay of Bengal, but some of the original partners in these activities have pulled out despite high Bangladeshi expectations.

TABLE 6.30   BANGLADESH: INDUSTRIAL PRODUCTION BY SECTOR

1973/74=100	All	Manufacturing	Mining	Electricity
1980/81	145	143	144	210
1981/82	146	143	177	240
1982/83	139	136	186	271
1983/84	146	142	220	296
1984/85†	151	145	229	344

Source: Bureau of Statistics
Note: †provisional

Heavier industry embraces shipbuilding, iron and steel (there is a solitary steel mill at Chittagong and cement production, with the latter two doing less well in recent years.

With only about 2% of the population enjoying access to electricity it is not surprising that Bangladesh has amongst the world's smallest appetites for commercial energy. However, in 1983, primary energy production of slightly less than 3 mn tonnes of coal equivalent satisfied only slightly more than 60% of demand, and in 1983/84 fuel imports cost US$161 mn (9% of imports and 20% of export revenues).

Sri Lanka

In 1984 GDP grew by 5.1% in real terms almost duplicating the performance of the previous year. These figures represented something of a deceleration of GDP growth as the average for 1978 and 1979 was 7.2%. They were, however, still substantially better than the 2.9% annual average registered during the first three-quarters of the 1970s.

As elsewhere on the Indian Sub-Continent, the economy is principally agricultural based, with that sector providing one-quarter of GDP, and almost half of all jobs. What industry there is is dominated by the processing of farm products; such activities account for about one-third of all manufacturing output.

TABLE 6.31   SRI LANKA: GDP EXPENDITURE

Rs bn						
	1970	**1980**	**1981**	**1982**	**1983**	**1984**
Private consumption	9.9	53.4	68.8	79.2	94.9	111.2
Public consumption	1.6	5.7	6.3	8.2	9.9	11.9
Gross domestic fixed capital	2.4	20.8	23.3	30.2	35.3	38.4
Changes in stocks	0.2	1.6	0.3	0.2	0.2	0.2
GDP	14.1	81.5	98.7	117.9	139.9	161.7

Source: Central Bank of Ceylon (CBC)

The introduction of a new national accounts series in 1982 makes overall historical comparisons between economic structures difficult, but it is clear that the manufacturing and service (retail trade, financial

TABLE 6.32   SRI LANKA: GDP BY SECTOR

Rs bn

	1982*	1983*	1984*	1984 % share
Agriculture, forestry and fishing	25.0	32.2	40.2	29.0
Mining	2.2	2.8	3.2	2.3
Manufacturing	13.6	16.0	20.9	15.1
Construction	8.0	9.8	11.2	8.1
Electricity, gas, etc.	1.1	1.4	1.6	1.2
Transport and communications	10.7	12.6	15.5	11.2
Commerce	19.7	21.8	27.2	19.7
Financial services and real estate	2.2	2.3	2.8	2.0
House ownership	3.3	3.7	4.0	2.9
Public administration and defence	2.9	4.1	5.3	3.9
Services (n.e.s.)	4.6	5.4	6.3	4.6
TOTAL GDP	93.2	112.0	138.2	100.0

Source: CBC
Note: *provisional

services, transport and communications) sectors have benefited while the farm sector has declined in proportional significance.

As regards Sri Lankan agriculture, there is the 'wet zone' and there is the rest. Only the south-western quarter of the island enjoys enough rain to sustain agriculture on a nationally significant scale, and agriculture on the rest of the island is limited to irrigated areas by the ferocity and duration of the annual drought. Of particular significance in this context is the Accelerated Mahaweli River Diversion scheme, started in 1980, which will help irrigate 593,052 ha of currently arid land whilst at the same time doubling electricity generating capacity. By the beginning of 1985 almost 70% (392,529 ha) of the target area was under cultivation.

Agriculture is dominated by just three crops—tea, rubber and coconuts—all of them 'cash crops' and therefore grown with the export market specifically in mind. The three cover 40% of the 13.8 mn hectares cultivated, with paddy covering another 44%. About 60% of the tea, 30% of the rubber and 10% of the coconut acreage is state-owned. Other minor crops include coffee, cocoa, cashew nuts, maize and various spices.

Sri Lanka is the world's third largest tea producer after India and China, but has suffered a prolonged period of declining output (1981 notwithstanding) which culminated in a 1983 crop of 179 mn kilograms, a 20-year low. In 1984 the crop recovered by 16.2% to 208 mn kg, just short of the 1981 level. Underlying weaknesses remain and the government has embarked upon a five-year programme of restoration at a cost of US$130 mn, but by the end of 1984 only 18% of total tea acreage had been replanted.

TABLE 6.33   SRI LANKA: CASH CROP OUTPUT

	1980	1981	1982	1983	1984†
Tea (mn kg)	191.4	210.1	187.8	179.3	208.0
Rubber (mn kg)	133.2	123.9	125.2	140.0	142.0
Coconut (mn nuts)	2,026.0	2,258.0	2,521.0	2,313.0	1,982.0

Source: CBC
Note: †provisional

Rubber production too has been making a gentle recovery, largely powered by firmer prices. In 1983 output grew by 12% to 140 mn kg, though this represented a more humble (5.3%) gain on 1981's crop. In 1984 a further though very small gain of 1.4% was registered. The area under rubber fell quite sharply between 1980 and 1981 (shrinking by 9.7% to 205,300 ha) and has yet to recover. A US$16 mn replanting and maintenance programme has been initiated with World Bank backing, and by the end of 1984 about 85% of the total rubber acreage had been replanted.

It is characteristic of the coconut industry that production oscillates particularly violently as a result of the forces of price and weather. And in 1984, as a result of the delayed malevolence of the 1983 drought, the crop fell by 14.3% (to 1,982 mn nuts). In 1983 the fall had been 8.3%, after 11%-plus growth in 1981 and 1982.

So far during this decade both the area cultivated for paddy and the yields associated with it have grown steadily. In 1984 a harvest of 2.42 mn tonnes was 13.5% higher than the 1980 crop, whilst the area sown was,

TABLE 6.34   SRI LANKA: PRINCIPAL FOOD CROPS

'000 tonnes	1981	1982	1983
Rice (paddy)	2,229	2,156	2,200
Maize	24	24	25
Millet	14	14	15
Potatoes	66	77	80
Sweet potatoes	159	153	160
Cassava	526	573	570
Dry beans*	7	7	7

Source: FAO
Note: *estimate

at 990,000 ha, 17.2% more expansive and yields were 5.1% more favourable at 7,600 kg/ha (despite a 15% fall from 1983's 8,911 kg/ha).

In the late 1950s the manufacturing sector accounted for just 6% of GDP, but average annual real growth of 10% took the sector's share to 10% at the beginning of the 1970s, and 16% by 1984. Nonetheless industrial activities continue to be concentrated in the western province (80% of the total) and around the capital, Colombo, in particular.

The industrial sector is dominated by state-run concerns (operated through 28 state industrial corporations) and is largely oriented towards consumer goods production. However, the private sector has been offered a welcome degree of liberalisation by the present government, and relatively recent additions to the nation's industrial activities (such as an oil refinery, a small steel mill and textiles and clothing plants) have shifted the sector's focus somewhat.

Indeed, the oil refinery's activities now account for about half of all industrial output, so that during 1983, when it was undergoing maintenance work, real industrial output growth fell to 0.8%, only to recover to 12% in 1984 when the installation was re-opened.

However, the private industrial sector continues to be Sri Lanka's most dynamic, and in 1984 it grew by 26%—more than twice the rate for the sector as a whole—and this despite energy shortages.

The government has also tried to encourage greater production for

TABLE 6.35   SRI LANKA: INDUSTRIAL CAPACITY UTILISATION

%	1980	1981	1982	1983	1984†
Food, beverages and tobacco	70	66	77	73	75
Textiles, clothing, leather goods	70	87	94	98	99
Wood and wood products	89	81	92	95	93
Paper and paper products	68	75	70	71	76
Chemicals, petroleum, plastics etc.	79	76	77	63	68
Non-metallic mineral products	82	83	85	77	75
Basic metal products	62	53	33	25	17
Fabricated metal products, machinery and transport equipment	58	68	83	81	84
Manufactures n.e.s.	70	69	73	81	87
TOTAL	73	74	76	74	75

Source: CBC

Note: †provisional

TABLE 6.36   SRI LANKA: INDUSTRIAL PRODUCTION

Rs mn	1980	1981	1982	1983	1984†
Food, beverages and tobacco	3,899	4,496	5,246	6,998	8,623
Textiles	1,923	3,040	3,863	5,136	7,565
Woo and wood products	289	315	361	522	640
Paper and paper products	476	626	725	901	907
Chemicals, petroleum, coal, rubber and plastic products	9,416	12,015	13,099	11,888	14,328
Non-metallic mineral products	1,156	1,250	1,370	1,468	1,829
Basic metal products	478	428	262	302	199
Fabricated metal products, machinery and transport equipment	620	782	904	1,129	1,456
Manufactures n.e.s.	54	58	74	90	106
TOTAL	18,311	23,010	25,904	28,434	35,653

Source: CBC

Note: †provisional

export markets with the creation of an Investment Promotion Zone (IPZ) run by the Greater Colombo Economic Commission. By the end of 1984 of the 112 firms that had signed contracts 74 were up and running, employing 29,251 people (12.3% more than in 1983), and generating exports worth Rs 3,537 mn (US$139 mn), 46% higher than in the previous year.

The construction sector is relatively small, with a 1984 contribution to GDP of about 8.5%. After 10% per annum growth during 1978–81 this sector has all but stagnated in recent years as the Mahaweli irrigation/power programme neared completion and the Urban Development Authority scaled down its operations. In the private sector building approvals granted by the Colombo Municipal Council have declined sharply since 1982.

Tourism is an important revenue earner for Sri Lanka, and between 1976 and 1982 the number of tourists grew by an annual average of 24%. In 1982 total earnings from a total influx of 407,230 reached Rs 3,050 mn, 22% up on the previous year. However, the inter-communal violence that broke out in mid-1983 did considerable harm to Sri Lanka's image overseas, and arrivals fell by 17% to 337,530 whilst revenues fell 5% to Rs 2,896 mn. In 1984, according to provisional figures, arrivals and revenues fell for the second year running, by 6% and 5% respectively. Even when measured by the number of nights spent by tourists, the sharp reductions are clear; down by 22% and 11% in 1983 and 1984 respectively.

Sri Lankans' principal energy source is firewood, though in commercial terms oil provides two-thirds of total energy needs, though most (66%) electricity is generated by hydro-electric means. A sharp rise in demand

TABLE 6.37   SRI LANKA: ELECTRICITY OUTPUT/CAPACITY

	1980	1981	1982	1983	1984
Installed capacity (mW)	421	501	561	592	812
of which: Hydro	331	371	371	402	542
Thermal	90	130	190	190	270
TOTAL GENERATED (mn kWh)	1,669	1,872	2,066	2,114	2,600

Source: Review of the Economy—CBC

in 1979 prompted some new hydro projects, and in 1984 installed capacity was increased by 37% from 592 mW to 812 mW. More than 60% (140 mW) of the additional capacity came from the Accelerated Mahaweli Diversion Programme.

IV   Standard of living

According to the World Bank's classification of national economies all four Indian Sub-Continent countries are of the 'Low Income' variety. But when viewed from the prosperity of an 'Industrial Market Economy' even this term seems an understatement of the true scale of deprivation. In countries such as these any meaningful analysis of living standards must concentrate on qualitative, rather than quantitative, indicators. In addition the low income group hides wide variations between countries.

Bangladesh and Pakistan perform consistently badly across a wide range of indicators, despite Pakistan having the highest per caput GNP at US$390; US$60 higher than Sri Lanka, 50% higher than India (the low income average of US$260), and three times that of Bangladesh. GNP per caput among industrial market economies was US$11,060 in 1983.

Pakistanis and Bangladeshis are substantially more likely to die young than Indians and especially Sri Lankans. Infant mortality among infants under one year is a massive 132 per thousand in Bangladesh and 119 per thousand in Pakistan; figures that are respectively 76% and 59% higher than the low income average of 75. (For industrial countries the figure is 10 per thousand.)

Not surprisingly therefore, overall life expectancies are very low in Pakistan and Bangladesh, where both men and women can expect to live just 50 or so years (10 years or 20% shorter than the low income average). Indian males at 56 years come somewhat closer to the 58 year average, though women's life expectancy of 54 years is six below the 60 year average.

In addition India, Pakistan and Bangladesh all suffer some degree of calorie deficiency. For Pakistanis it is marginal; they receive 99% of the necessary calorific minimum (2,300 calories per day). In India the situation is worse (93%), however Bangladesh suffers more with daily calorie intake of 1,922 per day, or just 83% of the minimum requirement.

The Sri Lankans appear to fare best of all with GNP per capita 50%

higher than the category average. Also Sri Lankans look forward to nine (men) and eleven (women) extra years (the overall death rate of 6 per thousand is half the low income average and even one-third lower than for industrial economies), and have an infant mortality rate of 37 per thousand—half the low income average.

V Foreign trade

On the Indian Sub-Continent only India itself escapes the blight of over-dependence on a few principal (and frequently 'primary') export products. For Pakistan it is cotton/cotton products and rice (26% and 15%, respectively, of total 1983/84 exports), for Sri Lanka tea, rubber and coconut (42%, 9% and 6% in 1984), for Bangladesh jute/jute products and tea (51.3% and 8.4% in 1983/84).

India

India has a highly diversified export base, however the export sector is quite small in comparison to total economic activity; exports represent approximately 5% of GDP, imports 7%–8%. Whilst tea still accounted for 5% of exports in 1983/84, at a much higher level of sophistication, engineering goods accounted for 7%. Jute, which contributed 20% to total export earnings in 1960/61, was worth just 2% in 1983/84.

Over the past 30 years or so foreign trade has been progressively under-emphasised as economic development proceeded along a path of import substitution behind protective walls that undermined industrial efficiency and positively deterred agricultural improvement. More recently there has been a greater awareness of the benefits of an expanding export sector, not least of all to satisfy India's high-technology and foreign exchange needs. Consumption and capital goods imports have been progressively reduced leaving raw materials and intermediate goods (notably petroleum and uncut diamonds) as the principal import products.

In 1983/84 the US was still India's principal supplier (11.4%) but only just, having seen its share slide from almost 28% at the beginning of the 1970s. And though imports from the EEC have increased their share (though West Germany and the UK, the main European suppliers, have enjoyed only slight improvements), it is Japan, the Middle East (notably Iraq and Saudi Arabia) and the USSR that have seen the strongest growth.

TABLE 6.38 INDIA: PRINCIPAL EXPORT PRODUCTS

	1970/71		1980/81		1981/82		1982/83		1983/84†	
	Rs mn	%	Rs mn	%	Rs mn	%	Rs mn	%	Rs mn	%
Agricultural etc.	4,870.1	31.7	20,566.6	30.6	22,211.3	28.5	—	—	—	—
of which										
Tea	1,482.5	9.7	4,255.0	6.3	3,952.0	5.1	3,075.3	4.1	5,013.7	5.1
Cashew nuts	570.6	3.7	1,401.3	2.1	1,815.0	2.3	1,339.7	1.5	1,566.2	1.6
Oil cakes	554.2	3.6	1,250.8	1.9	1,178.5	1.5	1,493.5	1.7	1,462.9	1.5
Fish and fish preparations	305.3	2.0	2,170.2	3.2	2,849.0	3.6	3,494.5	3.9	3,273.0	3.3
Ores and minerals	1,640.2	10.7	4,135.6	6.2	4,587.9	5.9	—	—	—	—
of which: Iron ore	1,172.8	7.6	3,033.3	4.5	3,577.5	4.5	3,737.9	4.2	3,853.4	3.9
Manufactures	7,719.7	50.3	37,468.1	55.8	43,696.3	56.0	—	—	—	—
of which:										
Textiles	1,454.0	9.5	9,325.8	13.9	10,471.4	13.4	—	—	—	—
Jute yarn and goods	1,904.4	12.4	3,299.5	4.9	2,580.1	3.3	2,027.6	2.3	1,645.2	1.7
Engineering goods	1,304.1	8.5	8,150.1	12.1	9,388.7	12.0	7,861.6	8.8	6,882.7	7.0
Mineral fuels and lubricants	126.0	0.8	278.5	0.4	2,248.9	2.9	1,719.0	1.9	3,619.6	3.7
Others	995.6	6.5	4,658.2	6.9	5,314.6	6.8	—	—	—	—
TOTAL	15,351.6	100.0	67,107.0	100.0	78,059.0	100.0	89,077.5	100.0	98,653.0	100.0

Source: Economic Survey 1984/85
Note: †provisional

TABLE 6.39   INDIA: DIRECTION OF TRADE

% breakdown

	Exports		Imports	
	1970/71	1983/84†	1970/71	1983/84†
European Community	18.2	17.3	19.5	24.1
of which: West Germany	2.1	3.8	6.6	7.1
UK	11.1	5.6	7.8	7.3
North America	15.3	15.1	34.9	13.4
of which: Canada	1.8	0.9	7.2	2.2
USA	13.5	14.1	27.7	11.4
Asia and Oceania	15.2	9.5	7.4	10.3
of which: Australia	1.6	1.0	2.2	0.9
Japan	13.3	8.4	5.1	9.2
Middle East	6.4	8.9	7.7	20.6
of which: Iran	1.7	1.2	5.6	5.0
Iraq	0.6	0.6	0.2	5.0
Kuwait	1.0	1.2	0.3	1.7
Saudi Arabia	0.9	2.5	1.5	6.8
Eastern Europe	21.0	16.3	13.5	12.5
of which: USSR	13.7	13.2	6.5	10.5
Developing Countries	19.8	15.8	14.6	15.2
of which: Africa	8.4	3.2	10.4	2.7
Asia	10.8	12.4	3.3	10.3
Latin America	0.6	0.2	1.0	2.2
TOTAL	100.0	100.0	100.0	100.0

Source: Economic Survey 1983/84

Note: †provisional

The pattern of India's exports has changed little over the past 15 years. But amongst the few notable changes have been: a halving of the UK's share from 11.1% in 1970/71 to 5.6% in 1983/84; a drop in Japan's share from 13.3% to 8.4%; a five-point fall to 16.3% in exports to Eastern Europe; and a four-point reduction to 15.8% in exports to non-Middle Eastern developing countries.

Since the late 1970s there has been a very sharp increase in the trade deficit, which rose from US$125 mn in 1977/78 to US$2,239 mn in the following year and US$4,166 mn in 1979/80; a 33;fold dollar increase in just two years.

TABLE 6.40   INDIA: BALANCE OF PAYMENTS

US$ mn

	1971/72	1979/80	1980/81	1981/82	1982/83
Imports (cif)	−2,678.0	−11,821.8	−15,862.3	−15,484.0	−15,428.5
Exports (fob)	2,090.9	7,656.0	8,316.3	8,658.8	9,452.8
Balance	−587.1	−4,165.8	−7,546.0	−6,825.2	−5,975.7
Invisible receipts	492.3	4,957.2	6,736.0	5,921.4	5,847.0
Invisible payments	−677.5	−1,743.6	−1,995.6	−2,238.3	−2,712.3
Balance	−185.3	3,213.8	4,740.4	3,683.1	3,134.7
Current account	−772.4	−945.6	−2,805.6	−3,142.1	−2,841.0

Source: Economic Survey 1984/85 (all data 'preliminary')

As import growth has dramatically outstripped exports, private transfers in particular have been of considerable importance in saving India from an even sharper deterioration of the current account; though the deficit nonetheless grew to US$2,841 mn by 1982/83—three times the 1979/80 level. Much if not all of this deterioration can be attributed to the second oil shock of 1979/80, when the annual cost of India's imported oil more than doubled from US$3 bn in 1979 to US$6.2 bn a year later.

Pakistan

With the narrow export product base and heavy dependence on foreign oil that is so typical of the region, Pakistan is also no stranger to large external deficits. As in the case of India, the two oil shocks did much to erode the external position, and since the first OPEC price hike Pakistan's merchandise deficit has widened from US$336 mn (1973/74) to some US$3.8 bn in 1984/85. Between 1979 and 1980 the cost of energy imports doubled from US$682 mn (15.9% of merchandise imports) to US$1,442 (26.5%). The largest single import remains petroleum/petroleum products, though more recently falling world oil prices and rising domestic production have helped lower the bill.

Meanwhile export performance has been erratic at best (despite many incentives) and is still heavily dependent on cotton and rice despite some degree of diversification. In the decade to 1980 the proportion of total exports accounted for by primary commodities fell from 48% to 27%, whilst for manufactures it rose from 39% to 55%.

TABLE 6.41 PAKISTAN: BALANCE OF PAYMENTS

Rs mn

	1980/81	1981/82	1982/83
Merchandise exports	27,706	24,669	33,502
Merchandise imports	−55,079	−61,127	−71,413
Trade balance	−27,373	−36,458	−37,911
Invisible credits	7,504	9,248	11,588
Invisible debits	−12,103	−14,406	−19,203
Invisible balance	−4,599	−5,158	−7,615
Net private transfers	22,196	25,690	39,212
Net public transfers	2,721	4,433	4,250
Current account balance	−7,055	−11,493	−2,064

Source: Pakistan Statistical Yearbook

The sixth five-year plan set a 1984/85 export target of US$3.3 bn, but only US$2.4 bn was realised. Foreign exchange reserves have also been hit by falling workers' remittances, which have been falling from a peak of US$2.9 bn (another US$1 bn or so entered Pakistan through unofficial channels) since 1982/83.

TABLE 6.42 PAKISTAN: PRINCIPAL IMPORTS AND EXPORTS

Rs mn

	1981/82	1982/83	1983/84
Exports			
Rice	4,128	3,629	5,688
Cotton fabric and yarn	5,838	6,887	7,787
Surgical instruments	252	287	4,300
Garments and hosiery	1,294	2,305	3,402
Carpets and rugs	1,680	1,915	2,323
Leather	1,152	1,311	1,972
Raw cotton	2,938	3,985	1,967
TOTAL (incl. others n.e.s.)	29,239	34,675	37,326
Imports			
Mineral fuels and lubes	18,046	20,529	19,161
Non-electrical machinery	6,845	8,801	10,126
Transport equipment	5,170	5,424	6,307

TABLE 6.42   PAKISTAN: PRINCIPAL IMPORTS AND EXPORTS *(continued)*

Rs mn	1981/82	1982/83	1983/84
Iron and steel and assoc. manufactures	4,163	3,052	3,414
Electrical goods	1,687	2,590	3,066
Tea	1,093	1,676	2,567
Drugs and medicines	1,222	1,390	1,850
TOTAL (incl. others n.e.s.)	58,563	68,164	76,718

Source: Pakistan Economic Survey

TABLE 6.43   PAKISTAN: DIRECTION OF TRADE

	1980/81 %	1981/82 %	1982/83 %	1983/84 %
Exports				
Iran	7.8	3.1	12.3	16.0
USA	6.0	7.2	6.0	8.7
Japan	6.4	8.5	8.2	8.6
Saudi Arabia	6.0	7.4	9.3	7.8
UAE	—	—	8.2	7.6
West Germany	4.3	3.9	4.5	4.8
UK	4.0	5.1	4.8	4.4
Kuwait	1.7	2.0	1.4	1.9
China	8.8	5.9	4.9	1.8
Hong Kong	3.9	4.6	4.4	1.3
Imports				
Japan	11.6	12.3	13.4	14.3
USA	10.9	8.8	9.7	11.4
Saudi Arabia	12.8	14.3	13.3	9.9
Kuwait	8.0	9.7	9.4	8.1
UK	6.2	6.3	6.4	6.7
West Germany	5.0	5.9	5.7	6.4
UAE	—	—	5.6	5.7
Malaysia	—	—	3.1	4.2
China	3.3	3.2	2.6	2.5
Australia	—	—	1.4	1.0

Source: State Bank of Pakistan

The country's dependence on oil has led it to foster closer trading links with the Middle Eastern oil producers, and Iran in particular. In 1983/84 Iran took 16% of Pakistan's exports whilst Saudi Arabia and the UAE took 7.8% and 7.6% respectively. But signs are that the Middle East's proportion was much smaller in 1984/85, and Pakistan is seeking again to reinforce such links. Other important export markets in 1983/84 were Japan (8.6%), and the US (8.7%). Pakistan's principal non-oil suppliers are Japan (14.3%), the US (11.4%), the UK (6.7%) and West Germany (6.4%).

Bangladesh

Bangladesh's external balances have been chronically weak since before independence. The economy is dependent on imports for almost all essential goods (not least of all food—17% of imports in 1983/84), whilst the export base is both narrow—effectively still reliant on jute/jute products and tea despite efforts to diversify—and faced with declining export prices and volatile world primary products markets.

During the 1980s the visibles deficit has consistently been around the US$1.4 bn—US$1.6 bn mark, with the singular exception of 1983 when weaker merchandise and invisible imports combined with a 65% surge in private transfers to reduce dramatically the current account deficit. However in 1984 previous trends reverted with a US$1.4 bn trade

TABLE 6.44   BANGLADESH: BALANCE OF PAYMENTS

US$ mn	1980	1981	1982	1983	1984
Merchandise exports	793	791	768	724	932
Merchandise imports	−2,353	−2,435	−2,221	−1,931	−2,340
Trade balance	−1,560	−1,644	−1,453	−1,207	−1,408
Invisible credits	288	253	247	252	281
Invisible debits	−551	−561	−594	−523	−600
Invisible balance	−263	−308	−347	−271	−319
Net private transfers	301	402	394	650	473
Net public transfers	765	536	749	769	730
Current account balance	−757	−1,014	−657	−59	−524

Source: IMF—International Financial Statistics

deficit, translating into a US$524 mn current account shortfall as total net transfers and the invisibles deficit once again returned to average levels (US$1.2 bn and US$319 mn respectively).

The terms of trade have moved sharply against Bangladesh ever since independence, with the worst shifts coming after the oil price rises of 1973 and 1979; mineral fuels imports accounted for 20% of the total import bill in 1983/84. In 1984/85 firmer prices for commodity exports and weaker world oil prices should have helped Bangladesh to a favourable shift in the terms of trade, but this will have proved short-lived with tea and jute prices falling again before the end of 1985.

Current account deficits have shown some improvement of late, largely because of increases in remittances from Bangladeshis working

TABLE 6.45   BANGLADESH: PRINCIPAL IMPORTS AND EXPORTS

mn taka	1981/82	1982/83	1983/84
Exports			
Raw jute and cuttings	2,000	2,580	2,730
Jute goods	6,282	7,920	8,711
Tea	812	1,101	1,700
Hides and leather goods	1,073	1,581	2,198
Fish and preparations	1,004	1,673	2,031
Newsprint etc.	106	61	2
Spices	1	6	11
TOTAL (incl. others n.e.s.)	12,387	18,016	20,136
Imports			
Wheat	3,914	3,425	3,716
Rice	1,123	1,830	876
Mineral fuels	7,104	4,440	4,036
Chemicals	4,564	4,253	5,572
Machinery and transport equipment	7,148	9,609	8,511
Basic manufactures	8,016	6,716	8,967
TOTAL (incl. others n.e.s.)	38,697	37,473	42,661

Source: National Statistics

221

abroad (mostly in the Middle East), but they still have to be funded by large tranches of aid, IMF drawings, and (indirectly) food aid from the US. An export promotion zone has been established south of Chittagong—the first factories started production in late 1984—and others are planned. But even if Bangladesh could expand and diversify its exports to a significant extent, it is ill-prepared (in infrastructural and educational terms) for industrialisation and the speed with which it would run up against developed countries' protectionist barriers (especially in the area of textiles).

TABLE 6.46   BANGLADESH: DIRECTION OF TRADE

	1982/83 %	1983/84 %	1984/85 %
Exports			
USA	11.7	13.3	18.9
Iran	6.4	10.4	5.1
Italy	1.3	8.6	6.7
Pakistan	7.9	8.1	5.3
Japan	6.1	7.7	6.8
UK	4.6	6.0	5.2
USSR	5.8	1.8	3.7
China	3.5	1.7	0.9
Sudan	3.6	1.6	1.3
Imports			
Japan	11.3	11.6	21.1
USA	12.6	11.1	18.0
Singapore	10.9	9.0	22.0
Australia	1.1	5.2	4.0
UK	3.7	4.4	5.4
West Germany	3.5	3.7	6.5
South Korea	4.0	3.4	8.2

Source: Bangladesh Economic Survey/Monthly Statistical Bulletin

Sri Lanka

Sri Lanka's trade and current account deficits have enjoyed a considerable strengthening in the last few years. On the visible account the provisionally calculated Rs 10,797 mn (US$424 mn) 1984 deficit was

TABLE 6.47 SRI LANKA: BALANCE OF PAYMENTS

Rs mn

	1980	1981	1982	1983	1984*
Merchandise exports (fob)	17,603	20,507	21,098	25,038	37,198
Merchandise imports (cif)	−33,915	−36,121	−41,420	−45,201	−47,995
Trade balance	−16,312	−15,614	−20,322	−20,163	−10,797
Invisible balance	859	80	−395	−1,416	−1,736
Private transfers	2,260	3,918	5,494	6,441	7,031
Official transfers	2,281	3,118	3,379	4,016	5,154
Current account balance	−10,912	−8,498	−11,844	−11,122	−348

Source: CBC
Note: *provisional

TABLE 6.48 SRI LANKA: PRINCIPAL IMPORTS AND EXPORTS

Rs mn

	1982	1983	1984
Exports			
Tea	6,335	8,296	15,772
Rubber	2,420	2,852	3,301
Coconut	345	433	304
Copra	57	74	72
Dessicated coconut	600	902	1,177
Gemstones	685	941	706
TOTAL (incl. others n.e.s.)	21,124	25,183	36,541
Imports			
Rice	925	765	197
Flour	62	108	28
Sugar	955	1,985	1,346
Petroleum products	11,506	11,023	10,681
Machinery and equipment	5,604	5,261	5,335
Wheat	1,787	2,340	2,471
TOTAL (incl. others n.e.s.)	36,876	42,021	46,913

Source: Sri Lankan Customs

barely more than half the size of the previous year and the current account's Rs 348 mn (US$14 mn) 1984 shortfall was a small fraction of the Rs 11,122 mn (US$473 mn) registered in 1983. This recovery has occurred against a backdrop of declining revenues from tourism and an increasingly heavy debt servicing burden. According to the Central Bank of Ceylon's calculations (which admittedly differ markedly from IMF statistics) the invisibles balance slipped into deficit for the first time in 1982 and has deteriorated steadily (to a deficit of Rs 1,736 mn in 1984) ever since.

In rank order, Sri Lanka's principal export markets are the US, Egypt, West Germany, the UK and Japan; whilst its main suppliers are Japan, Iran, the US, Singapore, India, Saudi Arabia and the US.

TABLE 6.49   SRI LANKA: DIRECTION OF TRADE

	1981 %	1982 %	1983 %	1984 %
Exports				
USA	13.3	13.9	17.3	19.1
Egypt	3.0	7.0	6.9	6.3
West Germany	5.3	5.4	6.1	4.8
UK	6.2	6.4	4.9	4.9
Japan	3.1	4.8	4.8	4.2
Iraq	2.8	4.5	4.5	7.0
Imports				
Japan	13.6	13.4	16.4	16.5
Iran	6.4	10.2	9.7	2.9
UK	5.9	5.8	6.2	4.6
Singapore	5.2	5.3	7.6	5.5
India	4.0	3.6	6.0	6.0
USA	6.8	5.7	6.0	8.8

Source: IMF—Direction of Trade Yearbook

VI   Foreign indebtedness

Of the four countries within the Indian Sub-Continent India is by far and away the largest—in terms of both population (seven and a half times larger than Pakistan's 99 mn or so) and GDP (almost six times larger than Pakistan's US$31 bn). Therefore it is no surprise to discover that India's debt burden is, in absolute dollar terms, many times that of the region's next largest debtor, Pakistan.

As for its neighbours, foreign aid has been of considerable importance to India. But whilst a public external foreign debt total of approximately US$25.5 bn in 1984 is a considerable sum, it nonetheless represents the smallest proportional debt burden on the sub-continent and, since much of it was contracted on concessional terms (90.4% of the disbursed total in 1974 and still 82.4% a decade later), the burden of debt servicing is also small in both regional and global terms.

India

TABLE 6.50   INDIA: FOREIGN PUBLIC DEBT

US$ mn	1979	1980	1981	1982	1983
Outstanding disbursed debt*	15,796	17,576	17,976	19,513	21,277
of which: Multilateral	5,298	6,720	7,801	9,126	10,459
Official bi-lateral	10,163	10,320	9,417	9,252	9,168
Supplier credits	171	130	101	73	89
Financial markets	165	406	658	1,062	1,561
Total debt service	1,033	1,056	1,025	1,150	1,323
of which: Multilateral	174	193	202	252	342
Official bi-lateral	766	773	737	721	704
Supplier credits	66	52	39	35	37
Financial markets	26	39	47	142	240
Principal (%)	62.5	64.1	63.1	58.7	58.2
Interest (%)	37.5	35.9	36.9	41.3	41.8

Source: World Bank

Note: *components may not sum due to individual roundings.

In 1984 India's US$25.5 bn foreign public debt represented slightly less than 13% of GDP whilst a servicing bill of approximately US$1.5 bn absorbed just 10% or so of goods and services export revenues. For its sub-continental neighbours: Pakistan's US$9.5 bn debt was equivalent to approximately one-third of GDP and cost almost one-third of total export revenues to service; Sri Lanka's US$2.2 bn foreign debt was equivalent to more than 40% of GDP and absorbed slightly more than 11% of export revenues to service; and finally Bangladesh, whose US$4.2 bn foreign debt was also equivalent to one-third of GDP and absorbed 15% of export revenues to pay a US$180 mn servicing bill.

Of the four, India is the only country to experience a deterioration in the terms of its borrowings over the last decade, and this is a reflection of increasing recourse to private capital markets as the economy—and thus the country's international credit rating—strengthened. Looking at the terms associated with new commitments, in 1983 India faced a 5% average interest rate, almost three points higher than a decade earlier, maturities shorter by 10%, grace periods shorter by 20%, and the proportion accounted for by grants down from 62% to 41%.

Pakistan

TABLE 6.51   PAKISTAN: FOREIGN PUBLIC DEBT

US$ million	1979	1980	1981	1982	1983
Outstanding disbursed debt*	7,999	8,760	8,812	9,164	9,466
of which: Multilateral	1,540	1,819	1,902	2,158	2,352
Official bi-lateral	6,096	6,394	6,399	6,573	6,733
Supplier credits	171	176	143	120	120
Financial markets	192	391	368	313	260
Total debt service	511	592	533	537	831
of which: Multilateral	109	103	115	108	144
Official bi-lateral	295	356	255	282	562
Supplier credits	52	50	44	43	35
Financial markets	55	84	119	106	90
Principal (%)	58.3	58.3	62.7	60.4	66.8
Interest (%)	41.7	41.7	37.3	39.6	33.2

Source: World Bank
Note: *components may not sum due to individual rounding.

75% of Pakistan's aid is acquired through the Aid to Pakistan Consortium of western industrial nations and multilateral organisations (the other 25% coming from Saudi Arabia and the Gulf). The country suffered a small increase in average interest rates but a 46% lengthening of average maturities (to 36 years), and a 41% lengthening of grace periods (to 8.5 years).

Bangladesh

TABLE 6.52   BANGLADESH: FOREIGN PUBLIC DEBT

US$ mn	1979	1980	1981	1982	1983
Outstanding disbursed debt*	2,845	3,521	3,852	4,295	4,185
of which: Multilateral	1,084	1,385	1,621	1,878	2,157
Official bi-lateral	1,607	1,989	2,086	2,272	1,877
Supplier credits	128	118	109	99	97
Financial markets	26	30	36	46	53
Total debt service	84	76	98	111	143
of which: Multilateral	14	13	16	28	43
Official bi-lateral	50	38	55	62	76
Supplier credits	13	21	22	16	12
Financial markets	7	3	5	6	11
Principal repayments (%)	50.7	52.7	52.3	56.7	55.9
Interest repayments (%)	49.3	47.3	47.7	43.3	44.1

Source: World Bank

Note: *components may not sum due to individual rounding.

Bangladesh is the poorest (and least creditworthy) of the grouping, with a per caput GDP figure of US$131—barely more than half the Indian level. The country's shuffling struggle to edge closer to solvency is one of Himalayan proportions and, with seemingly ever-wider external deficits, the rates of expansion of Bangladesh's debt and debt service totals over the five years to 1983 are, at 47% and 70% respectively, second only to Sri Lanka's. The Bangladeshi 'resource deficit' is a comprehensive one, and thus so is the composition of the annual aid package; in 1984 food aid made up US$3 bn of a US$16.4 bn total.

In recognition of the painfully slow pace of economic progress in Bangladesh, the last ten years have seen a further softening of already very soft terms for new debt commitments. By 1983 the average interest rate had dropped another point to 1.7%, average maturities had lengthened by almost 30% to 39 years, grace periods were 20% longer

227

at 9 years, and, with the grant element up to 70% (from 55%), the proportion of the disbursed total contracted on concessional terms had risen to 94% from 77% a decade earlier.

Sri Lanka

TABLE 6.53   SRI LANKA: FOREIGN PUBLIC DEBT

US$ mn	1979	1980	1981	1982	1983
Outstanding disbursed debt*	1,111	1,344	1,610	1,965	2,205
of which: Multilateral	281	336	374	445	539
Official bi-lateral	767	866	917	976	1,077
Supplier credits	63	55	67	168	145
Financial markets	—	88	253	376	444
Total debt service	77	84	93	138	167
of which: Multilateral	11	11	10	12	15
Official bi-lateral	46	54	47	46	57
Supplier credits	19	16	15	13	32
Financial markets	1	4	21	66	63
Principal (%)	63.0	60.3	46.9	49.7	48.4
Interest (%)	37.0	39.7	53.1	50.3	51.6

Source: World Bank

Note: *components may not sum due to individual rounding.

The country has the unenviable distinction of having the fastest growing debt and debt service burdens of the four countries that make up the sub-continent. During the five years to 1983, and as a consequence of galloping current account deficits, total disbursed foreign public debt almost doubled, whilst the cost of servicing it increased by 117%. By way of compensation the decade to 1983 has seen a considerable softening of terms for Sri Lanka, with average interest rates dropping from 5.1% to 1.9%, maturities and grace periods trebling to 40 years and 10 years respectively, and the proportion of new commitments accounted for by grants rising from 27% to 70%.

Chapter Seven

OUTLOOK

I Introduction

Most Asian economies appear to be entering into periods of uncertain growth, at least in the medium term. Reflecting the volatility of the international economic environment, the Asian economies have experienced a wide amplitude of fluctuation in their recent economic growth, as shown in Figures C, D and E. Even the Indian Sub-Continent economies, which are supposed to be less vulnerable to external economic fluctuation, have displayed significant swings in their growth. Furthermore, the existing international economic environment is anything but growth-inducing. In 1985 the industrial countries grew by just over 2%, hardly effective as the world's locomotive in terms of pulling other economies along for higher growth. The growth of world trade was also disappointing, with only 2.9% increase in volume terms, which obviously did not offer a viable source of growth for the open Asian economies.

Thus most Asian economies started to decelerate in their growth in 1985. Economic growth of the NICs plummeted abruptly in 1985. The economic down-turn was also sharp for ASEAN, with the Philippine economy collapsing into −4% growth in 1984, and Singapore plunging into negative 1.7% growth in 1985. The growth of the Indian Sub-Continent economies has similarly drifted downwards, even though these economies depend more on domestic demand than external factors as their main source of growth. The immediate challenge faced by these Asian economies is therefore how to restore their past growth momentum and maintain it on a more stable basis. To succeed in this they have to weather the unfavourable international economic climate as well as come to grips with their domestic structural economic problems.

II The uncertain international economic setting

There is considerable uncertainty concerning the emerging international economic order but that which is likely to prevail in the medium term is going to be difficult for the Asian economies from the standpoint of

229

economic growth. First, there is growing protectionism in the developed countries as a result of their protracted recession. With the rate of unemployment in the industrial countries continuing to increase, coupled with their failure to achieve positive structural adjustments in their manufacturing sector, their protectionist sentiments begin to mount. Increasingly the industrial countries have resorted to non-tariff barriers (e.g. quotas, voluntary export restraints and 'orderly' marketing arrangements) as the main instruments of their trade protection against the manufactured imports from LDCs. The best known and the most elaborate system of protection devised in the industrial countries against labour-intensive imports from LDCs is the 25-year old Multi-Fibre Arrangements (MFA, renewed in August 1986 for another 5 years) which imposes a severe restriction on the growth of textile exports from LDCs to the industrial countries. Besides textiles and clothing, the industrial countries individually or in a group (e.g. EEC) have also entered into bilateral arrangements with several Asian NICs in order to restrict their exports of other labour-intensive products, e.g. footwear, and even their more skill-intensive manufactures such as colour TVs and consumer electronics.

Restrictive trade policies on the part of the industrial countries will certainly curtail the growth potential of all the export-oriented Asian economies, though the impact will be far more serious on the NICs than on ASEAN or the Indian Sub-Continent. But some ASEAN countries like Thailand and Malaysia, and Indian Sub-Continent countries like India will also stand to lose in the new round of trade curbs on textiles and clothing. The other ASEAN economies face additional protectionist barriers against their resource-based exports, with the tariffs often escalating according to the stages of processing.

The next unfavourable international development is the collapse of the prices of primary commodities, including petroleum and gas. To be sure, the impact of the general decline in the prices of primary commodities differs with various Asian economies. While the plummeting of oil prices is a general blessing to most Asian economies which are energy-deficient, it hurts the few oil exporting countries, namely, Indonesia, Malaysia, Brunei and Burma, especially Indonesia which used to derive some 70% of its total export earnings from the export of oil and gas. By comparison, the slump in the non-oil primary commodities has in various ways adversely affected all the ASEAN countries and most of the countries on the Indian Sub-Continent. The prices for most non-oil primary products have since 1985 decreased on average by more than a third, bringing about a sharp deterioration in the terms of trade for the resource-based Asian economies, especially the ASEAN countries. The weak primary commodity prices have in fact been the major factor for the recent economic downturn of ASEAN, though the same is considered as the beneficial factor for the resource-poor NICs. In particular, South Korea and Taiwan are currently reflating their economies on the back of cheap oil and cheap raw materials.

The future path of oil prices is difficult to predict at the present time, though the downward pressure is likely to remain in the medium term. Low oil prices will encourage more synthetic substitition (which is basically energy-intensive activities) and will therefore further depress the demand for the natural primary commodities. As for the general movement of the non-oil primary commodity prices in the near future, it is even more difficult to pinpoint. Apart from the supply-side factors, the crucial determinant in the change of primary commodity prices comes from the demand from the industrial economies, which are in the throes of a major structural transformation, moving away from basic manufacturing to high-tech industries or modern services which inherently need less raw materials from the LDCs. Thus it is difficult to foresee a return to the conditions of the raw material boom of the early 1970s. Such a scenario does not augur well for the resource-rich ASEAN economies.

Lastly, the international financial situation has deteriorated for most Asian economies, which need to continue importing capital from the advanced countries in order to fill their domestic resource gaps or to stabilise their balance of payments crises. But the external financing situation in terms of availability of various forms of financial flows to the Asian economies will become much tighter. The problem is aggravated partly by the current international debt crisis, with many LDCs having difficulty in servicing their debt and hence discouraging future private capital inflow; and partly because of widening fiscal deficits in the traditional capital-exporting countries. At present, the problem of indebtedness does not appear to be serious for Asia as a whole, because its average debt-service ratio in 1986 is only 12.3%, as compared with 32.3% for Africa and 43.5% for the Western Hemisphere. However, debt-service difficulties have already affected the Philippines and a number of low-income countries on the Indian Sub-Continent as a result of the sluggish growth of their exports. The latter countries have also been hit by the dwindling of their overseas workers' remittances in recent years due to recession in the Middle East.

231

On the whole, the worsening international financial situation will hit the Indian Sub-Continent countries, which are heavily dependent on capital imports for their development, more than either the NICs or ASEAN; just as the upsurge of protectionism affects the NICs more than the others while the declining primary commodity prices have more adverse effects on ASEAN than the others. In various ways and in varying degrees, the emerging international economic environment has become less supportive of Asia's continuing development efforts.

III The imperative of structural adjustment

Even for the most open and outward-looking economies, growth does not depend exclusively on external demands. Domestic sources of demand are just as important, and are more critical now that the external economic environment has grown less favourable. To recapture their past growth momentum, most Asian economies will have to undergo the necessary structural adjustments in their domestic economies.

From a longer perspective, the kind of structural adjustments envisaged will have to be more fundamental and more far-reaching than are required merely for boosting short-term domestic economic growth. Most Asian economies have now reached the critical phase in their industrialisation processes, and they have to undertake extensive structural transformation in order to sustain long-term growth. Thus all the NICs have in recent years launched economic restructuring measures, such as 'Industrial Diversification' in Hong Kong, 'Industrial Upgrading' in Taiwan, and 'Industrial Sophistication' in South Korea. All are primarily aimed at promoting higher value-added and more skill- or capital-intensive industries. But the action required also involves a range of measures and policies pertaining to productivity growth, manpower training, R & D programmes, new patterns of labour relations and new styles of management. Successful economic restructuring for the NICs will ultimately mean upgrading of their economies to become fully industrial countries.

For ASEAN, the nature of institutional transformation and structural adjustments will be a little different, as the main thrusts of the change for ASEAN are still concerned with policies and measures designed to consolidate or continue their efforts towards economic diversification. The current recession in their primary commodity sector has once again brought home the clear message that the ASEAN economies must step up their industrialisation progress in order to reduce their dependency on the volatile primary exports. On the industrial front, specific measures must be undertaken to accelerate the transition from import substitution to export expansion, e.g. by lowering the overall levels of effective protection.

As for the Indian Sub-Continent, both the magnitude and priority of the adjustment policies will again be different from the other two groups. Some of these low-income countries are still in the process of coming to grips with the basic development issues of poverty, unemployment and the provision of basic needs, which can be more effectively dealt with not by simple redistribution but by strong economic growth. To induce higher economic growth, the governments of these countries need to introduce more liberalisation measures on the one hand and to re-orient their economies to be more outward-looking on the other. Such crucial policy reorientation will enable the Indian Sub-Continent economies to exploit the international forces for their economic growth as well as to improve their overall operational efficiency through greater exposure to the world market forces.

IV Opportunities from regional initiative

One way to meet the challenge of the emerging international economic order is for the various Asian countries to form regional groupings. But the inherently wide political, economic and social diversity of the Asian countries will render any effective regional co-operation efforts exceedingly difficult. So far the only viable Asian grouping in existence is ASEAN, which was formed in 1967. During the past 10 years, ASEAN has made serious attempts at regional economic co-operation by preferential trading arrangements and regional industrial complementation schemes. But the actual results have been quite disappointing.

ASEAN's lack of conspicuous success in intra-regional economic co-operation is nevertheless made up for by its success in the area of 'extra-regional' co-operation. Over the years ASEAN has been successful in developing a unified perception on many regional and international economic issues, e.g. on protectionism, which affect ASEAN as a region. It has maintained formal dialogues with advanced countries for improving bilateral economic relations. In short, the effectiveness of ASEAN as a group is due to its collective framework within which it operates its external leverage *vis-à-vis* other country groups in order to secure a better deal for itself. Thus ASEAN continues to enjoy high political visibility, despite its slow progress towards substantive internal co-operation.

Apparently encouraged by the success of ASEAN, the Indian Sub-Continent has recently moved to form its own regional grouping, the South Asian Association for Regional Co-operation (SAARC), which includes Bangladesh, Bhuttan, India, the Maldives, Nepal, Pakistan and Sri Lanka. The first meeting of the heads of state of the SAARC was held at Dhaka in December 1985. Primarily to give institutional expression to a long-felt desire for co-operation among the Indian Sub-Continent countries, SAARC will probably follow ASEAN's approaches to regional co-operation with more emphasis on achieving some external political clout rather than going for substantial economic integration, which is in any case difficult to realise for developing economies.

In contrast, the NICs as a group are politically isolated and without a common institutional structure. Economically, however, the NICs are increasingly integrated with China and Japan, and are quite complementary to the resource-rich ASEAN. This gives rise to a strong possibility of a *de facto* sub-regional economic integration based on the Asia-Pacific region, i.e. comprising, Japan, China, the NICs and ASEAN. Already there is a high degree of economic inter-dependence among these Asia-Pacific countries in terms of trade and investment flows, apart from the fact that they are potentially high performance economies. Continuing economic growth in future will certainly bring these economies, largely complementary to each other, closer still even in the absence of a political framework for regional co-operation. Should this emerge in future, it could constitute a formidable economic sub-region to rival North America and Western Europe.

FIGURE C   RECENT ECONOMIC GROWTH OF THE NICs

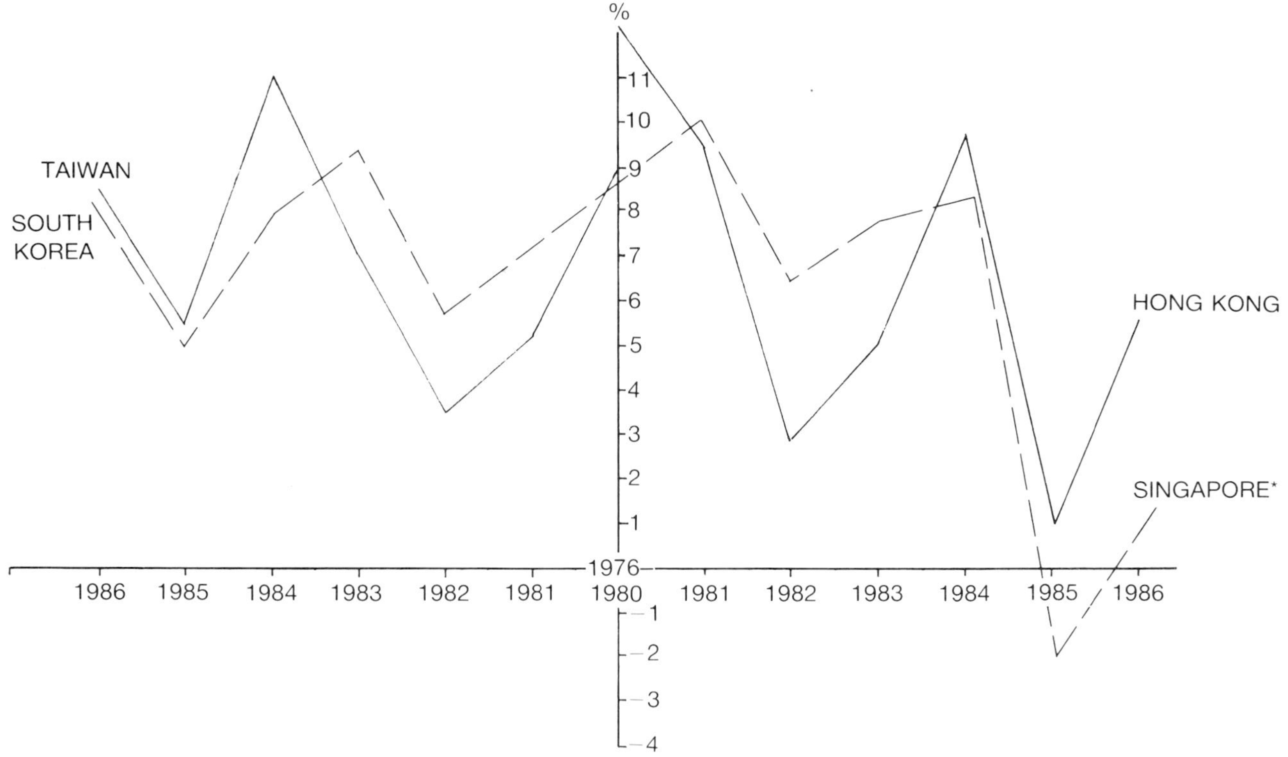

Note: * Under 'ASEAN'

235

FIGURE D RECENT ECONOMIC GROWTH OF ASEAN

FIGURE E   RECENT ECONOMIC GROWTH OF SOUTH ASIA

FACT FILE

FACT FILE TABLES

TABLE 1   POPULATION DISTRIBUTION

	Population ('000)	Area ('000 sq km)	Persons per sq km	% urban
Bangladesh	99,200	144	689	17
Burma	36,392	677	54	29
Hong Kong	5,466	0.4	5,119	92
India	750,900	3,288	228	24
Indonesia	165,153	1;905	87	24
Kampuchea	6,388	181	35	9
North Korea	21,200	121	175	62
South Korea	42,400	99	429	62
Laos	3,679	237	15	16
Macao	420	16	26	91
Malaysia	15,190	329	46	31
Pakistan	93,290	796	117	29
Philippines	54,350	301	181	39
Singapore	2,750	0.6	4,583	100
Sri Lanka	15,990	66	242	26
Taiwan	19,260	36	535	50
Thailand	51,300	514	100	18
Vietnam	60,650	350	184	20

Sources: IMF/National Statistics

TABLE 2   TRENDS IN POPULATION SIZE

	1980	1982	1984	1986 estimates
Bangladesh	88,660	92,590	96,750	99,200
Burma	33,880	35,910	37,610	38,101
Hong Kong	5,040	5,230	5,364	5,596
India	663,600	716,880	745,010	759,910
Indonesia	146,360	153,040	159,890	167,200
Kampuchea	6,747	6,646	7,149	6,388
North Korea	18,900	19,200	21,200	23,500
South Korea	38,120	39,330	40,580	42,400
Laos	3,756	3,983	4,033	3,585
Macao	318	350	400	420
Malaysia	13,760	14,400	15,190	15,700
Pakistan	82,580	87,760	93,290	99,500
Philippines	48,320	50,740	53,170	54,500
Singapore	2,414	2,472	2,529	2,570
Sri Lanka	14,747	15,189	15,606	15,990
Taiwan	17,300	18,300	18,850	19,260
Thailand	46,455	48,490	50,396	51 300
Vietnam	53,500*	55,990	58,307	60,650

Sources: IMF, UN, National Statistics
Note: *Estimate

TABLE 3   VITAL STATISTICS, 1983

	Births (per '000)	Deaths (per '000)	Male life expectancy (years)	Female life expectancy (years)	Adult literacy (%)
Bangladesh	44.8	17.5	55	54	29
Burma	37.9	12.7	59	61	66
Hong Kong*	14.5	4.8*	73	78	90
India	33.8	11.9	46	45	38
Indonesia	30.7	13.0	51	54	36
Kampuchea	45.5	19.6	42	45	41
North Korea	30.5	7.4	63	67	95
South Korea*	23.0	6.2	63	69	93
Laos	40.6	15.5	48	51	85
Macao*	19.4	4.6	63	67	90
Malaysia	29.2	5.8	67	72	60
Pakistan	42.6	15.2	59	59	24
Philippines	32.3	6.9	63	66	83
Singapore	16.2	5.3	69	74	85
Sri Lanka	26.2	6.1	66	69	85
Taiwan	—	—	75	78	94
Thailand	28.6	7.9	58	64	86
Vietnam	31.2	10.1	57	61	87

Source: United Nations/Estimates
Note: *1984

TABLE 4   POPULATION BREAKDOWN, BY SEX

	Year	Total ('000)	Male %	Female %
Bangladesh	1982	92,585	51.5	48.5
Burma	1983	35,306	49.6	50.4
Hong Kong	1981	4,987	52.2	47.8
India	1981	703,300	51.7	48.3
Indonesia	1980	146,776	49.7	50.3
Kampuchea	1962	2,499	58.0	42.0
North Korea	1986	21,200	—	—
South Korea	1980	37,436	50.1	49.9
Laos	1985	3,585	51.0	49.0
Macao	1984	420	52.0	48.0
Malaysia	1980	13,436	50.2	49.8
Pakistan	1981	84,253	52.5	47.5
Philippines	1980	48,098	50.2	49.8
Singapore	1985	2,558	50.9	49.1
Sri Lanka	1981	14,848	51.0	49.0
Taiwan	1984	19,260	51.0	49.0
Thailand	1980	44,824	49.8	50.2
Vietnam	1986	60,650	—	—

Sources: United Nations/National Statistics

TABLE 5   EMPLOYMENT/UNEMPLOYMENT

	Year	Labour force ('000s)	% of population	Unemployed ('000s) latest year	% of labour force
Bangladesh	1983	32,750	33.0	11,300	34.5
Burma	1984/85	14,792	40.6	710	4.8
Hong Kong	1985	2,879	48.8	98	3.4
India	1984	300,000*	40.3	23,500	7.8
Indonesia	1983	59,599	37.4	6,000	10.0*
Kampuchea	1985	4,095	37.5	—	—
North Korea	1984	8,000*	37.7	—	—
South Korea	1984	14,984	36.9	465	3.1
Laos	1985	1,863	52.0	—	—
Macao	1985	185	44.0	—	—
Malaysia	1985	5,576	36.7	10,500	7.0
Pakistan	1983/84	27,600	29.6	1,078	3.9
Philippines	1983	19,212	35.3	1,191	6.2
Singapore	1984	1,175	45.9	39	3.3
Sri Lanka	1981	4,120	27.9	1,194	14.0
Taiwan	1985	7,650	39.7	359	4.7
Thailand	1985	26,900	52.4	592	2.2
Vietnam	1985	24,240	44.4	3,000*	12.4

Source: National Statistics
Note: *Estimates

TABLE 6   EMPLOYMENT, BY SECTOR

% breakdown	Year	('000s)	Agri-culture	Services	Industry & construction
Bangladesh	1983	21,450	68.0	24.0	8.1
Burma	1984/85	14,792	63.5	25.2	10.0
Hong Kong	1985	2,879	2.0	60.4	30.5
India	1984	300,000*	71.0	18.3	10.7
Indonesia	1986	54,000*	48.0	30.0*	10.0*
Kampuchea	1962	2,499	80.3	14.5	2.0
North Korea	1984	8,000*	45.0	15.0	40.0*
South Korea	1984	14,984	26.0	48.0	23.0
Laos	1983	1,863	72.0	18.0	10.0
Macao	1985	185	1.0	60.0	39.0
Malaysia	1985	5,576	35.5	41.9	22.6
Pakistan	1984/85	28,192	51.8	33.2	15.0
Philippines	1983	19,212	51.4	34.6	14.0
Singapore	1984	1,175	7.5	56.4	36.1
Sri Lanka	1984	4,120	45.0	44.0	11.0
Taiwan	1984	7,308	17.6	40.6	41.8
Thailand	1984	26,900	67.3	23.9	8.7
Vietnam	1985	24,240	70.0*	20.0*	10.0*

Source: National Statistics
Note: *Estimates

TABLE 7   GROSS DOMESTIC PRODUCT

	Currency (millions)	1983	1984	1985	GDP per capita, latest year	GDP US$ mn
Bangladesh	Taka	288,400	349,900	397,750	4,210	14,203
Burma	Kyat	49,784	54,042	—	14,369	6,891
Hong Kong	HK dollar	183,315	232,700	234,560	43,253	30,072
India	Rupee (bn)	1,398	2,132	2,343	2,861	174,000
Indonesia	Rupiah (bn)	73,698	85,914	—	537,000	79,994
Kampuchea	Riel	—	—	—	—	—
North Korea	Won (bn)	20,957	—	20,700*	988,538	19,700
South Korea	Won (bn)	59,603	67,126	—	1,654,000	81,168
Laos	Kip	18,047	17,557	—	4,531	765
Macao	Pataca	7,300*	8,000*	8,320*	20,000	1,000
Malaysia	Ringgit	69,910	79,634	78,000	5,135	32,165
Pakistan	Rupee	365,770	418,770	453,946*	4,489	27,264
Philippines	Peso	384,690	549,670	623,100	11,458	32,740
Singapore	S dollar	35,171	38,733	36,800	15,244	15,930
Sri Lanka	Rupee	121,571	152,615	159,483	9,974	7,594
Taiwan	NT dollar (bn)	2,044	2,278	2,395	125,221	60,987
Thailand	Baht	924,250	991,560	1,047,560	20,420	39,831
Vietnam	Dong	—	—	—	—	—

Sources: National Statistics/IMF
Note: *Estimates

TABLE 8   GDP BREAKDOWN, BY SECTOR

	Year	Agriculture	Services	Industry & construction
Bangladesh	1984/85	48.4	37.7	13.9
Burma	1983	48.0	39.0	22.0
Hong Kong	1984	0.5	69.7	29.8
India	1983/84	39.8	39.1	21.1
Indonesia	1983/84	26.4	17.2	21.4
Kampuchea	1986	75.0*	20.0*	5.0*
North Korea	1985	50.0*	30.0*	20.0*
South Korea	1984	14.7	55.2	30.1
Laos	1984	82.2	7.7	9.9
Macao	1985	1.0	66.5	33.5
Malaysia	1985	29.3	43.3	27.4
Pakistan	1984/85	24.7	55.6	19.7
Philippines	1984	26.2	49.1	24.7
Singapore	1984	0.8	73.2	26.0
Sri Lanka	1984	29.0	45.5	25.5
Taiwan	1985	1.0	56.9	36.1
Thailand	1984	23.1	50.0	26.9
Vietnam	1985	75.0*	15.0*	10.0*

Source: National Statistics
Note: *Estimates

TABLE 9   SECTORAL DEVELOPMENT, 1973–83

Average annual growth rates, 1973–1983	GDP	Agriculture	Manufacturing	Services
Bangladesh	5.2	3.2	−8.1	7.4
Burma	6.0	6.6	6.1	5.1
Hong Kong	9.3	1.1	−8.2	9.8
India	4.0	2.2	4.3	6.1
Indonesia	7.0	3.7	12.6	9.0
Kampuchea	—	—	—	—
North Korea	—	—	—	—
South Korea	7.3	1.5	11.8	6.8
Laos	—	—	—	—
Macao	4.5	−1.0	3.5	6.0
Malaysia	7.3	4.4	−8.7	8.2
Pakistan	5.6	3.4	7.0	6.3
Philippines	5.4	4.3	5.0	5.2
Singapore	8.2	1.5	7.9	8.1
Sri Lanka	5.2	4.1	3.4	6.0
Taiwan	8.6	1.3	11.1	8.5
Thailand	6.9	3.8	8.9	7.6
Vietnam	5.0	—	—	—

Sources: World Bank/National Statistics/Estimates

TABLE 10   INFLATION RATES

% per annum	1982	1983	1984	1985
Bangladesh	12.5	9.4	10.5	10.7
Burma	5.3	5.7	4.8	6.8
Hong Kong	10.5	9.9	8.1	3.2
India	7.9	11.9	8.3	5.1
Indonesia	9.5	12.4	10.4	4.7
Kampuchea	—	—	—	—
North Korea	—	—	—	—
South Korea	7.3	3.4	2.3	2.5
Laos	—	—	—	—
Macao	9.6	8.9	5.6	3.0
Malaysia	5.8	3.7	3.9	0.3
Pakistan	5.9	6.2	6.6	5.8
Philippines	10.1	10.0	5.0	12.0*
Singapore	3.8	1.2	2.6	0.4
Sri Lanka	10.9	14.0	16.6	14.4
Taiwan	3.4	1.8	0.2	0.4
Thailand	5.2	3.7	0.9	2.4
Vietnam	90.0*	50.0*	50.0*	50.0*

Sources: IMF/National Statistics
Note: *Estimates

245

TABLE 11   EXCHANGE RATES, 1980–86

Unit of currency per US dollar, yearly averages at market rates

	1980	1983	1984	1985	June 1986
Bangladesh	20.7	26.2	25.5	34.1	35.7
Burma	6.8	8.2	8.8	7.8	7.3
Hong Kong	5.1	7.8	7.8	7.8	7.8
India	7.9	10.5	12.5	12.2	12.5
Indonesia	626.8	994.0	1,074.0	1,125.0	1,131.0
Kampuchea	n.a.	4.0	4.0	4.0	4.0
North Korea	—	0.9	0.9	0.9	0.9
South Korea	659.9	795.5	827.4	890.2	886.6
Laos	10.0	30.0	35.0	35.0	35.0
Macao	8.1	8.1	8.1	8.1	8.1
Malaysia	2.2	2.3	2.4	2.4	2.6
Pakistan	9.9	13.5	15.4	16.0	16.8
Philippines	7.5	11.1	16.7	18.7	20.5
Singapore	2.1	2.1	2.1	2.1	2.2
Sri Lanka	18.0	25.0	26.3	27.4	28.0
Taiwan	35.0	40.1	39.5	39.9	36.8
Thailand	20.6	23.0	27.2	26.7	26.3
Vietnam	9.0	10.5	11.2	12.0*	11.8*

Sources: IMF/National Statistics
Note: *Official rates: The tourist rate was amended in April 1985 to US$1.00=D 100. Black market rate was around D 350.

TABLE 12   INTEREST RATES

	Type	1980	1981	1982	1983	1984	1985
Bangladesh	Discount rate	10.5	10.5	10.5	10.5	10.5	10.5
Burma	n.a.	—	—	—	—	—	—
Hong Kong	Lending rate	—	16.5	10.5	13.5	11.0	7.0
India	Bank rate	9.0	10.0	10.0	10.0	10.0	10.0
Indonesia	Money market	12.9	16.3	17.2	13.2	18.6	10.3
Kampuchea	n.a.	—	—	—	—	—	—
North Korea	n.a.	—	—	—	—	—	—
South Korea	Discount rate	16.0	11.0	5.0	5.0	5.0	5.0
Laos	n.a.	—	—	—	—	—	—
Macao	12 month deposits	—	—	9.6	8.8	8.4	—
Malaysia	Discount rate	4.5	4.5	5.1	5.2	5.1	—
Pakistan	Bank rate	10.0	10.0	10.0	10.0	10.0	10.0
Philippines	Discount rate	11.0	—	—	—	—	—
Singapore	Money market	11.0	11.5	7.9	7.1	7.7	—
Sri Lanka	Bank rate	12.0	14.0	14.0	13.0	13.0	11.0
Taiwan	Rediscount rate	11.0	11.8	7.8	7.3	6.8	5.3
Thailand	Discount rate	16.6	14.3	12.0	14.9	11.0	11.0
Vietnam	n.a	—	—	—	—	—	—

Sources: IMF/National Statistics

246

TABLE 13   TRENDS IN GROSS FIXED INVESTMENT

	Currency (millions)	1981	1982	1983	1984
Bangladesh	Taka	—	—	254,700	—
Burma	Kyat	8,635	10,044	9,054	10,052
Hong Kong	HK dollar	56,050	57,792	55,250	56,900
India	Rupee	294,700	347,800	401,800	449,500
Indonesia	Rupiah (bn)	11,553	13,467	21,668	22,566
Kampuchea	Riel	—	—	—	—
North Korea	Won	—	—	—	—
South Korea	Won (bn)	13,208	15,676	18,605	20,176
Laos	Kip	—	—	—	—
Macao	Pataca	—	—	—	470*
Malaysia	Ringgit	20,365	23,457	25,363	26,658
Pakistan	Rupee	42,970	49,170	56,740	63,760
Philippines	Peso	79,290	86,030	95,250	105,590
Singapore	S dollar	11,988	14,795	16,623	—
Sri Lanka	Rupee	23,279	30,207	35,312	38,427
Taiwan	NT dollar	494,047	488,618	472,305	484,386
Thailand	Baht	189,070	179,900	205,990	228,800
Vietnam	Dong	—	—	—	—

Sources: IMF/National Statistics
Note: *New investment only

TABLE 14   PRIVATE SECTOR CONSUMPTION

	Currency (millions)	Year	Total consumption	Per capita
Bangladesh	Taka	1982/83	254,700	2,750
Burma	Kyat	1984	46,028	1,223
Hong Kong	HK dollar	1984	158,376	29,526
India	Rupee (bn)	1983	1,337	1,795
Indonesia	Rupiah (bn)	1983	49,231	317,005
Kampuchea	Riel	—	—	—
North Korea	Won (bn)	—	—	—
South Korea	Won (bn)	1984	40,381	952,382
Laos	Kip	—	—	—
Macao	Pataca	—	—	—
Malaysia	Ringgit	1985	39,382	2,508
Pakistan	Rupee	1984	341,450	3,660
Philippines	Peso	1985	491,460	9,018
Singapore	S dollar	1984	38,733	15,316
Sri Lanka	Rupee	1984	111,235	7,128
Taiwan	NT dollar	1985	1,158,802	61,475
Thailand	Baht (bn)	1985	655,240	13,002
Vietnam	Dong	—	—	—

Sources: IMF/National Statistics

TABLE 15   GOVERNMENT SPENDING

	Currency (millions)	Year	Total spending	% of GDP
Bangladesh	Taka	1982/83	21,300	7.4
Burma	Kyat	1984/85	6,448	11.8
Hong Kong	HK dollar	1984	18,384	7.4
India	Rupee (bn)	1984	449	21.1
Indonesia	Rupiah (bn)	1983	7,791	10.9
Kampuchea	Riel	—	—	90.0*
North Korea	Won (bn)	—	—	—
South Korea	Won (bn)	1984	7,137	10.6
Laos	Kip	—	—	—
Macao	Pataca	1985	2,129	26.5*
Malaysia	Ringgit	1985	11,750	15.1
Pakistan	Rupee	1984	50,310	12.0
Philippines	Peso	1985	42,830	6.9
Singapore	S dollar	1984	4,307	7.8
Sri Lanka	Rupee	1984	11,935	7.8
Taiwan	NT dollar	1985	356,445	14.9
Thailand	Baht	1985	140,500	13.4
Vietnam	Dong	—	—	—

Sources: IMF/National Statistics
Note: *Estimate

TABLE 16   GOVERNMENT FINANCE: BUDGET DEFICIT AS A PROPORTION OF GDP

	Currency (millions)	1984	%	1985	%
Bangladesh	Taka	4,591	1.3	6,239	1.5
Burma	Kyat	−338	7.2	—	—
Hong Kong	HK dollar	−600*	0.2	100	0
India	Rupee	−183,020	8.6	−204,390	8.7
Indonesia	Rupiah	−296,800	5.8	−281,800	—
Kampuchea	Riel	—	—	—	—
North Korea	Won	0	0	0	0
South Korea	Won	−841,300	1.3	−945,000	1.5
Laos	Kip	−910	5.2	—	—
Macao	Pataca	291	3.6	1	0
Malaysia	Ringgit	−7,075	8.9	−5,999	7.7
Pakistan	Rupee	−37,800	7.9	−39,000	7.5
Philippines	Peso	−9,828	1.8	−11,188	1.8
Singapore	S dollar	2,088	5.4	595	1.6
Sri Lanka	Rupee	−13,632	8.9	—	—
Taiwan	NT dollar	0	0	0	0
Thailand	Baht	−33,183	3.3	−39,159	3.7
Vietnam	Dong	−20,500	—	—	—

Sources: IMF/National Statistics
Note: *1983

TABLE 17   MERCHANDISE EXPORTS 1981–85

US$ million, fob	1981	1982	1983	1984	1985
Bangladesh	790	768	723	931	999
Burma	475	393	378	366	—
Hong Kong	2,147	1,954	2,063	2,838	30,154
India	8,437	9,226	9,770	9,460	—
Indonesia	23,348	19,747	18,689	20,754	18,583
Kampuchea*	4	5	6	—	—
North Korea	537	1,015	900	—	—
South Korea	20,671	20,879	23,204	26,335	26,442
Laos	19	40	43	36	—
Macao	497	560	703	935	910
Malaysia	11,675	11,966	13,683	16,407	15,265
Pakistan	2,730	2,341	2,877	2,480	2,648
Philippines	5,722	5,021	5,005	5,391	4,629
Singapore	19,662	19,435	20,429	22,662	21,500
Sri Lanka	1,063	1,014	1,061	1,462	1,303
Taiwan	22,408	21,776	25,028	30,185	30,466
Thailand	6,902	6,835	6,308	7,338	7,059
Vietnam	232	285	317	—	—

Sources: National Statistics/IMF
Note: *USSR and OECD countries only; excluding countertrade

TABLE 18   MERCHANDISE IMPORTS 1981–85

US$ million, fob	1981	1982	1983	1984	1985
Bangladesh	2,435	2,221	1,931	2,340	2,300
Burma	371	408	276	601	—
Hong Kong	2,432	2,196	2,252	2,864	29,821
India	14,149	14,046	13,868	15,006	—
Indonesia	16,542	17,854	17,726	15,254	12,583
Kampuchea*	111	86	102	—	—
North Korea	640	1,215	1,110	—	—
South Korea	24,299	23,473	24,967	27,461	26,461
Laos	110	132	135	98	—
Macao	513	555	673	820	782
Malaysia	11,780	12,719	13,251	13,426	11,593
Pakistan	5,656	5,744	5,592	6,234	5,925
Philippines	7,946	7,667	7,490	6,070	5,111
Singapore	25,785	26,196	26,252	26,734	24,535
Sri Lanka	1,695	1,794	1,723	1,699	1,960
Taiwan	20,883	18,130	18,760	20,952	19,249
Thailand	8,931	7,565	9,169	9,236	8,403
Vietnam	1,002	1,107	1,216	—	—

Sources: National Statistics/IMF
Note: *USSR and OECD countries only; excluding countertrade

TABLE 19   TRADE BALANCE

US$ million, fob

	1981	1982	1983	1984	1985
Bangladesh	−1,644	−1,453	−1,207	−1,408	−1,300
Burma	104	−15	102	−235	—
Hong Kong	−501	−365	−243	487	321
India	−5,711	−4,820	−4,098	−4,516	—
Indonesia	6,806	1,893	963	5,500	5,876
Kampuchea*	−106	−81	−96	—	—
North Korea	−103	−202	−210	—	—
South Korea	−3,628	−2,594	−1,763	−1,036	−19
Laos	−90	−92	−92	−62	—
Macao	−16	5	30	115	128
Malaysia	−105	−753	432	2,981	3,277
Pakistan	−2,926	−3,403	−2,715	−3,754	−3,277
Philippines	−2,224	−2,646	−2,485	−679	−482
Singapore	−6,123	−6,762	−5,823	−4,071	−3,035
Sri Lanka	−632	−780	−664	−237	−657
Taiwan	1,825	3,646	6,268	9,233	11,217
Thailand	−2,029	−731	−2,861	−1,898	−1,344
Vietnam	−770	−822	−899	—	—

Sources: National Statistics/IMF
Note: *USSR and OECD countries only; excluding countertrade

TABLE 20   CURRENT ACCOUNT BALANCE OF PAYMENTS, 1980–1985

US$ million

	1980	1981	1982	1983	1984	1985
Bangladesh	−757	−1,014	−656	−60	−529	−578
Burma	−350	−314	−499	−344	—	—
Hong Kong	−1,226	−1,599	−1,012	−500	1,410	2,179
India	−1,785	−2,698	−2,524	−1,953	−2,560	—
Indonesia	2,864	−566	−5,324	−6,338	−2,114	−1,632
Kampuchea	—	—	—	—	—	—
North Korea	—	—	—	—	—	—
South Korea	−5,321	−4,646	−2,650	−1,606	−1,372	−887
Laos	−54	−58	−65	−76	−52	—
Macao	—	—	—	—	—	—
Malaysia	−285	−2,486	−3,601	−3,497	−1,660	−669
Pakistan	−921	−914	−802	25	−1,195	−1,106
Philippines	−1,917	−2,096	−3,212	−2,751	−1,268	8
Singapore	−1,507	−1,478	−1,206	−819	−727	−253
Sri Lanka	−657	−446	−549	−466	7	−556
Taiwan	−913	519	2,248	4,412	6,976	9,294
Thailand	−2,070	−2,569	−1,003	−2,874	−2,111	−1,547
Vietnam	—	—	−898	−926	—	—

Sources: IMF/National Statistics

250

TABLE 21 EXPORTS, BY CATEGORY

Percentage of total exports

	Year	Agriculture	Mining & quarrying	Manufac-turing
Bangladesh	1983	32.6	0.1	67.4
Burma	1983	36.0	25.0	39.0
Hong Kong	1983	0.6	0.2	99.2
India	1980	25.2	14.9	59.9
Indonesia	1983	10.5	72.6	16.8
Kampuchea	1984	80.0*	25.0*	5.0*
North Korea	1984	5.0*	80.0*	15.0*
South Korea	1981	5.2	0.4	94.4
Laos	1983	75.0*	15.0*	10.0*
Macao	1981	1.7	0.2	98.1
Malaysia	1982	23.9	28.2	47.9
Pakistan	1983	17.1	0.4	82.6
Philippines	1982	12.0	10.6	77.3
Singapore	1983	8.0	1.8	90.3
Sri Lanka	1982	57.1	4.1	38.8
Taiwan	1984	0.9	0.0	99.1
Thailand	1983	33.7	5.1	61.2
Vietnam	1985	60.0*	15.0*	25.0*

Sources: IMF/National Statistics/Estimates
Note: *Estimates

TABLE 22 IMPORTS BY CATEGORY

Percentage of total imports

	Year	Food, beverages, tobacco	Indus-trial supplies	Fuels	Machin-ery	Trans-port equipment	Con-sumer goods
Bangladesh	1983	18.9	43.4	10.5	14.7	8.3	3.9
Burma	1977	6.7	42.3	1.9	27.6	15.3	5.5
Hong Kong	1983	11.4	41.3	6.6	16.2	3.2	20.8
India	1981	7.9	33.9	43.6	11.4	2.0	1.2
Indonesia	1983	7.1	30.6	24.8	26.6	8.4	2.2
Kampuchea	—	—	—	—	—	—	—
North Korea	—	—	—	—	—	—	—
South Korea	1981	9.7	35.4	29.7	16.0	7.1	1.8
Laos	1983	0.7	—	—	22.1	—	—
Macao	1981	10.9	58.7	6.5	5.6	2.5	15.6
Malaysia	1982	9.7	28.4	15.0	29.4	10.3	6.4
Pakistan	1983	13.2	29.6	28.2	17.2	8.6	3.2
Philippines	1982	7.2	28.8	26.4	17.1	5.3	2.1
Singapore	1983	6.2	23.7	31.2	20.7	7.8	9.4
Sri Lanka	1982	12.4	27.3	31.3	12.1	9.8	6.6
Taiwan	1985	44.5	18.1	16.4	15.1	—	—
Thailand	1983	3.1	35.4	24.1	21.4	8.1	3.8
Vietnam	—	—	—	—	—	—	—

Source: IMF

TABLE 23 EXPORTS BY DESTINATION, 1985

US$ mn	Industrial-ised countries	Africa	Other Asian	Europe	Middle East	USSR, East Europe	Others
Bangladash	47.9	11.4	14.6	3.3	15.3	6.5	0.7
Burma	22.0	18.4	45.9	0.3	2.4	4.5	2.1
Hong Kong	54.3	1.3	37.2	0.3	2.5	0.6	1.1
India	59.1	2.6	10.0	1.4	8.8	17.7	0.2
Indonesia	80.0	0.5	14.1	0.4	1.0	0.5	1.7
Kampuchea	—	—	85.0*	—	—	12.0*	—
North Korea	—	—	80.0*	—	—	15.0*	—
South Korea	70.0	2.1	13.3	1.4	6.2	0.0	3.3
Laos	9.5	0.0	95.0*	0.2*	—	4.5*	—
Macao	71.0	0.2	27.1	0.5	0.8	0.3	0.1
Malaysia	54.6	0.3	38.3	0.7	1.8	1.4	0.4
Pakistan	49.5	5.7	18.5	1.6	18.1	5.6	1.1
Philippines	73.7	0.1	19.7	1.9	1.5	0.8	0.4
Singapore	46.5	2.3	39.4	1.1	5.6	1.3	2.0
Sri Lanka	50.8	1.7	11.3	1.2	22.9	4.0	1.2
Taiwan	67.0	0.4	14.4	4.6	2.9	0.0	10.7
Thailand	56.4	3.8	27.3	0.8	7.5	1.4	0.7
Vietnam	30.0	0.8	56.0	4.2	0.0	—	0.2

Sources: IMF/National Statistics
Note: *Estimates

TABLE 24 IMPORTS BY ORIGIN, 1985

US$ mn	Industrial-ised countries	Africa	Other Asian	Europe	Middle East	USSR, East Europe	Others
Bangladesh	43.3	0.2	28.2	0.9	10.1	3.1	0.4
Burma	61.7	2.2	25.7	0.2	0.1	9.6	0.0
Hong Kong	48.8	1.1	38.9	0.1	0.8	0.4	0.8
India	54.1	1.7	11.4	1.5	18.9	8.8	3.1
Indonesia	77.2	1.1	13.0	0.2	3.9	0.2	1.4
Kampuchea	0.0*	0.0*	90.0*	—	—	10.0*	—
North Korea	2.0*	0.5*	85.0*	0.2*	0.0*	10.0*	—
South Korea	64.5	1.0	12.0	1.2	9.5	0.0	5.5
Laos	2.0*	0.0*	90.0*	0.5*	0.0*	5.0*	—
Macao	4.9	0.1	92.9	0.5	0.3	0.3	0.1
Malaysia	61.5	0.4	29.9	0.2	3.9	0.4	0.9
Pakistan	54.8	2.0	14.5	1.4	25.1	1.1	1.1
Philippines	53.8	0.2	28.4	0.2	12.3	0.3	1.3
Singapore	49.0	0.8	31.9	0.3	13.9	0.2	0.5
Sri Lanka	46.0	2.0	23.5	1.3	21.7	0.8	1.5
Taiwan	49.7	1.0	6.7	9.7*	10.1	0.0	—
Thailand	59.7	1.2	24.9	0.6	7.9	0.7	1.5
Vietnam	42.5	0.0	37.2	6.8	0.0	—	0.7

Sources: IMF/National Statistics
Note: *Estimates

252

TABLE 25   FOREIGN INDEBTEDNESS AND LIQUIDITY, 1984/85

US$ mn	Total foreign debt	% of GNP	% of foreign exchange receipts	International currency reserves
Bangladesh	5,600	43.8	7.1	368
Burma	3,000	43.5	—	63
Hong Kong	6,180	19.0	0.2	—
India	24,000	13.8	14.9	5,034
Indonesia	23,500	29.4	15.7	4,702
Kampuchea	—	—	—	—
North Korea	1,400	—	—	—
South Korea	45,000	55.4	18.0	6,800
Laos	414	—	—	—
Macao	0	—	—	—
Malaysia	17,900	55.7	13.6	3,470
Pakistan	11,800	36.8	17.5	912
Philippines	25,400	77.6	37.5	574
Singapore	1,100	69.1	1.3	10,291
Sri Lanka	3,100	52.5	8.8	505
Taiwan	10,100	17.6	6.9	15,664
Thailand	14,800	35.1	24.1	1,890
Vietnam	6,000	—	—	—

Source: National Statistics

TABLE 26   TOTAL EDUCATION EXPENDITURE AS % OF GDP PRODUCT AND TOTAL GOVERNMENT EXPENDITURE

	Year	US$ million	% current	% capital	% of GNP	% of government expenditure
Bangladesh	1983	195.3	70.9	29.1	1.4	18.9
Burma	1977	71.5	96.6	3.4	1.6	14.6
Hong Kong	1983	756.5	90.6	9.1	2.9	25.0
India	1981	5,188.4	98.7	1.3	3.2	13.7
Indonesia	1981	1,434.7	—	—	2.2	9.3
Kampuchea	—	—	—	—	—	—
North Korea	—	—	—	—	—	—
South Korea	1983	3,699.4	75.8	24.2	5.1	23.0
Laos	1980	2.4	—	—	0.5	1.3
Macao	—	—	—	—	—	—
Malaysia	1982	1,959.5	78.8	21.2	7.5	22.0
Pakistan	1983	604.8	75.9	24.1	2.0	4.9
Philippines	1982	692.7	81.4	18.6	2.0	12.0
Singapore	1982	634.8	72.4	27.6	4.4	9.6
Sri Lanka	1983	16.4	89.0	11.0	3.0	7.1
Taiwan	—	—	—	—	—	—
Thailand	1983	1,534.8	79.7	20.3	3.9	20.0
Vietnam	—	—	—	—	—	—

Sources: United Nations/National Statistics

253

TABLE 27   HEALTH CARE FACILITIES

	Year	Hospital beds ('000)	Population per hospital bed	Population per doctor	Average daily calorie supply as % of requirements (1983)
Bangladesh	1983/84	18.7	5,309	6,378	84
Burma	1984/85	25.6	1,488	4,680	113
Hong Kong	1985	24.6	4,593	1,210	128
India	1981	340.8	1,338	3,690	87
Indonesia	1983/84	103.5	1,430	11,530	110
Kampuchea	1985	17.9	399	14,128	88
North Korea	—	—	83	430	126
South Korea	1981	63.8	636	2,990	126
Laos	1982	9.0	401	18,400	97
Macao	1982	1.4	309	2,593	—
Malaysia	1984	36.8	413	1,320	121
Pakistan	1983	52.2	1,903	3,480	106
Philippines	1984	70.6	753	7,970	116
Singapore	1985	8.0	316	1,150	121
Sri Lanka	1981	44.0	354	7,170	102
Taiwan	1984	61.0	307	1,268	125
Thailand	—	—	823	7,100	104
Vietnam	1981	120.8	460	4,190	90

Sources: National Statistics/World Bank/UNESCO

TABLE 28   TRANSPORT STATISTICS

	Main ports	International airports	Railways (km)	Total roads (km)	Paved (km)
Bangladesh	2	2	2,750	4,623	4,200
Burma	3	1	2,000	27,000	23,067
Hong Kong	1	1	70	1,323	1,323
India	10	6	64,000	632,455	24,140
Indonesia	6	3	8,600	155,000	39,000
Kampuchea	2	1	612	13,351	10,087
North Korea	2	1	4,400	20,280	365
South Korea	4	1	6,007	50,850	16,350
Laos	5	1	0	21,300	7,200
Macao	1	0	0	45	45
Malaysia	9	5	20,917	43,818	33,980
Pakistan	2	4	8,775	101,300	34,000
Philippines	4	1	1,143	162,924	98,000
Singapore	1	1	26	2,569	2,569
Sri Lanka	4	1	1,944	27,000	19,000
Taiwan	5	2	4,800	19,306	18,000
Thailand	2	3	3,800	34,700	11,000
Vietnam	3	2	3,000	347,200	41,000

Sources: National Statistics/Estimates

TABLE 29   MEDIA INDICATORS, 1984

	Radios ('000)	Per 1,000 population	TVs ('000)	Per 1,000 population	Telephones ('000)	Per 1,000 population
Bangladesh	770	8	84	1	143	1.5
Burma	864	23	6	2	53	1.4
Hong Kong	2,710	510	1,195	225	2,350	438.1
India	45,000	61	2,096	3	3,300	4.3
Indonesia	22,000	138	3,500	22	9,114	5.7
Kampuchea	900	131	60	9	—	1.0
North Korea	4,100	193	1,050	50	5	1.4
South Korea	18,000	451	7,000	175	4,800	130.0
Laos	400	95	—	—	7	4.0
Macao	100	329	1	25	40	95.3
Malaysia	6,500	437	1,425	96	1,350	88.9
Pakistan	7,000	78	1,100	12	553	5.7
Philippines	·2,342	45	1,350	26	850	15.6
Singapore	681	272	472	188	1,000	363.6
Sri Lanka	1,800	117	50	3	74	4.6
Taiwan	10,500	545	5,200	270	4,228	219.5
Thailand	7,200	146	840	17	500	9.7
Vietnam	6,000	10	2,250	39	—	—

Sources: UNESCO/National Statistics

TABLE 30   TOURIST ARRIVALS

	1982 '000	1983 '000	1984 '000	1985 '000	Year	Visitors' expenditure (US$ mn)
Bangladesh	54	80	103	145	1985	20
Burma	30	30	29	—	1984	9
Hong Kong	2,600	2,900	3,200	3,440	1985	1,900
India	1,288	1,305	1,253	—	—	—
Indonesia	592	639	683	—	1984	519
Kampuchea	—	—	—	—	—	—
North Korea	—	—	—	—	—	—
South Korea	1,150	1,195	1,297	—	1984	366
Laos	—	—	—	—	—	—
Macao	3,500	3,750	4,170	3,995	1984	1,911
Malaysia	2,400	2,681	2,950	—	1983	1,200
Pakistan	29	365	410	—	1983	202
Philippines	891	861	700	715	—	—
Singapore	2,900	2,800	2,991	2,910	1984	1,183
Sri Lanka	407	338	317	—	1984	101
Taiwan	1,111	1,167	1,227	1,195	1985	1,045
Thailand	2,210	2,190	2,300	—	1984	1,004
Vietnam (1973)	79	—	—	—	—	—

Sources: National Statistics/Estimates

LIST OF TABLES

258

INDIAN SUB-CONTINENT

INDEX

267

DATE DUE